Dragon Suit

Dragon Suit

The Golden Age of Expatriate Executives in China

Gábor Holch

BEP

BUSINESS EXPERT PRESS

Leader in applied, concise business books

Dragon Suit: The Golden Age of Expatriate Executives in China

Copyright © Business Expert Press, LLC, 2024

Cover design by Hisna Nur Azizah

Interior design by Exeter Premedia Services Private Ltd., Chennai, India

First published in 2023 by
Business Expert Press, LLC
222 East 46th Street, New York, NY 10017
www.businessexpertpress.com

ISBN-13: 978-1-63742-485-8 (paperback)
ISBN-13: 978-1-63742-486-5 (e-book)

Business Expert Press International Business Collection

First edition: 2023

10 9 8 7 6 5 4 3 2 1

To my wife, Yimin. Writing takes patience, and
I have little. I put hers to the test instead.

Description

Worldwide businesses leaders who try to comprehend China's unavoidable impact on their livelihoods often ignore the most important voices: those of expatriate managers with years of experience in the country. Based on interviews with China-based corporate executives over five years, *Dragon Suit* brings to life the country's swarming cities, recent economic tsunami, unstoppable middle class, endemic pollution, intermittent Internet, confusing culture, and endless opportunities.

This book is a rare insight into the way global firms select, relocate, manage, motivate, and reward top managers in the world's most populous market. CEOs, C-suite executives, and senior managers recall their careers since China's early 2000s reform period until a notable 2014 policy paper declared "the end of a golden age for foreign business in China," and beyond to the present day.

Dragon Suit addresses crucial questions for international business:

- How did China become a key market for global firms?
- Why are most foreign managers unprepared for its challenges?
- Why did the country's near-million foreigners begin to leave in the mid-2010s, and who will replace them?
- Most importantly, how can managers, entrepreneurs, experts, and students prepare for an increasingly China-facing future in business?

Keywords

China; business in China; business management; international business; intercultural; expatriate; expat life; leadership; global mobility

Contents

Foreword

Why does my friend Gabor Holch publish a book about expatriate executives in China right now, at such a precarious time? Some may think this book is a brave effort but off sync with recent developments between China and the world. But in my opinion, *Dragon Suit* could not have come at a better time. To explain why, allow me to illustrate the topic of Western expats in China in the widening contexts of my own story, the history of my firm in China, and finally the likely direction of the entire country.

The company that I am heading in Beijing, the German chemical giant BASF, established its first operations in Shanghai during the Qing dynasty, in 1885. The year before the First World War broke out, China represented 17 percent of the conglomerate's global sales. Over a century later, in 2021 China accounted for 15 percent of our global sales, but the pie itself had become an order of magnitude greater, resulting in a business worth an astounding 12 billion euros for us in China alone. From our first incorporation in the country until now, BASF executives have accompanied China through recurring cycles of triumph and disaster, and consequently enjoyed a front-row seat to the most impressive economic comeback story of the 20th century.

Such sagas of countries and corporations are made possible by the determination of visionary entrepreneurs. They are people with the willingness to take risks and endure uncertainties, and so they benefit from the wealth of rich social interactions and the rapid speed of business development that this grand nation can offer. Gabor and I are proud members of that community, although we represent different generations within it—I first arrived in China in August 1982, Gabor exactly 20 years later in 2002. We both spent the following two decades weathering China's frequent ups-and-downs while helping our businesses ride the waves, along with a growing number of multinational businesses in the country.

In recent years, doing business in China has undeniably become harder, with mounting challenges from geopolitical conflicts and rising nationalism in the PRC. Newly arising suspicions have both distorted the views that many Europeans have of China and clouded the judgment of many Chinese about Europe. At the time of writing, China's zero-tolerance approach to COVID-19 gravely inhibits human engagement and has become a major headwind for the further development of the Chinese economy. The foreigners who once followed promising career opportunities to China often vote with their feet: Europeans are in danger of becoming virtually extinct in China, with numbers dropping to levels unseen since the 1990s. Meanwhile, polls indicate that China's popularity in Europe has plunged to historic lows.

But my long experience in China taught me that such hardships always indicate the beginning of another cycle, with new headaches and prospects. As I write this in August 2022, BASF is in the process of establishing a 10-billion-dollar production site in China's southern province of Guangdong, the largest overseas investment in the company's history. Thousands of foreign businesses across a wide array of sectors, from pharmaceutical through automotive to professional services, continue to thrive in a tougher environment which, however, still offers virtually endless opportunities.

It is therefore more important than ever that curious minds, regardless of whether they are in Europe, China, or elsewhere, understand the intricacies and complexities of conducting business in the world's second largest market, as well as the ramifications of China's push to establish its economic champions in Europe. Nothing helps to convey these messages better than first-hand accounts from expats who have lived the experience of doing business in China. Their stories are important because they remind us not to lose sight of the long-term prospects of China, a continent-sized country we have successfully engaged for decades.

Forty years of living and working in the country have convinced me time and again that Chinese people are resilient and have a proven *comeback gene*. Because of this, I believe the biggest risk associated with doing business in China is not to be there at all. May everyone who reads *Dragon Suit* become part of this exciting journey!

Shanghai, August 25, 2022
—Joerg Wuttke, Chief Representative, BASF China and President
EU Chamber of Commerce in China

Acknowledgments

I would like to thank everyone who appears in *Dragon Suit*, whether under their real name or, according to their wishes, an approximate pseudonym. I deeply appreciate the time, thought, and care they dedicated to my project.

I am grateful to the friends who painstakingly peer-reviewed my book: Weirong Li, Kyle Hegarty, Peter Hill, and Michael Wenderoth. Going beyond the already ambitious task of reviewing an entire manuscript under time pressure, they contributed original ideas that I did my best to include in the final version.

I am indebted to educators at ELTE Budapest, the Central European University and the Diplomatic Academy of Vienna for starting me on a global journey, and mentors who helped me develop into a leadership consultant, speaker, and writer: Prof. Albrecht Schnabel, Rob Wagenaar, the late Francois Rouen, Hans Werner Hagemann, Katalin Ferber, and Shelley Weiner.

Any merit of *Dragon Suit* includes the dedication of colleagues and business partners at my Shanghai-based consultancy and our affiliated firms, including Wang Yuhai, Gabor Nagy, Tracy Zang, Rik Vodeb, Magnus Omstedt, Christine Xue, Bethany Jeanfreau, Jack Guo, Zoltán Aszalós, Csaba Toth, Sinto Llobera, Fabrizio Ullivi, Jamie Chang, Richard Kang, and many others.

I gained invaluable knowledge, experience and wisdom from clients who became friends over time, including executives featured in this book, but also Luo Fei, Akyazici Oemer, Balázs Vizi, David Lee, Jürgen Ries, Gohar Siddiqui, Szilárd Bolla, Massimo Meloni, Gábor Szórád, and others. I am also grateful to the thousands of managers who shared their ideas at my workshops, coaching sessions, keynote speeches, and panel discussions.

Much of what I know about intercultural existence comes from amazing friends like Áron Zsigmond, Philippe Tremblay, Naobumi Obara,

Barbara Ürögdi, Rich DeForno, Nicky Almasy, Rosanna Terminio, Gustavo Araujo, Claude and Fiona, Niels and Lindsey, and others.

Dragon Suit would have been impossible without my agent Nigel Wyatt, and the dedicated team of Business Expert Press.

The whole undertaking would be meaningless without an amazing family that taught me curiosity and respect toward other people's thoughts, feelings, living memory, and written legacy: Mom and Dad, my sister Nikoletta, and my late Aunt Klára.

Introduction:
Why *Dragon Suit?*

I checked, and then I checked again: nobody had written a book called *Dragon Suit*. Why not? Ever since I moved to central Shanghai two decades ago, I saw them every day: sharply dressed men and women who confidently went about their multimillion-dollar business. I passed by as they discussed issues of importance over designer lunches. I stepped out of the way as they dashed from chauffeured cars into glitzy office towers. Most importantly, I met them daily as a leadership coach and consultant. Was I really the only one who mentally labeled them Dragon Suits?

Chinese people use the dragon as their cultural icon because dragons are believed to be everywhere and still remain a mystery—think Loch Ness Monsters in every lake. Like the dragon, China is unavoidable: I challenge you to look around you right now without spotting anything made in China or, if you are in a crowded bookstore, airport, or café, someone from China. Yet, despite thousands of dragon-titled books, films, lectures, and businesses, the world's most populous country managed to remain a mystery to most people.

Yes, managed. Like the dragon, China has carefully managed its exposure so that everyone can admire its power without knowing too much about it. China is the world's biggest and most misunderstood story. And that is where the suits come in. Because while heads of state, global CEOs, investors, traders, journalists, talk show hosts, office workers, and pub-goers make hit-and-miss attempts to understand and explain this omnipresent force, there is someone who might help them. That person is a current or former expatriate manager in China—a *Dragon Suit*.

This book started as a series of interviews I made with executives who had spent years in China's vast metropolises managing factories, warehouses, stores, clinics, recruitment, sales, and research operations. Their accounts of why they accepted jobs in China, their first impressions, their daily life, their professional trials and triumphs, their struggle with bad air, restricted Internet and culture shock, their promotions to ever-higher leadership positions, personal growth, and eventual departure are fascinating as they are.

But beyond the personal journeys, their revelations explain why China emerged from obscurity to global dominance in a quarter century and why international firms are determined to do business in, or at least with China. Why it prefers to erect Great Walls that restrict the movement of information, goods, and people in and out of the country while its presence is felt in virtually every household in the world. Why, while it claims to be a land of harmony, it is so often embroiled in conflict with the outside world and itself.

Most importantly, the Dragon Suits who appear in this book teach us how to get on well, or at least much better, with China. They learned the hard way, over a long time. Once they returned to their countries or moved elsewhere, they already helped hundreds of colleagues, bosses, customers, or suppliers who were understandably mystified by China's uniqueness. But although Dragon Suits are scattered across the world and may be closer to you than you think, I strongly believe that by sharing their stories and opinions, we can make an increasingly China-facing world a little bit easier place.

Since I settled in China in the sizzling summer of 2002, I have spent most of my working days demystifying the leadership cultures of East and West to one another. I have worked with European and American CEOs in Asia, Asian executives at Western firms, and people of various nations and professions who somehow found themselves entangled in the thrilling exchange between China and the world. But *Dragon Suit* is not a business manual. It is a collection of first-hand insights into what some experts call the *golden age* of foreign business in China. It also reveals why the same people think the *golden age* is over, and what we can expect of the new era that people doing business with China are about to inaugurate.

CHAPTER 1

Signing Up

The Golden Age of Foreign Business in China

To all appearances, 2014 was a great year to be an expatriate manager in China. Twenty-five years after the country started re-engaging with the capitalist world, people had the cash and appetite for all things foreign. Wristwatches, bicycles, and television sets were the trinity of middle-class aspirations no more: Chinese people wanted Rolexes, BMWs, and multiplex cinemas featuring Hollywood blockbusters. The omnipotent Communist Party's curious new leader, Xi Jinping, unhesitatingly tackled the chief concern of foreign investors: corruption. Not only did shady demands from government officials drop dramatically almost overnight—it seemed to happen without the expected economic slowdown of anticorruption clampdowns. Doubling down on the previous administration's development spree, the new leadership made sure that airports and railway stations, factories and wind turbines, Apple Stores, and luxury malls kept sprouting from the ground. President Xi toured the world, and few doubted he was after foreign investment, know-how, and guidance. Before the end of the year, Australian Prime Minister Tony Abbot would praise visiting Xi Jinping for his commitment to full democracy in China by 2050.[1]

The Free Trade Agreements (FTA) that President Xi churned out around the globe meant new opportunities for the China branches of multinational corporations that employed most foreigners. Some polls

---

[1] N. Woodley. November 2014. "Prime Minister Tony Abbott Praises Chinese President Xi Jinping's Commitment to Democracy, But Tourism Industry Not Convinced by FTA," *ABC News*. www.abc.net.au/news/2014-11-18/praise-for-chinese-president/5898212?nw=0.

had recently named China as the most desirable expat destination in the world, mainly for the money to be made there. "Jobs like mine in China exist because investors abroad are concerned about working in an environment with communication and cultural differences," the BBC quoted a Fortune 500 firm's foreign executive. "My role is to mitigate those fears and make people feel good about their investments."[2] But there was more, the article continued. As Chinese firms explored global opportunities, they would need foreign talent to replicate the success stories of China-bound multinational investment in reverse. With China's outward investment growing tenfold over a decade,[3] a steady source of expatriate jobs at local firms looked secure. It was in this upbeat atmosphere that the European Union Chamber of Commerce in China, a prestigious lobbying institution, declared in one of its annual publications: "The 'golden age' for business in China is drawing to a close."[4]

The paper in question, *The European Business in China Position Paper*, was far from mainstream media. Its few thousand print copies and several times as many digital downloads were limited to China-watchers with an appetite for data and the attention span to digest it. But the Position Paper was a trusted resource among China's expat executive and expert communities, Eurocrats in Brussels and China-facing businesspeople worldwide. Moreover, EU Chambers all over Asia were hives of networking activity, and the message was sufficiently dramatic to spawn a self-replicating meme. "Is the golden age over for multinationals in China?" Hong Kong's *South China Morning Post* asked days after the Position Paper's launch.[5] The question soon echoed through hotel auditoriums,

---

[2] K. Martinez-Carter. November 2013. "The Best—and Worst—Countries for Expats?," *BBC*. www.bbc.com/worklife/article/20131122-an-expats-home-away-from-home.

[3] L. Zhou. January 2015. "China's Overseas Investments, Explained in 10 Graphics," World Resources Institute. www.wri.org/insights/chinas-overseas-investments-explained-10-graphics.

[4] European Union Chamber of Commerce in China. September 9, 2014. "European Business in China Position Paper 2014/2015," p. 5.

[5] E. Tse and P. Pan. August 2014. "Is the Golden Age Over for Multinationals in China?," *South China Morning Post*. www.scmp.com/comment/article/1581467/golden-age-over-multinationals-china.

conference rooms at investment banks, consultancies and law firms from Shanghai to Guangzhou, Shenzhen, Beijing, and beyond. It soon scrolled onto global screens through a wide range of worldwide publications, including predictable ones like *Industry Week*,[6] and more unlikely ones like *The Christian Science Monitor*.[7]

Global firms had enjoyed a spectacular run in China for three decades. Why would it end? Sure, some managers frantically wired their money and their firm's money abroad. A few packed their bags and posted vitriolic "Why am I leaving China?" blogs, which will appear in later chapters. But apart from a panic-stricken minority, the prophecy hardly stopped anyone else from going about its feverish business. Foreign executives plotted investment strategies from high-rise offices that flickered with reflections of skyscrapers and multilevel intersections. Mid-managers and specialists from scores of nations bent over machines, microscopes, and balance sheets in factories and logistical centers. Spouses tried to communicate with local housekeepers. Their children waved from American-style school buses to Chinese kids hurried to class in BMW SUVs or by pedaling grandparents. Millions of local workers ran offices for foreign firms, assembled, loaded, and offloaded their manufactures, drove and polished their trucks and sedans, booked their meeting rooms, flights, hotels, restaurants, and doctor's appointments, cooked their meals, delivered their packages, and cleaned their shimmering swimming pools at serviced apartment compounds. Aspiring expats kept nurturing China dreams: jobs applications were at all-time highs.

And yet, almost imperceptibly at that time, the tide was turning in China. Or, more precisely, it was returning. The joint authors of the study at the European Union Chamber and consulting firm Roland Berger had

---

[6] K. Olsen. September 2014. "Businesses in EU Say China's Promised Reforms Moving too Slowly," AFP. www.industryweek.com/the-economy/article/21963586/businesses-in-eu-say-chinas-promised-reforms-moving-too-slowly.

[7] P. Ford. March 2015. "Nokia Exit: Is China's 'Golden Age' of Foreign Investment Over?," *The Christian Science Monitor*. www.csmonitor.com/World/Asia-Pacific/2015/0309/Nokia-exit-Is-China-s-golden-age-of-foreign-investment-over.

spotted the storm clouds earlier than most, but their conclusions became more evident with each passing year. By 2017, well over half of the surveyed executives agreed that the *golden age* for multinational firms in China was in fact over.[8] Did that mean anything? Was it mere resentment from the West as some observers claimed? After all, recent international bestseller *When China Rules the World* sold over a million copies in previous years, catapulted its British author Martin Jacques on a lucrative keynote speaking career, and set the tone on China's rise for many who listened.[9] And if the Chamber survey's authors turned out to be right after all, what would follow? Would the future vindicate Gordon Chang instead, whose book, *The Coming Collapse of China*, had created quite a stir around the same time Jacques published his? To understand the parallel narratives of this still inconclusive debate, we have to revisit the origins of China's epic collapse in the early 20th century and heroic return as an international business location at the dawn of the new millennium.

From Zero to Hero

Calling China's recent *reform and opening* a zero-to-hero success story is not a figure of speech: the People's Republic of China (PRC) did start the new millennium from virtually nothing. How China found itself without foreigners has been interpreted in many ways, but the basic facts are seldom debated. China's relationship with outsiders had always been troubled and mostly restricted to a handful of cities and towns along the eastern coast. When the victorious Communist Party declared a PRC in 1949, one of its outspoken aims was to purify the land from *imperialist* practices, and most activities pursued by foreigners fell under that category. Mao's regime rid the country of most things foreign, starting with Western and Japanese interests, then followed by Soviet and South-East Asian interests, including brotherly Socialist nations like Vietnam and Cambodia. As a consequence, external trade and investment plummeted.

---

[8] European Union Chamber of Commerce in China. May 31, 2017. "European Business in China Confidence Survey 2017," p. 30.
[9] M. Jacques. 2009. *When China Rules the World: The End of the Western World and the Birth of a New Global Order* (London: Penguin Books).

The cross-border movement of people ground to a near halt. Predictably for a vast continental power, the price of isolation was poverty: per capita gross domestic product (GDP) between 1949 and the 1980s remained alarmingly low.[10]

By the late 1950s, what remained was a handful of diplomats, leftover advisors, and technicians from the Soviet Union and other Leninist states, and a thinning streak of international business travelers, journalists, academics, entertainers, and self-declared Maoists. "Aside from a Polish shipping agency and a Pakistan International Airways office that opened in 1964, there were only three resident foreign firms by the end of 1965, all of them British," historian Robert Bickers described once-cosmopolitan Shanghai under Mao's xenophobic regime.[11] Few foreigners entered the country, but there was little to find anyway. Tourism, culture, and education ground to a halt, as did business. In 1978, the private sector accounted for less than 1 percent of economic activity.[12] Shanghai had lost the entirety of its previous population of 30,000 non-native residents.[13] Shum Chun, a bustling southern trading and entertainment hub until the late 1930s, emptied out so thoroughly that even today, many journalists believe it had been an insignificant fishing village until its eventual resuscitation as Shenzhen.[14]

China's seclusion has bewildered the world's politicians and businesspeople alike. "There is no place on this small planet for a billion of its

---

[10] Data Commons Place Explorer. n.d. "Gross Domestic Product Per Capita in People's Republic of China." https://datacommons.org/place/country/CHN?utm_medium=explore&mprop=amount&popt=EconomicActivity&cpv=activitySource%2CGrossDomesticProduction&hl=en# (accessed July 31, 2022).

[11] R. Bickers. 2017. *Out of China: How the Chinese Ended the Era of Western Domination* (London: Allen Lane), p. 332.

[12] K. Brown. 2018. *China's Dream: The Culture of Chinese Communism and the Secret Sources of its Power* (Cambridge: Polity), p. 42.

[13] F.N. Pieke. November 2019. "How Immigration Is Shaping Chinese Society," *MERICS*, Exhibit 2. https://merics.org/en/report/how-immigration-shaping-chinese-society.

[14] P. French. January 2021. "Myth Busting: Shenzhen's Sleazy Past as Short-Lived Gangster and Gambling Hub Shum Chun," *The South China Morning Post*. www.scmp.com/magazines/post-magazine/long-reads/article/3117505/myth-busting-shenzhens-sleazy-past-short-lived.

potentially most able people to live in angry isolation," wrote Senator Richard Nixon in 1967, five years before he would embark on his epic visit as the U.S. president.[15] But under the reign of a Chairman Mao who refused to travel abroad, spoke no foreign languages, and was now deeply suspicious of anything non-Chinese, there was little the world could do. Then, as economist Stephen Radelet cynically wrote, "in 1976, Mao single-handedly and dramatically changed the direction of global poverty with one simple act: he died."[16] The floodgates separating a resource-rich but impoverished nation from a commerce-thirsty world cracked open, and the resulting deluge was a spectacular affair. Three years after Mao's death, Beijing designated hubs of illicit market exchange between Guangzhou and Hong Kong as the first special economic zones (SEZs).[17] Guangdong, Shanghai, Shenzhen, Xiamen, and Tianjin—one after another enclave was carved out of a bankrupt socialist economic landscape to host investment-wielding, tax-paying, job-creating capitalist ventures from abroad. The 1980s saw French winemaker Rémy Martin, German automotive firm Volkswagen, and many others do the previously unthinkable: establish joint ventures with state-owned firms, lease land, and build factories in what many still called *Red China*. PepsiCo, Rado, Metro Group, and McDonald's promoted products that remained unknown to most locals for years and unaffordable for decades.

Between Deng Xiaoping's 1992 Southern Tour, a symbolic pilgrimage to new SEZs around Hong Kong, and the early 2000s, inflows of goods, services, and investment grew 10-fold. Carefully selected locals proudly went to work in shiny new complexes for global firms and their

[15] J.W. Graver. 2016. *China's Quest: The History of the Foreign Relations of the People's Republic of China* (Oxford and New York, NY: Oxford University Press), p. 290.

[16] S. Radelet. 2016. *The Great Surge: The Ascent of the Developing World* (New York, NY: Simon & Schuster), p. 35.

[17] T. Zhou. March 2021. "Leveraging Liminality: The Border Town of Bao'an (Shenzhen) and the Origins of China's Reform and Opening," *Cambridge University Press*. https://www.cambridge.org/core/journals/journal-of-asian-studies/article/abs/leveraging-liminality-the-border-town-of-baoan-shenzhen-and-the-origins-of-chinas-reform-and-opening/45A171DCD475824FD726C999250845D2.

suppliers. Along with foreign investment came the people: amazed locals rubbed shoulders with overseas Chinese and foreign entrepreneurs the way costumed extras mingle with technology-wielding film crews. Party cadres, local government officials, and state-owned firm directors dusted off China's ancient networking culture to wine and dine foreign investors in hotels, karaoke parlors, and girlie bars still run mostly by the People's Liberation Army at the time. The people exchange went both ways. Communist Party officials, previously relying on third-hand accounts of the outside world, have now embarked on overseas study tours to factories, labs, conferences, as well as wine regions, beach resorts, and Disneyland. But lurking under this new current of economic and social activity was a profound ideological dilemma yet to be resolved. How to import capitalist prosperity without the dangerous ideas that accompanied it?

By the time China started its cautious integration into an essentially capitalist world order, its political elite had spent half a century consolidating a system where the Communist Party represented the population in all aspects of life. It had fought for the people, built for the people, bought and sold, hired and fired, voted for the people, and decided the size, life quality, and routines of their homes, families, communities, and dreams. If there were to be re-engagement, it had to be micromanaged, and unfold on the Party's terms. The first steps had been scarce and cautious, "feeling each stone while crossing the river" in Party patriarch Deng Xiaoping's frequently quoted words. Government policies assigned a handful of selected cities as exclusive gateways for inward investment, and an internal residence permit system ensured that locals who entered, worked, and lived in those model communities were handpicked just as cautiously. But despite their best efforts, the Party cadres in charge of *reform and opening* began to lose control of the forces they had unleashed. What was worse, Deng Xiaoping's death in 1997 emboldened conservatives in the Party to openly question whether the great reformer's dream would actually turn into Mao's nightmare: ideological degradation and political revisionism.

Most foreigners at that time arrived and remained in Beijing, Shanghai, Canton, and a few other top-tier cities—they still do. In a twist of ironic historical déjà vu, newly created development hubs were almost invariably previous concession ports: semicolonial entities run by major international powers until their discontinuation in the early 20th century. Thanks to Deng's reforms, the standard of living around SEZs once again dashed ahead of the country in general, and showed little resemblance to mainstream China. Shanghai Pudong New Area and an upgraded Guangzhou-Shenzhen conurbation boasted high-speed railways and automated electronics factories when steam-powered locomotives in the Western provinces still chugged past peasants hauling wooden ploughs behind water buffaloes. The fortunate few permitted to migrate to those futuristic places sent home multiple times the average salary and still kept some for themselves. Each major development area created more wealth than the rest of the country combined. This further raised the country's status in the eyes of global investors and expat managers. But for the Party, the solution started to resemble the problem. Recreating previous treaty ports was not what they had in mind.

There was more. For half a century, secrecy had been at the core of the culture of the People's Republic. Resident diplomats used to guess the importance of cadres from their distance from successive paramount leaders in photographs. Power stations, factories, and airfields were hidden deep inside the country, far from seaports, essential resources, and available labor. Mystery surrounded the ownership structure of not only state-owned firms but also newly created private businesses like Huawei. Reform presented a danger that alarmingly resembled Western spying. As foreign corporations created local joint ventures and Chinese state-owned companies incorporated brass-plate firms in the British Virgin Islands and other tax havens, Global accounting firms like PriceWaterhouseCooper (PWC) and Ernst & Young (EY) gained a deep insight into China's affairs. Reintegration into the economic and political institutions of the wider world also attracted unwelcome attention and deeply resented criticism. The 1995 United Nations World Conference on Women in Beijing elevated China's stature as a member state but also triggered condemnation of its human rights record. To many Party cadres, negotiations toward the country's World Trade Organization (WTO) membership painfully resembled great powers arrogantly dictating terms as they had done a century before.

Questioning China's eventual economic rise might sound absurd today, but at the time success seemed far from certain. "I met a senior partner of

PriceWaterhouseCooper Sydney in 2000," said Leigh, previously senior auditor to PWC, then managing director to an international consulting agency, as we sat in a central Shanghai café emptied out by the descending COVID-19 epidemic in early 2020. Born in China and taken to Australia as a child, he had guided Western companies through China's commercial and cultural labyrinths for over 20 years. "He said to me, 'you know, everybody talks about the China market, but I don't see the potential'. That's when it occurred to me that with my Chinese-born background, I could serve as the missing link." He was right. Shortly afterward, the People's Republic marched onto the global commercial stage and took over the show. Nobody at any company with international outreach doubts its strategic importance anymore. In the early 2000s, businesspeople excitedly counted how many firms in the Fortune Global 500 list were present in China. In a few years, nearly a 100 of them *were* Chinese.

A quarter century of development established the PRC as a global economic powerhouse. In the early 1980s, when my father worked there for Hungarian industrial firm Tungsram, the PRC had been only marginally friendlier to foreign investment, people, and ideas than today's North Korea. As I arrived with two light suitcases in 2002, the size of China's economy still matched France's, decent bread, cheese, and wine were rare even in major cities, and cocktails were served with a twist of Chinese characteristics. But the nation had started to "embrace the world with open arms," its motto for joining the WTO the previous year, gearing up to the *coming-out parties* of the 2008 Beijing Olympic Games and the 2010 Shanghai World Expo. Exposure brought more investment, and the realization of national ambitions. China overtaking the UK as the world's second largest economy had been a widely ridiculed vision of Mao Zedong in the 1950s.[18] By 2010, China had beat the current contender Japan and rose to second place. The World Bank included the Mainland in its annual Ease of Doing Business Index.[19] In 2013, the

[18] N. Chung-Huang. 1958. *China Will Overtake Britain* (Peking: Foreign Languages Press).

[19] The International Bank for Reconstruction and Development and The World Bank. June 1, 2009. "Doing Business 2010." www.doingbusiness.org/content/dam/doingBusiness/media/Annual-Reports/English/DB10-FullReport.pdf.

illustrious HSBC Expat Explorer Survey named it the most attractive expat destination in the world.[20]

Accidental Ambassadors

What goes up must come down, an old saying warns. Proverbs find their ways through generations for a reason, but some become such commonplaces that we seldom consider their meaning anymore. China's stellar economic rise is an excellent example. For nearly a quarter century, the People's Republic boasted double-digit growth in all significant economic areas and modernized every aspect of its people's lives at a pace that evoked time-lapse video footage. People at all strata of society and business happily surfed its waves of growth toward a better future, from smallholding peasants to CEOs and university deans. Expats were among the beneficiaries of that bonanza, breaking previously unimaginable sales, production, and growth records. Riches seemed within reach as long as they managed to show up at work in the morning. China's gluttonous consumer market rescued entire global sectors that had been neglected by slowing consumption and new priorities in advanced economies, from flavored sodas to luxury purses and SUVs. In the midst of this adrenaline-infused celebration of globalized commercialism, why would anyone expect the waves to calm and curves to slacken?

But what goes up must come down, and at the time of writing, China is once again rescripting all essential elements of the nation's interaction with the outside world, from flight operations and visa policies for incoming and outgoing travelers to the way foreign firms may invest in China and PRC corporations can list on foreign stock exchanges. Some see this as the coming collapse of China as an expat career and investment destination and point to data that later chapters will present and discuss in detail. They remind us that in the late 2010s, the PRC engaged in trade wars with virtually all of its major trading partners. The pandemic years saw a steep plunge in China's global image, often labeled as *soft power*,

---

[20] K. Martinez-Cortez. November 2013. "The Best—and Worst—Countries for Expats?," *BBC.* www.bbc.com/worklife/article/20131122-an-expats-home-away-from-home.

and the share of foreign firms plotting to relocate some of their operations doubled during the same period. Such pessimists wield new vocabulary items like *decoupling* and *expat exodus* to highlight a growing trend to see this new emerging power as a danger rather than opportunity. Unpredictability in China, they claim, is killing business.

Others claim that such gloom about the future of foreign money, ideas, and people in China rests on a selective reading of the data. They point out that the PRC's trade war adversaries remain its top trading and investment partners and remind that investment to China from some of the most bitterly critical countries actually increased during the past half decade. Yes, the age of privileged foreign firms and managers thriving under state protection may be over, and expats may be sad to part with their tax exemptions and benefit packages. The implicit conclusion of this reasoning is that the enclaves known as SEZs have never been sustainable; perhaps they were necessary evils at an early stage of China's economic development. At corporate meetings and conferences, most of which take place in a dozen cities along the Eastern shoreline, such debates often boil down to contests on who knows more about China. Visiting executives challenge resident experts, foreigners challenge locals, and juniors question their seniors if they dare. They seldom conclude that instead the entirety of China, about which few of them really know or care, it would be more constructive to start from the microcosms that foreigners can understand and influence.

Natives of Shanghai and Guangzhou mockingly claim that if their cities were independent countries, their national wealth would rival that of Sweden. Counterfactuals are hard to debate, but the undoubtable concentration of riches, infrastructure, and open-minded people in a handful of China's coastal cities is obviously what made them livable for expats. For most foreigners, the *real China* always lingered beyond legal, digital, and cultural demarcations that separated top-tier cities from the national mainstream. With the exception of Guangzhou and Shenzhen where one could take daytrips to Hong Kong and Macau, a two-hour drive from any other foreign enclave strands visitors with incomprehensible food served in confusing ways, few people who speak foreign languages, cultural hiccups, staring eyes, and an uncomfortable realization of the abyss separating China from both the world and the nation's convenient showcase cities. But the same geographic reality, combined with China's long absence from global circulation and its restricted Internet, also insulates its expats from the outside world. The result is a strange dual isolation from both local and overseas realities. And yet, its expats are the key to understanding this curious country.

Despite its pivotal role in international commerce, politics, and history, China is among the least understood and most misunderstood countries in the world. That is partially due to indifference abroad, but the main reason is the several generations of its people who diligently kept foreigners away from their territories, or when that was impossible, at least their cultural core. While fascinated by the outside world and voracious learners of imported ideas, Chinese people have always been protective of their way of life and suspicious of foreigners. Most visitors experience glaring politeness but little intimacy. Restrictions on the inflow of foreign beliefs and people are not recent phenomena either: the Middle Kingdom long maintained that attitude with sometimes tacit, and sometimes vocal popular support. As a result, most Chinese people have incomplete information about life beyond the significant physical, digital, and mental borders that separate them from the world, which is equally ignorant about them. That, as the BBC interviewee earlier pointed out, entrusts foreigners living in China with special responsibilities. Whether they like it or not, every single foreigner in China represents at least a nation—often an entire continent or simply the rest of planet Earth.

The first decade after my 2002 arrival in China was characterized by the nearly universal celebration of *reform and opening*—an all-encompassing integration project on all levels, from Party politics to payment apps. Beijing's *Three Represents* policy encouraged foreign-educated entrepreneurs to join the Communist Party. Clunky state-owned firms and newly forged private companies forged global expansion plans on government budgets. Foreigners were welcomed as catalysts of China's global return, entered the country in the tens of thousands, and started new lives there. Then, toward the mid-2010s, China's indicators of international exposure first reached their apex, then turned around. In a growing economy that increasingly relied on domestic markets, the contribution of foreign investment to national wealth tumbled.[21] Resuming Party control over all

---

[21] "China Foreign Direct Investment 1979-2022." n.d. *Macrotrends*, table 2, '% of GDP'. www.macrotrends.net/countries/CHN/china/foreign-direct-investment.

media reduced the population's access to outside data, ideas, and entertainment.[22] The number of expats plateaued and then started decreasing accordingly. As China drifted away, complaints about the world misunderstanding it became louder. "The West needs to understand that China's people are not a monolith," columnist Brian Wong demanded in late 2021.[23]

China remained a mystery well into the 21st century for a number of reasons. One is its already mentioned preference for polite secrecy. Another is that frantic reengagement since the 1990s never managed to compensate for its previous isolation. An optimistic assumption of nearly a million foreigners just before the pandemic was still a homeopathic drop in the ocean of 1.5 billion people, about 0.07 percent according to the Mercator Institute for China Studies.[24] A 2017 Gallup study named it among the five least accepting countries for migrants, right behind Zambia and Honduras.[25] Nearby Japan and South Korea hosted several times as many foreigners, and in terms of population percentage even North Korea ranked ahead of the PRC.[26] It did not seem that way, because most foreigners gathered in the commercial centers of a handful of cities. The 2010 national census found over two-thirds in Beijing, Shanghai, or the Guangzhou-Shenzhen conurbation.[27] The 2020 census showed a similar

[22] J. Woetzel. July 2019. "China and the World: Inside the Dynamics of a Changing Relationship," *McKinsey Insights*. www.mckinsey.com/featured-insights/china/china-and-the-world-inside-the-dynamics-of-a-changing-relationship.

[23] B. Wong. December 2021. "The West Needs to Understand That China's People Are Not a Monolith," *Nikkei Asia*. https://asia.nikkei.com/Opinion/The-West-needs-to-understand-that-China-s-people-are-not-a-monolith.

[24] T. Speelman. December 2020. "Chinese Attitudes Toward Immigrants: Emerging, Divided Views," *The Diplomat*. https://thediplomat.com/2020/12/chinese-attitudes-toward-immigrants-emerging-divided-views/.

[25] N. Esipova, J. Fleming, and J. Raw. "New Index Shows Least-, Most-Accepting Countries for Migrants," *Gallup*. https://news.gallup.com/poll/216377/new-index-shows-least-accepting-countries-migrants.aspx.

[26] Wikipedia. n.d. "List of Sovereign States and Dependent Territories by Immigrant Population," *Wikipedia*. https://en.wikipedia.org/wiki/List_of_sovereign_states_and_dependent_territories_by_immigrant_population (accessed July 12, 2022).

[27] SAMPi. October 24, 2018. "China Expat Population: Stats and Graphs," *SAMPi*. https://sampi.co/china-expat-population-statistics/.

picture.[28] Nearly 90 percent of the principal offices of multinational firms were in the same three locations, a 2022 British Chamber survey found.[29] A million people concentrated in a combined land area smaller than Portugal can hardly be expected to bridge a continent-sized nation with the rest of the globe.

Even if we assume that expats do their absolute best as mediators, China's frantic pace of development and frequent political upheavals often undermine their efforts. Accurate information on China has always been scarce, and that remains true even as half of the world's population walks around with NASA-grade data terminals in their pockets. Most books, articles, videos, and courses on doing business in China follow cartoonish clichés of Confucians, Taoists, and Maoists performing *Transformer*-style conversions into electronic gadgets, skyscrapers, and high-speed trains. As China developed and its smartest people became international opinion leaders, the contemporary reality of a culturally heterogeneous and rapidly changing modern China gradually found its way into publications, lectures, and training programs. But even they suffer from a universal handicap: most are out of date by the time they roll off the press. The country changes too fast, too much in defiance with linear trends and predictions. Over time, poor visibility causes headaches and fatigue. Throughout my two decades of leadership consulting in China, I often heard the psychologically understandable but professionally damaging opinion: there is nothing to understand here—just do as the Chinese do and "feel each stone while crossing the river."

But China is neither unknown nor unknowable. While a conclusive business manual may never exist, thousands of people arrive in the country each year, inhale its equally intoxicating air and culture, eat its food, work with its people, and succeed well enough to make it one of the most profitable markets on Earth. Those are the people I train, coach, and advise.

---

[28] L. Lei. May 2015. "China Embraces Increasing Foreign Residents," *China Daily*. http://global.chinadaily.com.cn/a/202105/12/WS609b14c5a310 24ad0babd49f.html.

[29] British Chamber of Commerce in China. n.d. "British Business in China: Sentiment Survey 2020-21." www.britishchamber.cn/en/business-sentiment-survey/.

Over the years, I listened to their triumphs and tribulations as business leaders, professionals, parents, and friends. I attended their crisis meetings and ribbon-cutting ceremonies. I joined their weekend getaways and learned their strange twin language. I also realized that they were the best source of the scarce practical business advice for successful enterprise. The best academic research on China comes from abroad, due to the country's poor library network, restricted Internet, and politically embedded publishing and academic institutions. But the best books, articles, and speeches on getting things done in or with China come from foreigners who have recently lived there. They are busy engineering, financial, or managerial professionals, which means they do not share their invaluable insight as often as the world would need it. Their voices inspired *Dragon Suit*.

Although the reader may draw important practical conclusions on how to explore business opportunities in China, run projects and teams, make better strategic decisions, and even how to engage Chinese business partners in an increasingly virtual age, *Dragon Suit* is not a leadership manual. I deliberately maintain a subjective vantage point: that of individual expatriates who spent at least a few years in China, usually as managers of multinational firms. I include the voices of executive coaches, advisors, or psychologists as they explain essential aspects of expat life and work. I present current events and research as a backdrop for the professional and personal lives of foreign managers in China: their aspirations, challenges, successes, and lessons learned. The structure of the book follows the typical sequence of an expatriate manager's journey into and away from China: accepting an opportunity to relocate, first impressions, the delight and difficulties of expat life, working with local colleagues and eventually leading them, and finally, one way or another, leaving the country behind.

The rest of Chapter 1 places China's expatriates into a wider economic and historical context, and shows how my interview subjects arrived in the country. Chapter 2 presents an inside look at China's expat communities, reveals the beauties and benefits of their lifestyle, as well as how they conquer challenges like bad air, Internet restrictions, and culture shock. Chapter 3's focus is on work, from each expat's first day at the office and onward to how foreigners adapt to local work cultures and why some perform better than others. Chapter 4 elaborates on leadership responsibilities, from the basics of learning local hierarchies and networking to the often-unexpected challenge of political interference in foreign business in China. Finally, Chapter 5 enumerates the events that ended a *golden age* for foreign business in China: local managers replacing expats, the country's changing global relations, and trends that will shape who China's next generation of expats will be, what they can achieve there, and what they can learn from previous Dragon Suits.

Why Go to China?

China Is the New America

The stories of expats in China invariably start before they set foot on its soil. When I interview them, I open with a question about those personal prehistories: "What was your first reaction when the possibility of going to China first came up?" The diverse answers I heard over the decades gradually revealed three typical candidate mindsets—the cheerful, the scornful, and the clueless. Some raced through all three at once, like Vale Minerals Asia-Pacific Finance Manager Renata Santos and her husband, Serpa China Logistics Assistant Nicola Vilardo. I had coached Renata in intercultural leadership but did not know their back-story yet. "When we were offered Shanghai, we had reservations about going to China. We heard strange things about it: like that people ate dogs there," they told me over coffee at their Shanghai high-rise home in 2022. But Renata and Nicola did not leave it at that. They investigated in their native Brazil for people who had a more nuanced familiarity with China. "In a few days, Nicola told me about his conversation with someone who had worked at Huawei, including in China. Apparently, he said, Shanghai is the new New York."

There are many reasons why China recently rose from obscurity among expat destinations to rivalling economic powerhouses like Switzerland or Japan, tropical havens like the Philippines, and even combinations of both, like Singapore. Some are simply different ways of pointing out that China is enormous. Size matters in business, and this nation casually rewrites the Guinness Book of World Records on a daily basis. Apart from size, population and historical firsts like iron working, navigation instruments, paper, gunpowder, and more, modern China is practically its own sole competitor in engineering wonders like skyscrapers, train lines, power generation, and big data processing. Since its global return, China has held up half the sky: it makes half the world's steel, coal, aluminum, and glass. It used more cement between 2011 and 2013 than the United States over the entire 20th century, and its unused steel capacity exceeds the total annual production of Japan, India, the United States, and Russia, combined.[30] It consumes half of the world's pork and antibiotics, economists report, and does half its online shopping. In recent years, China annually added the equivalent of Romania to its urban population,[31] and the gross domestic product of Australia to its own. It can toast its successes with 34 billion liters of locally brewed beer every year, easily the largest output in the world.[32]

Statistics like these should be consumed with care, but they do convince worldwide businesspeople that, as the McKinsey institute recently put it, the future is Asian.[33] For money-makers, there might not be a similar breakthrough until the coming colonization of extraterrestrial markets, and those will probably be more modest. For prospective expat executives, that represents much more than an abstract discussion on opportunities for the global economy. The pay, promotion, and reputation of managers are tied to growth figures, which in turn largely depend on the surrounding environment. "When we talk to China CEOs of the world's largest companies, they soon reveal a typical reason why they want to be in China: to be corporate heroes," Shaun Rein, consultant and author of three business books on China, told me in late 2019 at the Shanghai office of his brainchild, China Market Research. "Twenty

[30] L. Patey. 2021. *How China Loses* (Oxford: Oxford University Press), p 117.

[31] C. Textor. February 2022. "Urban and Rural Population of China From 2011 to 2021," U.S. Department of Agriculture Foreign Agricultural Service. https:// apps.fas.usda.gov/newgainapi/api/Report/DownloadReportByFileName?file Name=China%20Beer%20Market%20Overview_Beijing%20ATO_China%20 -%20People%27s%20Republic%20of_01-04-2022.

[32] E. Covert. January 4, 2022. "China Beer Market Overview," *Statista*. www .statista.com/statistics/278566/urban-and-rural-population-of-china/.

[33] McKinsey Insights. May 24, 2019. "Why the Future Is Asian," *McKinsey Insights*. www.mckinsey.com/featured-insights/asia-pacific/why-the-future-is-asian.

years ago, China represented less than one percent of revenues for most Fortune 500 companies. Now it is the biggest market in the world: it generates sixty percent of Qualcomm's sales, nearly half for Texas Instruments, it is KFC's largest market and second largest for Starbucks after the United States. It is a must-win country: if you don't engage China, you cannot engage the world."

A gold rush of such magnitude can present endless opportunities, but it does not suit all talents and temperaments equally. "If I can make it there, I'm gonna make it anywhere"—the conditional in Sinatra's lyrics is important. Finding one's bearings and getting down to work, creating functioning processes, teams, organizations, and support networks, competing and supporting others in such an environment requires commitment, focus, and perseverance that far exceed the comfort and competencies of managers in most home markets. As a coach who supports managers before and during expat assignments, I know many executives who launched spectacular global careers after their China tenures. But even more returned with an aching yearn for normalcy, and many who quit before the end of their assignment. "If I can make it there"—because most cannot. Nobody expressed that spirit more eloquently than Attila Hilbert, Human Resources Vice President for Greater China and North Asia at Danone, as we sipped tea in the global food giant's office nested between Shanghai's Pudong New Area and yet undeveloped fields below. "You should set sail for Shanghai with the same mentality as one left for New York at the turn of the century. You must have the same curiosity, open mind and above all, determination. Otherwise, there is no need for you here."

Send Your Best People

That sort of conditionality has always been an essential feature of China's approach to the outside world, including the period since its reforms in the 1990s. The state, which is the sole guardian of the nation's resources, has raised entry barriers for organizations and individuals alike. Seeing those barriers, most foreigners intuitively understood the country's proposition. In rankings of expat destinations, as later chapters reveal, China has measured up with top economies in terms of income and career development, but poorly in most other aspects of life. Combined with the size and complexity of its markets, its unique culture and politics, this has meant that expats had to brace for a tough but potentially lucrative and rewarding ride there. Big projects meant dramatic leaps in responsibility as soon as they arrived. Engineering supervisors who had previously led a handful of people were soon in charge of hundreds or thousands, with plans to double the workforce annually. Managers previously purchasing spare parts and the occasional replacement machine upped their games to multimillion-dollar greenfield investment projects. Some executives brokered land leases big enough to engulf their home cities.

For decades, each multinational firm that entered China had to break new ground in one way or another—introducing new products, testing previously unknown strategies, or breaking the ice for entire sectors. Volkswagen and Buick resuscitated China's automotive industry, AIA private insurance services, Japanese industrial conglomerates upgraded its electronics sector and invested in its budding information technology firms. IBM is the secret ingredient to China's computer manufacturing capacity, Apple (including its own secret ingredient Qualcomm) to its mobile phone development and production. Firms like Siemens, General Electric, Mitsubishi, and BorgWarner ushered it from Soviet-style power stations into an age of renewable energy. During the two decades since I arrived, KFC and McDonald's fast-food restaurants graduated from being curiosities with endless queues outside to daily necessities with menus tailored to Chinese regional tastes. Foreign managers in charge of them worked without precedents or best practices. Mainland China had been a fully state-run economy before, and over time, it became increasingly apparent that, despite predictions, its developmental trajectory would not replicate the examples of Japan and *Asian Tigers* such as South Korea or Singapore. Dragon Suits could not just be implementers—they had to be innovators.

"Send your best personnel to China," corporate manual *China CEO* suggested in 2011.[34] On the employer side of the equation, this forced multinational firms to choose very carefully before they placed the weight

[34] J.A. Fernandez and L. Underwood. 2011. *China CEO: Voices of Experience From 20 International Business Leaders* (New York, NY: John Wiley & Sons), p. 6.

of their China businesses on a specific candidate's shoulders. Without precedents even vaguely resembling the size, complexity, and importance of China, there were no traditional ways of telling someone's readiness for the challenge, including performance at previous overseas assignments. On the side of the candidates, however, it created the perception that an appointment to a China office was a stamp of approval in itself, a sign that appointees were destined for greater things. General Electric CEO Jack Welch declared in no uncertain terms why people with untamed ambition should head East. "The Jack Welch of the future cannot be like me," he told the Harvard Business Review in 1999, nearing his retirement. "I've spent my entire career in the United States. The next head of GE will be somebody who has spent time in Bombay, in Hong Kong, in Buenos Aires."[35] With that remark, he joined a winding narrative of leaders who believed that the answers and opportunities their firms needed lay somewhere beyond the Eastern horizon.

Ages and Voyages

Faraway Islands of Foreignness

"Traveling is necessary, surviving is secondary"—the do-or-die spirit of this Latin quote (Navigare necesse est, vivere non est necesse) from ancient Roman Consul and conqueror Pompeius Magnus inspired generations of Western explorers. Their longing for the unknown triggered early versions of globalization, but the stakes were high. From antiquity through the era of the great discoveries, nearly half of those who embarked on intercontinental journeys perished on the way. Out of those who safely arrived, another half never made it back alive. Even a century ago, Westerners in the Orient kept falling victim to violent encounters, tropical illnesses, and mysterious afflictions that their dumbfounded doctors recorded as *melancholy* and *homesickness*. Some embarked for conquer, some for commerce, but whatever their dreams were, until recently, they set sail against

---

[35] J.S. Black and H. Gregersen. MarchApril 1999. "The Right Way to Manage Expats," *Harvard Business Review*. https://hbr.org/1999/03/the-right-way-to-manage-expats.

horrifyingly unpredictable odds. If you wonder whether it was worth it for anyone else than the lucky survivors themselves, look around right now and spot things that zigzagged between multiple continents before they reached you through an unprecedented network of multinational corporations and cooperation: your mobile phone, furniture, clothes, or a bag of chips.

Centuries before Pompeius Magnus but well known to him, those who aimed for grand adventures at faraway lands consulted the Greek priestess we know today as the Delphi Oracle, whose cryptic motto was: "know thyself" (gnothi seauton). Beyond a careful examination of one's physical preparedness for journeys that were arduous and dangerous, the advice was essential because not everyone was emotionally prepared to part from familiar places and people. Until the invention of steam engines that could propel vehicles in defiance of mountain ranges, storms, and currents, expatriate existence inevitably meant years of separation from one's homeland. Few people traveled far and many perished, so expat communities were small. We might see their stories as adventures today, but thrills were not what those settlers wanted. Most were spurred by either fear or greed, running from war, the law or obsessed with getting rich fast. For the same reason, cultural integration was not among their priorities. From ancient Greek colonies through Ming dynasty Chinese settlements to 19th-century Western colonizers, arrivals tried to replicate their home architecture, cuisine, routines, and traditions. When they started building, fences and walls came first.

Westerners in China continued the tradition of fusing global expansionism with local isolationism. On the one hand, foreign settlements in 19th- and 20th-century China were incubators of modernization from which international and local entrepreneurs launched the first railways, postal, and customs services, lighthouses, telegraphs, electric grid, and much more. On the other hand, the installations were often meant to serve the residents of foreign enclaves themselves, with little regard to the well-being of the wider population. As recently as the 1930s, American journalist Edgar Snow, who would soon jump to world fame for interviewing a then obscure guerrilla leader named Mao Zedong in his Hunan hideout, ridiculed expatriate separatism. "As in other Chinese cities, the foreigners in Shanghai developed an insular culture, their own little never-never land of whisky-and-soda, polo, tennis, and gossip, happily quite unaware of the pulse of humanity outside the great city's silent, insulating walls."[36] Like him, many of today's expats criticize fellow foreigners for their bubbled-up existence, unaware that they are part of the same ecosystem, and how much they owe to it.

In fact, it would be hard to imagine China's foreigners without their bubbles. The fact that today's expats have transportation and communication technology at their fingertips should not cloud our judgment. Jet flights and videocalls do not change the fact that new arrivals have traded their families, home communities, and familiar ways of life for opportunities in China. Like companies, individuals have little collective experience to rely on during their preparations. In families from most advanced economies, finding someone who lived in China is no easy feat. Designated cities do a splendid job providing foreigners with a convenient cultural buffer to conduct daily life and business as they would at home. Enclaves also allow enterprising locals a chance to encounter relative cosmopolitanism, and for others, including state officials, the security of keeping foreigners at bay. But while islands of cosmopolitanism can absorb the shock of plunging into modern China's risk-ridden enormity and dynamism, they cannot mitigate it altogether. Today, just like in the old Delphi days, adventurers are advised to learn a bit about themselves before they set sail.

"There is no such thing as being unfit for a specific place like China, but someone can be unfit for expat life" Bronwyn Bowery-Ireland, CEO of the Lissom Group and one of Asia's most experienced executive coaches, told me in a Hong Kong café in summer 2019. She echoed the managers, recruiters, consultants, coaches, and relocation specialists who raise a cautionary hand to clients who just cannot wait to leap into the unknown. "You must start with some soul-searching before you embark on an expat mission. Are you open-minded enough? Are you flexible? Are you ready for adventure as well as some tough lessons about yourself?' Living abroad causes a disruption in self-management." The simple message wrapped in coaching lingo is that challenge, confusion, and

[36] K. Peraino. 2017. *A Force So Swift: Mao, Truman, and the Birth of Modern China, 1949* (New York, NY: Crown Publishing Group), p. 134.

self-doubt are not possible side effects of taking an expat job or accompanying an expat in a culturally challenging place; they are inevitable parts of the experience. Simply put, the first working day at a China branch is the beginning of an arduous journey, not its end.

Why Not Go to China?

A close, critical look in the mirror before accepting a job in China is necessary because frankly, there are just as many reasons to stay away. That is true about any possible destination, but as usual, China is different: scales are bigger, differences more dramatic, and reliable information scarcer. "From people who worked there before, I heard a lot of bad things, mainly about the pollution, the crowds, and the chaos," Renata Santos admitted. "I was even offered a paid visit to Shanghai, but I said no. I was afraid that if the country was as bad as I heard, I would refuse my first overseas appointment. I was terrified, but I wanted to take the career step." Attila Hilbert recalled a similar struggle. "In 2003, I actually named Russia and China as the places where I refused to relocate. At that time, Tiananmen Square and the one-child policy dominated the news about China. As I saw it, I did not want to live in a society that had so little respect for human life. But by the time I was offered my Shanghai post in 2015, people with experience in the country had helped me understand the wider context. In a society that still struggled with poverty and disorder, could I imagine a better way to run things? Or perhaps were my Western liberal values completely out of place there? That made me do some serious thinking."

Managers in charge of appointing expats are seldom aware how the chain reactions that start with individual appointments eventually determine the fate of the people, firms, and places involved. There is much talk of global villages, but serial expats are the ones who really live in them, and they are a competitive lot. Candidates compete for positions, projects, and budgets across continents. Companies compete for candidates, and countries compete for the investment of those companies. Like villagers anywhere, they gossip too, but their rumors spread faster, wider, and create more upheaval than usual town-square chatter. Stories of triumphs and fiascos reach worldwide offices almost instantly, adding to the folklore of a community where most newcomers replace someone they know at least from reputation. These stories build and destroy the reputation of expat destinations. News of juicy promotions, luxurious resorts, fulfilled families, and skyrocketing careers turn cities or countries into corporate bonanzas where human resource managers can pick the best talent available. Rumors of botched relocations, annoying regulations, bumpy roads, and endless overtime turn them into pariah places for candidates who missed boats for better shores and want extra cash as consolation.

Expats must pick jobs carefully. "Multinational firms are extremely political organizations, and that can keep ambitious managers from taking jobs abroad," Tony Shi, Asia-Pacific Executive Vice President at German automotive firm Benteler, told me in late 2018. As his leadership coach for two years, I could witness Tony as an ideal mentor with characteristic Chinese agility: he thinks, speaks, and acts at intimidating speeds unless he slow-motions himself into a fitting pace while instructing his team or interacting with European colleagues. "Foreigners coming to China must place their ambitions in the context of their long-term career plans. Many are rightly afraid that while they are abroad, someone will take their positions at home, and they will return to nothing." In other words, the big job, big life, and big money in China may come at the cost of status battles afterward. Returning expats and headquarters can both see the situation as unfair. "People at the home office find it difficult to imagine that returning expats need help readjusting after just a few years away," the *Harvard Business Review* wrote in 1999. "They don't see why people who've been given an extended period to explore the Left Bank or the Forbidden City should get a hero's welcome."[37]

Beyond a constructive career path, there is a lot more to consider. As interviewees will admit in later pages, candidates must weigh separation from family (sometimes closer, sometimes wider) against the financial future that a promising appointment can provide. They contrast their fear of the unknown and possible lifestyle disruption with cultural curiosity

---

[37] J.S. Black and H. Gregersen. MarchApril 1999. "The Right Way to Manage Expats," *Harvard Business Review*. https://hbr.org/1999/03/the-right-way-to-manage-expats.

and the experience to be gained. Destinations differ wildly, further complicating decisions. Appointments invariably come with disappointments, because locations never fulfill all expectations. One has a bad climate, but the people are lovely, and the money is good. Another sets a gutting pace but offers wonderful beaches nearby, and the money is good. A third has a judgmental population but amazing culture and nightlife, and the money is good. Yes, expats follow the money: research shows that at major Western firms, expats can earn up to double the income of home-based managers.[38] The result is a remarkable dynamic between places, jobs, and the people with sufficient talent, knowledge, and experience. Farther destinations imply harder challenges and higher expectations but also bigger compensation packages. Consequently, assignment to a distant and problematic business location guarantees an upward step not only in income but also recognition and prestige.

China offers the same mixed bag as expat packages in almost any country. Even long-term darlings of the global executive community rank unfavorably against some criteria. The 2021 HSBC survey gave Switzerland poor rankings in personal fulfillment, Singapore in work–life balance, New Zealand and Spain in career progression. Mainland China's 2021 HSBC rankings, the last before its disruptive *zero-COVID* policies, revealed problems with settling in (37th place in 2021), quality of life (37th), physical and mental well-being (35th), and work–life balance (35th). On the other hand, the country featured among the global top 10 in terms of fulfillment (7th), and reaching one's potential (5th), and nearly there in terms of career progression (11th).[39] Depending on personal preferences and priorities, that can be a promising or terrifying proposition. In the end, choosing between expat locations is like picking a profession or a life partner: it has as much to do with rational choices as it does with fickle human chemistry. But speaking of chemistry and

---

[38] A. Scofield. n.d. "New Research Shows Expats Earning Up To 900% More Than Local Employees," *Expat Focus*. www.expatfocus.com/employment/new-research-shows-expats-earning-up-to-900-more-than-local-employees-3159 (accessed July 12, 2022).

[39] HSBC. October 2021. "Expat Explorer Survey 2021," *HSBC*.www.expat .hsbc.com/expat-explorer/.

connections, polls highlight two persistent issues that have long repelled international talent from China: air pollution and Internet censorship.

Health is a priority for expats not only for their own and their family's sake but also as managers in charge of their workforce's safety, insurance, health care, and other costly commodities. As for connectivity, Chapter 2 will reveal how China's restricted Internet complicates personal and professional tasks, and even access to information on the country when candidates consider postings there. Many key factors defining expat life in the country have gone through ebbs, flows, and complete reversals in the past two decades: growth and opportunities in specific sectors, the cost and quality of living in different locations, and even China's official attitude toward the countries that often serve both as trading partners and sources of expats. But as Chapter 2 reveals, unhealthy air and restricted Internet have been constant annoyances to foreigners, only overtaken by COVID-19-related travel restrictions in recent years. However, the two issues followed different trends. Air quality, while still below the standards of advanced economies, has been improving. Internet restrictions, on the other hand, became more stringent, depriving foreigners of a few more digital lifelines to the outside world with each passing year.

How these annoyances affect individual expats depends on their expectations for work and life in a new location. Any advice must be taken with caution: one person's paradise may be hell for another. "Back in the US, I talked to someone who, after her first week in China, was just counting down until she could return to North America," said Briana, a senior human resources leader I coached during her first year in Shanghai at a global pharmaceutical firm. Admittedly, her colleague's rant had shaken her confidence in relocating. "As it turns out, she had a terrible misalignment between her desire to find a life partner and start a family, and local expats who were mostly either men who hung out in bars, or families where she did not fit in. That kept her from investing herself in China and make use of the opportunities there. I had to think hard whether her situation was relevant to my own." It could happen just as easily that an expat arrives in China in pursuit of someone's enthusiastic praises, and eventually hates every moment there. Matching people with places is essential. But short of mischievously throwing people in at the deep end and watching them sink or swim, how can employers predict the compatibility of individual expats with China's reality?

How Expats End Up in China

The way multinational corporations create, offer, and manage overseas positions says volumes about the conflicted human attitude toward faraway lands and cultures. Distance fascinates and frightens people at the same time. Travelers were traditionally of the naturally restless sort, lured by the siren song of adventure. The global supply chains of modernity have solved many problems and created many more. Today, international firms offer distant postings as promotion, and workers who crave for advancement accept them, each side trusting the other's insight and intentions. But many candidates are as unadventurous as can be, and multinational firms ship around couch potatoes as eagerly as their namesake vegetables. Reluctant accidental adventurers consider expat jobs a form of reward, but they also expect additional safety measures and compensation in exchange for their troubles. Technology takes care of the logistical aspect of transition: within a single day, new expats can reach the firm's most distant branch, type in their password, and get to work. But places are different, environments affect performance, change is hard, and not everyone weathers culture shock well.

Few people at Western headquarters have the linguistic, cultural, or political skills required in the PRC. Assigning new managers often resembles mutual trust falls where both candidates and decision makers hope the other would be there to catch them. Firms assign people with the most expertise and derring-do to take the job. Appointees take charge of local operations whose size can range from a few dozen to thousands of people, then hold on to their hats in China's wild winds of commercial, political, and social exposure. There is no roadmap for a shifting terrain and, once the firm has committed to a China entry, mostly no return. The candidates themselves are often unsure how they earned the privilege. "I first visited China in 2006," Henrik König recalled his arrival as a senior manager at ThyssenKrupp System Engineering. Before our 2019 interview, I had coached Henrik for two years as the incoming China CEO. "China was becoming the automotive center of the world, but in our firm's thirtieth-floor panoramic office in Shanghai, there were only ten people doing very little. I was part of a public relations delegation of sorts. I toured the country for two weeks and had an amazing time, but when my bosses back home asked me about the prospects of our China business, I said: 'It will never work'. That got me my first offer."

Without reliable standards to differentiate between great expat material and otherwise talented people with poor overseas potential, even relatively careful companies rely on willingness rather than ability. "Many companies send people abroad to reward them, to get them out of the way, or to fill an immediate business need," the above-quoted Harvard article continues. "Companies that manage expats wisely do not assume that people who have succeeded at home will repeat that success abroad. They assign international posts to individuals who not only have the necessary technical skills but also have indicated that they would be likely to live comfortably in different cultures."[40] Some expat careers with accidental beginnings triumphed later. "I ended up in China by coincidence," Markus Baumgartner, then General Manager for Miba Holding told me in 2019. "At a dinner after training program, someone asked me if I were interested in working for a China-based joint venture. It sounded like a great opportunity, and I agreed. Maybe I wasn't entirely sober."

Like Henrik König, Markus visited major customer sites in various cities, in his case Luoyang and Lijiang, before he took the job. His initial bravery proved justified: Markus spent nearly a decade in China before he became Miba's U.S.-based Head of Global Business Services. But happy endings are interesting exactly because they are uncertain, and whether someone intuitively feels ready for the task is a poor predictor of success. The findings of the Harvard article's authors are in line with my own interviews: far from everyone succeeds in riding China's perilous waves of growth and dynamism. Specific numbers at individual multinationals are closely guarded secrets of the firms, their executive search, and relocation service providers, but according to worldwide mobility provider Mercer's 2020 global survey, anywhere between 5 and 40 percent of international assignments fail each year due to poor adjustment to the new environment.[41] While other estimates are lower, even optimistic survey results

---

[40] J.S. Black and H. Gregersen. MarchApril 1999. "The Right Way to Manage Expats," *Harvard Business Review*. https://hbr.org/1999/03/the-right-way-to-manage-expats.

[41] P. Andrews. 2020. "Pre-assignment Health Screening –Avoiding Failed Assignments," *Mercer*. https://mobilityexchange.mercer.com/insights/article/pre-assignment-health-screening-avoiding-failed-assignments.

claim that one in 10 expats end their terms prematurely. It is a gamble, and companies go all-in with alarming frequency.

It appears that past track records and willingness to take on the China challenge are terrible justifications to appoint expats there. But are there any better ones? Successful individual placements, teams, and even entire China operations at certain firms suggest that there are. Moreover, the best practices that this book describes are widely available, have been used for over half a century, and do not demand unaffordable amounts of time, money, manpower, or other resources. Why, then, do global firms still send their expatriates on choppy overseas rides with unpredictable outcomes, perpetuating worrisome failure statistics? As it is often the case in human resource management practices, the reason is a systemic lack of balance between two equally tempting extremes: micromanaging talented people in some circumstances, and neglecting them in others. On the one hand, corporate managers who appoint expats routinely assume that, like modular buildings, machinery, and software, people can be shipped over, installed, and put to work without much fuss. On the other hand, the same decision makers dismiss the local cultural environment as something mysterious and impossible to quantify.

Both assumptions contradict management theory and practice, but that is almost beside the point. Most decision makers are secretly aware that matching the individual temperaments and talents of candidates with local circumstances dramatically reduces the risk of erroneous placements. But over two decades of intercultural leadership consulting also made me familiar with a wide range of excuses why companies refuse to use advanced tools to select, appoint, and promote expat managers. Chief among them are fears that new methods will complicate things and reduce available talent pools. Companies that spend millions on relocation, accommodation, equipment, insurance, education, and other services for expat families hesitate to assess the intercultural compatibility of the same people for the price of a decent dress shirt. That is a poor decision: a single manager with a strong personal mismatch to China's reality can result in massive loss of time, attention, reputation, and what really counts in business, money. Yes, personalized decisions can be more complicated in the short run. But smart human resource managers learn to appreciate the impact of their work on human lives, and seldom regret the time and money spent on carefully considered decisions.

According to old seafarer's wisdom, dolphins do not always carry struggling sailors toward the shore, but those who are hauled the opposite way to open seas never live to tell their stories. In a similar vein, the interviews that inspired this book reflect the experiences of Dragon Suits who remained, survived, and thrived in China, both professionally and personally. For them, as well as for the hundreds of coaching clients and thousands of workshop participants I have met since my arrival in 2002, the fulfillment of time spent in this awe-inspiring country clearly outweighs the frustrations. Another thing I learned from five years of interviews was that for people with the right fit, working in China was fun! Recollections of surprises large and small, joyous and ugly, from their children's initial adjustment to administrative wars with authorities, were accompanied by the eloquent chuckles, gasps, guffaws, and face-palms that print sadly cannot reflect. As we shall see in the following chapters, China's scale and challenges, combined with its optimism and dynamism, seem to bring out the best in open-minded people who are ready to push themselves to the next level.

CHAPTER 2

Settling In

First Impressions

"What did I expect?" Richard Eardley, Asia Managing Director for global recruitment firm Hays, echoed my question as we started the interview in the summer of 2019. Expat journeys begin long before the screeching tires of a newly appointed manager's flight touch down in a Chinese city. That watershed moment follows weeks or months of anticipation and preparation. Job descriptions are drafted, salary packages negotiated, kids pulled from schools, flights purchased, belongings boxed up, and shipped out in containers. Before relocation arrangements can even begin, candidates must face, digest, and accept the often-unexpected opportunity to work in China. Executives at my leadership workshops and coaching sessions often recalled hearing the news of such a possibility as the true beginning of their China story. Eventually, I made it a habit to start all my interviews by asking about that crucial moment, including the one with Richard. "What did I expect," he savored the sentence once more before he made up his mind. "I have no idea."

The admission might sound strange from the senior executive of a global firm that finds and moves thousands of talented people across continents each year. But cluelessness about China seems to be the rule rather than the exception at multinational headquarters. In advanced economies, one after another postwar generation lived their lives oblivious of the existence of People's Republic even as they purchased products from Japan, Korea, Taiwan, and even the carved-out territories of Hong Kong and Macau. Despite China's surging importance lately, many expats I met confessed that working there had hardly occurred to them before. Like many others, Renata Santos had another country in mind when she received the momentous offer. "My boss said, 'I know that you dream of an international assignment, and we might have just the right thing for you.' I was sure I would be offered Canada. When I heard China, I stiffened. I was completely terrified." Such shock is understandable in the light of widespread stereotypes about China: Mao-suited cyclers, red-bannered rallies, pollution, and dog soup. Those who dismiss such cartoonish generalizations are either left with equally meaningless clichés of the Great Wall, skyscrapers, and the Long March space mission or—nothing.

"China was a blank slate to me," Henrik König recalled. "Before that trip, I had never done business there or even met Chinese people." Thanks to the tour that ThyssenKrupp arranged, he eventually arrived better informed than most newly appointed managers. Chris, a European luxury fashion brand's Chief Financial Officer for Asia, told me in 2019 how it should not be done. "We have incoming expats whose only China experience was a Cantonese restaurant in Milan." That was probably an exaggeration. They had probably watched a documentary on ghost towns in Inner Mongolia, read a Forbes article on Chinese billionaires, and uttered a multilingual *no* to the tourist who asked if the parking meter accepted WeChat Pay. International firms find it nearly impossible to hire professionals with an elementary understanding of China's current reality. As opposed to Mexico, Japan, or even Russia, the People's Republic has been a blank area in the world's mental map for too long. Like Richard, most incoming managers simply do not know what to think. What is even more amusing is how this cluelessness may follow expats well beyond the first weeks of their assignment.

For two decades, I started leadership workshops, university lectures, and keynote speeches with an icebreaker I called *China in One Word* in homage to Yu Hua's brilliant book *China in Ten Words*. I ask the visiting business, government, or academic delegations to compress their first impressions about the country into a single word. Initial remarks usually express approval and admiration. *Dynamic. Growing. Futuristic. Booming. Amazing.* It would be hard to argue with that in a meeting room 30 floors above a multimillion metropolis or surrounded by a hipster-style shared space. Modern China is like a three-dimensional exaggeration, whether you count the number of construction cranes, the mileage of railroads under construction, or the amount of money poured into artificial intelligence research. Visitors are advised to take their usual concepts of employee numbers, project budgets, and so forth, and multiply them by 10. Increasingly, it is not only the biggest but also the first. It was first to bridge a sea island, create a national virtual currency and crack quantum encryption for satellites. Local mobile phone apps that receive, pay, transfer, and invest money with a few clicks are digital windows into the future.

Fans always speak first. Sceptics slowly struggle through bottlenecks of self-censorship. *Interesting* is a frequent turning point: its disingenuity signals that the hard stuff is ready to pour forth. *Confusing. Crowded. Stressful. Polluted. Brainwashed. Inhuman.* They have a point too. International media teems with eye-catching news of environmental degradation, Orwellian state surveillance, confusion, corruption, and coercion in China. In supermarkets and comedy shows, it stands for cheap knockoffs and the exploited laborers who produce them. While in the country, my audience typically follows a ruthless pace of visits and meetings with little heed to their jetlag, touristic curiosity, or biological needs. Dodging motorcycle couriers on pedestrian pavements, rubbing shoulders (and other body parts) on public transport, they often realize there is something odd about local people. Something uncomfortable to contemplate and hard to discuss, raising the disturbing suspicion of being a closet racist. I love *China in One Word* for the way its internal struggles reveal as much about the players as about the place. I watch each character unfold and guess their China-compatibility. Who among them is ready for more?

The question is relevant because occasional business visits can turn into longer-term assignments. First impressions reveal a candidate's ability to willingly take the China challenge and turn it into results. Foreigners with successful records in the country often recall how early insights guided them in solving problems later. Unfortunately, those insights also depend on when, how, and under what circumstances someone arrives in the country. And those circumstances can vary wildly indeed. Some expatriates I interviewed for this book were chauffeured from airports across top-tier cities to five-star compounds past saluting security guards. Others arrived in half-furnished factory lodgings closer in comfort to Beirut than Beijing. Some were on their first overseas assignment, others brought decades of experience from worldwide locations. Whichever way they saw it first, they judged China accordingly. As humans perceive new impulses through the filter of previous ones, mundane airport rides turned flashing images across car windows and the accompanying sounds, smells, smiles, frowns, sweaty crowds, or air-conditioned limousines into persistent judgment about what China was all about.

Relocation specialists take heed. Whenever I discuss the topic with those who send managers to China, I mention a few ways to make or break a newcomer's first few weeks. A simple airport pickup can determine if someone lands into utter disaster or endless enchantment. "The company sent us a driver to the airport," Renata told me. "I asked him in English what his name was. Instead of answering me, he called someone and started yelling into the phone. In minutes, I got a call from the HR lady, who said, 'What did you say to this guy?' I said nothing, I just asked his name. 'No, don't talk to him, he is really nervous around foreigners,' she snapped at me. The driver started a similar quarrel with the doorman at the hotel. I thought about my visa interview the next day. Was I going to get the same treatment there?" Contrast that with Briana's experience. "By the time I arrived, our relocation agency had set up my banking, Alipay and WeChat Pay accounts and arranged an apartment. I had no stress from the work side either. My local manager checked whether I had landed okay and got settled in. 'Tell me when you're ready to start working,' his welcome text read. It was a strange feeling because I was paid without doing much for a while. But I realised that this was not just about work: it was about a complete life experience."

However amazing a job relocation specialists do, factors like the climate are beyond their control. Most foreigner-friendly cities lie in subtropical zones, and even northern Beijing and Dalian have foully hot summers. Nevertheless, mainly to align with school schedules, too many expats land in China during the hottest months. Adding heat shock to the already overwhelming culture shock, jet lag, and generally stressful experience of relocation causes unnecessary suffering to all but a few reptile-blooded individuals. If you think this is a problem reserved for spoiled European and North American expats, think again. "Because of the heat, we hated the entire first six months," Renata and Nicola recalled with visible shivers. "We thought, since we were from Brazil, a bit of heat could not scare us. But at home, the air cools in the evening. Shanghai suddenly surrounded us with a kind a feverish sensation from which there was no escape." Foreigners who have made returns in different seasons can testify how easily such misery can be avoided. Architect Kristina Kinder described in her expat memoire how she plotted a more enjoyable second arrival in China than her first. "But this time, I decided that I won't hate it. This time it will be different. It's April. Shanghai is warm, sunny and friendly, but not too hot yet."[1]

Will ship-shape containers, seamless flights at temperate seasons, pleasant rides, flats, and offices guarantee that new arrivals are thoroughly prepared for starting anew in China? Based on the thousands of personal stories I heard, not at all. Regardless of the time, place, smoothness, or absurdity of their arrival, most expats agreed that preparing newbies for the magnitude, speed, and oddity of China is a fool's errand. Like its iconic symbol, the Great Wall, the country will make new arrivals gaze in speechless awe even after seeing it in books, documentaries, and hearing personal accounts. While times, circumstances, and people change with every single visit, certain features of arriving in China seem to persist across the centuries. Since early Western visitors like Marco Polo, countless foreigners experienced the daunting realization that somehow, this place intended to invite, impress, and intimidate outsiders at the same time. Today as when the Polos arrived, the country's engineering wonders play a crucial role in perpetuating that impression.

Seasoned expats recall their goose-bumpy airport rides past multilevel intersections and futuristic cityscapes. Henrik König of ThyssenKrupp boyishly pressed his nose to the car window at the sight of 2006 Shanghai. "The chauffeur picked me up at the terminal and sped me down perfectly built eight-lane highways. Everything was impeccable, even the hedges that separated traffic directions. I saw more luxury cars during that ride than at home in a year. It was incomparable to anything in Germany." As he approached the center, Henrik gradually noticed tricycles overloaded with construction material, scrap metal, and wastepaper, as rare in his homeland as the honking supercars behind them. Many expats describe the surreal sight of avenues, streets, and alleys teeming with strange scenes, as if people had been choreographed to act excessively Chinese. "On my first evening, I took a walk near my apartment," an

---

[1] K. Kinder. 2015. *Wonderlanded: Life as an Expat in China* (Amazon LLC), p. 3.

Italian executive I coached recalled his arrival in Chongqing city. "In a park between thirty-floor residential towers, among trees lit by colourful spotlights, hundreds of old people ballroom danced to melodies blasting from a portable amplifier. The whole area was swirling and reverberating. I felt like I was drugged."

He was not, but the city was on steroids. In the 1990s, one of the government's many mammoth projects had been the urbanization of a predominantly agrarian society. Its vision to increase the proportion of people registered as urban dwellers from around 30 percent to over half of the population by 2020 was realized ahead of schedule, and the process continues. But this neck-breaking rush for the cities disrupted normal life for tens of millions of people. Ancient villages were scattered into the wind, demolishing places of service, privacy, community, worship, and identity. Multigeneration family homes were commanded into sterile concrete apartment blocks. The population of Chongqing alone doubled from 10 to over 20 million within a few years. The highly photographic urban rituals witnessed by incredulous foreigners are attempts to recreate uprooted routines. Immigrants in their own cities, farmers, and laborers turn empty plots into vegetable gardens and marketplaces. Masters teach martial arts and ballroom dancing in parks and parking lots. Fortune tellers, acupressurists, barbers, and ear-cleaners serve their clients on pavements, under bridges, or wherever they can.

Detours Into Chinese Reality

Generations of expats have recalled taking the wrong turn into a time traveler's alley where a single block away from glitzy office towers, school-children scribbled homework at peeling desks, seemingly undisturbed by the nearby fishmongers, open-air barbers, and cheered-on card games. Such detours are reminders of the price Chinese people pay for their nation's economic long march but also of their determination to carry on toward a better future. One statistic quoted ad nauseam is that China lifted over 750 million people out of poverty in recent decades.[2] That,

---

[2] M. Rajagopalan. May 2016. "China to Relocate 2 Million People This Year in Struggle to Banish Poverty," *Reuters*. www.reuters.com/article/us-china-poverty-idUSKCN0Y10LF.

however, also implies that at the beginning of the reform period, half a century into the Communist Party's rule, three-quarters of the nation's near-billion inhabitants were poor. Suddenly relieved by the permission to ditch the Maoist ideal of equality in poverty, a traditionally enterprising population applied a combustive cocktail of state socialism and market capitalism to pick up the pace of modern times. They did, but speed is a costly and wasteful commodity. The Communist Party's once cherished goals of social equality, common prosperity, or at least the lack of resented elites soon fell victim to economic revival. Three decades of reform raised inequality from the level of the United Kingdom in 1990 to that of India, one of the highest in the world, by 2010.[3]

The streets that newly arrived foreigners walk during their first weeks in China are part of a gargantuan social experiment with uncertain outcomes, where locals and foreigners are equally at odds with ever-changing routines and realities. People, families, businesses, and communities concoct daily practices from ancient traditions, the legacy of semicolonial exposure at treaty ports, the revolutionary rituals imposed by the Communist Party, and recent ideals of middle-class prosperity. Most cities designated for Special Economic Zones (SEZs) have rich histories as foreign enclaves and deliberately follow routines imported from Europe, the United States, Japan, Russia, and beyond. The exotic rituals that result from this fusion create a pleasurable backdrop to a foreigner's initial experience in China. "If you walk around in the morning, before the shops and malls and restaurants open, you can see how all the employees line up in front of their shop," Kristina Kinder wrote. "They wear uniforms and get shouted at. In a chorus they shout back and then do gymnastics together. For me it is rather bizarre to see how obedient employees here are. I can't imagine doing this myself."

The good, the bad, the amazing, and the frightening in the *China in One Word* game are reflections of Beijing's determination to manually balance an enormous national boat's shifting cargo and agitated people as officials redraft and repopulate entire cities. Most prospective expats

---

[3] S. Zhou. January 2021. "Will China Fall Into the 'Middle Income Trap'?," *Contemporary China Studies*. https://link.springer.com/chapter/10.1007/978-981-15-6540-3_3#DOI.

have a general awareness that China is a challenging destination due to its ancient culture, long isolation, and recent upheaval. While that is true, they soon find out that they, like generations of foreigners before them, are spared most of the strife and randomness that characterize life for the local population. Being an expatriate with a large company is an unusually smooth way to experience an otherwise mystifying travel destination like China. Nobody expects incoming foreign employees to be able to speak Chinese, find their hosting city on the map, or know how banks work. They are high-maintenance but potentially lucrative corporate human resources (HR). Airport pickups, preassigned accommodation, shipped-in belongings, welcome committees of local colleagues, agents, and housekeepers are ways to ensure a smooth ride to the expat's first day in office. If all goes well, managers promptly get to work, kids go to school, and picture frames find their places on shelves. The faster that happens, the better the return on the firm's investment.

Smooth collaboration between the Chinese authorities of SEZs and the multinational investors who populate them enable expats to spend weeks, months, or even entire multiyear assignments protected from surrounding complexities. At times, the subjective expat perspective can be adorably simplistic. When the China Flexpat Podcast asked a German Operations Manager about the complexities of changing jobs in China, he said it was very simple. "You just give your passport to the Human Resources Manager and take a few photos."[4] Local colleagues who conjure such miracles stay hidden from many expats, who only realize the value of their protected existence when they venture outside. When they first arrived, the accommodation and office for Renata and Nicola were both in the Intercontinental Building. Their lived and worked within that sheltered space until they decided to explore the city. "One day we entered a restaurant and I asked for a small salad," Renata recalled. "The waiter said they only had large salads. We questioned how that was possible, but ordered one anyway. Later, they came back and told us they didn't have one of the ingredients. Okay, give us chicken wings then. In forty

[4] S. Thaerigen. n.d. "Podcast #81 First China Job—Better Job—Own Business," *China Flexpat* (Podcast). https://podcasts.apple.com/hk/podcast/china-flexpat/id1514659021?l=en&i=1000550923269 (accessed July 12, 2022).

minutes, they served the salad *and* the chicken wings. I started crying: I couldn't even order my food in an international restaurant!"

The main attraction of China for foreigners is the prospect of a great career, and most expats know where their priorities lie. They may photograph army-style hairdresser drills, try their basic Mandarin skills with souvenir vendors and fishmongers, take daytrips, and tell their stories to incredulous families on Skype, but mostly they remain within confined foreigner-friendly spaces. They prepare toast and cereals over international cable news just in time for the children's school bus and the company chauffeur. They pick up Starbucks before their first meeting, which typically happens in English. Spouses shop for familiar brands and take yoga classes with English-speaking trainers and patrons. Somewhere beyond the well-lit offices, schools, cafés, and gyms lie the mystifying alleyways of a *real China* often mentioned by long-serving expats. But foreigners were never supposed to live there. For centuries, the Middle Kingdom preferred visitors rather than residents however long they stayed, and offered them guided tours through manicured showcases rather than full immersion. To understand the status and role of expats in today's China, we must briefly revisit the country's traditional relations with emissaries of the outside world.

Expat Islands in the *Real China*

Shortly after my 2002 arrival in China, a charmingly fragile old lady approached me beneath a Shanghai supermarket's towering stacks of instant noodles and dried shrimp. *"Zdravstvujtye, menya zavut Masha"* (Hello, my name is Masha), she greeted me in cheerful Russian, a language I owed to my schooling under the late Hungarian Socialist Workers Party. We managed a brief chat, but after a few pleasantries, she walked away. Apparently, I paled in comparison with the handsome foreigner whose image I conjured up in her memory. Had she been half a century younger, Masha would have used English and called herself Mandy. Everything had changed around her in a few short decades, and she was not alone with her nostalgia. To early 2000s arrivals like myself, China appeared to have started anew less than a decade ago, seemingly from zero. By the time I met Masha, the ice-breaking expat generation of the 1990s already resented the disappearance of the cheerfully grease-smudged, beautifully vapor-clad noodle-soup kitchens more akin to American Chinatowns than today's Beijing or Shanghai. Some had moved to more authentic pastures in South-East Asia. New arrivals had moved into their jobs and homes, bringing their own hopes, fears, plans, and prejudices.

The foreigners who had returned to the Soviet Union, Eastern Europe, Cuba, and other fellow Leninist states before the sudden wave of globalization perpetuated a pattern as old as the Middle Kingdom itself. The land we now know as China was never the hermit kingdom of Western imagination. It had maintained millennia of extensive trade and diplomacy with northern nomads, empires beyond the Himalayas, realms along the trade routes we now call the Silk Road, and peoples accessible by sea from Malaya to Madagascar. But perhaps to avoid overexposure, successive ruling dynasties habitually tightened alliances in one direction while maintaining defensive caution in the other. As if following invisible north-south traffic lights, the early Qin and Han dynasties, known to the West mainly for the terracotta army in Xi'An, were preoccupied with northern neighbors. The Tang and Song dynasties a millennium ago represented China's technological and cultural apex, but their empires were gradually pushed southward by increasingly uncontrollable northern nomads. We should forgive 13th-century Venetian merchant Marco Polo for thinking Cathay was an undiscovered kingdom. The Song capital had just been raised to the ground as the Great Kublai Khan integrated former Chinese territories into his Mongolian empire.

The West forgot and rediscovered China in recurring cycles. Two hundred years after the Polos, 15th-century admiral Zheng He reached the Red Sea as the ambassador of a lost continent. His stranded settlers blended into local tribes after a Ming emperor banned seafaring. Sixteenth-century European Jesuits followed the abandoned sea routes to baptize the Ming ruler and turn China into God's model kingdom. The Mandarins, the court's Confucian elite, welcomed crash-courses in astronomy, clockworks, and cannon smelting but dismissed the Gospels. "If practical Western learning and technology were originally meant to be the spoonful of sugar disguising the bitter medicine of Christianity, Ricci's patients proved adept at guzzling the former and spitting out the latter," historian Julia Lovell wrote.[5] When 18th-century British merchants gained a foothold in Canton, China was still in a state of self-inflicted isolation. "We have never valued ingenious articles, nor do we have the slightest need of your country's manufactures," Emperor Qianlong declared to diplomat George Macartney.[6] He was a Manchu, a descendant of Northern invaders who enforced strict segregation from indigenous Han people through language, law, and practices like half-shaven heads for men and foot-binding for women. Some of the cannons aimed at Macartney's ships had been made centuries earlier by resident German Jesuit monks.[7]

The trading operations that the British East India Company and its successors developed after Western ambassadors like Macartney were the predecessors of today's multinational corporations. The documented atrocities of the infamous Opium Wars rightly appall today's readers, but in an era of much deadlier conflicts, they seemed like skirmishes. The Taiping Rebellion, China's contemporary civil war, claimed over 10 million lives, 100-fold the combined death toll of the two Opium Wars. The territorial concessions that resulted from the First Opium War ending with the 1842 Nanking Treaty were meagre anyway. Nineteenth-century foreign communities in China were small and hardly livable. Foreigners were confined to an area near Canton that could hardly host a holiday resort today. To comply with official restrictions on foreign women entering China, gentlemen left their families at home or settled them in Portuguese-held Macau. Keeping the men company were scant local servants, merchants, and rowdy crews from ships calling at the Canton port. The treaty ports forced open by the 1856–1860 Second Opium War were similarly underwhelming. "In 1870 there were 1,666 foreign residents in the Settlement at Shanghai, men outnumbering

---

[5] J. Lovell. 2007. *The Great Wall: China Against the World, 1000 BC–AD 2000* (New York, NY: Grove Press), p. 272.

[6] J. Lovell. 2011. *The Opium War: Drugs, Dreams and the Making of China* (London: Pan Macmillan), p. 87.

[7] T. Andrade. 2017. *The Gunpowder Age: China, Military Innovation, and the Rise of the West in World History* (Princeton, NJ: Princeton University Press), chap. 16, pp. 237–256.

women six to one, and there were 167 children," Robert Bickers wrote in *The Scramble for China.*[8]

Imperial prohibitions ensured physical and mental segregation between locals and foreigners, including criminal punishment for teaching non-natives Chinese. Other aspects of interaction, like moving in and out of concession ports and intimate relations between locals and foreigners, were kept in check by laws and traditions on both sides. But the promise of wealth and power from trade outweighed the influence of the imperial court: Mandarins and local middlemen known to Westerners as Compradors diligently colluded with foreigners to dodge restrictions. That deprived the Court of both influence and income, while foreign trading houses and their local allies gained both. When Canton's wealthiest Comprador known as Howqua died in 1843, his fortune exceeded the national treasury: he was probably the richest man on Earth.[9] The conspiracy turned concession ports into hubs of not only commerce but also technology, science, and culture in a fading empire. China's future was soon forged not at the Forbidden City but at the Hongkong Shanghai Banking Corporation (HSBC), Russell & Company, and the customs, postal, investment, and scientific institutions newly established by the Brits, Dutch, French, Americans, later Germans, Japanese, Russians, and others.

The Qing ruling house, China's last imperial dynasty, finally collapsed in 1911. The new Republic's mostly foreign-educated reformers once again looked beyond the southern seas for inspiration. From Beijing, the *northern capital*, government relocated to Nanjing, the *southern capital*, and invited advisors from Japan, the United States, and Germany. Siemens, Standard Oil, Pfizer, BASF, and scores of brands from the previously unwelcome West soon became household names in China's cities, for their reliable products as well as investment and job opportunities. The next decade became China's own Roaring Twenties with lamp oil, animal feed, and cigarette salesmen hassling the nation by day and spending their

---

[8] R. Bickers. 2012. *The Scramble for China: Foreign Devils in the Qing Empire, 1832-1914* (UK: Penguin), p. 311.

[9] W.T. Hanes and F. Sanello. 2002. *Opium Wars: The Addiction of One Empire and the Corruption of Another* (USA: Sourcebooks), p. 160.

earnings in tea houses and cabarets at night. The decade did not last long. The Second World War started early in China, with gradual Japanese occupation during the 1930s. The ensuing civil war between Republican and Communist forces sent foreigners packing, and despite their best hopes, most never returned. Mao Zedong, the Leninist leader of the new People's Republic of China (PRC) from 1949, admired Qin Shi Huang, builder of mines, iron smelts, roads, and emperor to the northern Qin dynasty. The tide turned northward again.

The Soviet Union proved a more willing sponsor to the new People's Republic than the United States or its Western allies, and China borrowed political and industrial blueprints from the USSR and worldwide Communist nations. Chinese leaders were educated in Moscow, Sofia, and Pyongyang. With the *Internationale* and "Proletarians of the world, unite!" on their lips, scientists, engineers, laborers, and soldiers arrived to reconstruct the Socialist sibling. But their numbers paled in comparison with China's previous exposure, especially after Stalin's 1953 death soured Soviet-Chinese friendship and resulted in another wave of foreign departures. "In 1964, the total number of resident Russians, formerly the largest of the foreign communities, was down to 1,326, most of them living in Xinjiang," Robert Bickers wrote. "There were 2,730 foreign nationals in Shanghai at the start of 1965, but 2,092 of these were African, Asian or Latin American students. There were only sixty-five others resident in the city who were not diplomatic staff. There were forty-two Britons in 1962 (most of them the elderly ethnically Chinese widows of British men), and five French nationals." The number of Europeans in Shanghai doubled, the account adds, when 30 foreign experts arrived to teach at the Shanghai Foreign Language Institute.[10]

Footholds and Bridgeheads

In a decade, a new current of accommodation reached China again. At his 1972 visit, President Richard Nixon assured an incapacitated Mao Zedong and his French-educated diplomatic adviser Zhou Enlai that

---

[10] R. Bickers. 2017. *Out of China: How the Chinese Ended the Era of Western Domination* (London: Allen Lane), p. 332.

America and its friends in Hong Kong, Taiwan, Japan, South Korea, and Singapore would help rescue a nose-diving state-planned economy. In a few years, Mao and Zhou were dead, the Soviets had left, and others arrived. In 1992, a nearly 90-year-old man with Masha's physique embarked on a well-publicized *Southern Tour* and institutionalized the country's latest economic about-face. The man was Party patriarch Deng Xiaoping, who had spent some of his formative years with Zhou in Paris, working among others at Peugeot and Schneider factories. His destination was the resuscitated Shenzhen, China's newly designated portal to the world. Nearby British colony Hong Kong acted as buffer, depot, and clearing house. Like once Marco Polo, foreigners who visited China in the new era of *reform and reopening'* thought that the country had long been closed to the world. When China turns, reversals tend to erase most traces of previous periods, including people, products, practices, and memories.

China's north-south cycles change according to the outcome of painstaking internal and international negotiations and reflect a determination to engage the outside world at the Middle Kingdom's own terms. The concept continues to surprise outsiders, even though many believe that its physical manifestation, the Great Wall, is visible from spaceships. Conditionality has always applied to foreigners in China's territory. Whether they were Persian caravans or princes from Ceylon, Dzungarian emissaries, or British bankers, their polite welcome took place at demarcated cantonments under close supervision. Silk Road trading stations had been as secluded from local life as Canton's infamous factory encampment or Beijing's Legation Quarters. Mao's guests from sister nations were so strictly isolated that most of them were unaware of other foreigners in the same city.[11] As Deng put it, open windows let in fresh air but also flies. Today's expat hubs represent the same tradeoff between ideological purity and the inflow of foreign funds. "Both before and after 1949 China's reception and treatment of diversity has not been predicated on ideas of shared rights," strategic think tank MERICS wrote in a 2019. "The aim

---

[11] J. Lovell. 2015. "The Uses of Foreigners in Mao-Era China: 'Techniques of Hospitality' and International Image-Building in the People's Republic, 1949–1976," *Transactions of the Royal Historical Society* 25 (Cambridge: Cambridge University Press) pp. 135–158.

was not to incorporate foreigners and other non-Chinese, but to insulate Chinese society from them."[12]

Depending on their taste, temperament, goals, and expectations, some foreigners are happier with their enclosures than others. Amateur orientalists with Confucian leadership manuals under their pillow may be disappointed to give up the tea-sipping, calligraphy-scribbling, kung fu-fighting kingdom of their daydreams for English-language curiosity courses in shopping malls. Fans in search of Red China can still find fading revolutionary murals in condemned alleys where senior citizens shuffle mah-jongg tiles, but not for long. Some yearn for a more authentic experience and follow Beijing's recurring *go-west* campaigns to Chengdu or Kunming. Many eventually return to Beijing, Shanghai, and Shenzhen. Demographic data suggest that for most foreigners, the system served its purpose. According to the 2010 census results that constituted the only reliable data source for a decade, over half of the country's 600,000 foreigners lived in Beijing, Shanghai, and Guangzhou, and very few away from south-eastern shores.[13] The 2020 census showed similar shares of the 850,000 foreigners living in the three top cities.[14] For most expats who have ever lived in the country, the conveniences and challenges of a handful of cities equal life in China.

Foreigners sometimes feel suffocated by China's expat hubs for a variety of reasons. Renata and Nicola became ever happier as they worked their way out of their corporate cocoon and befriended local middle-class families. Markus Baumgartner of Miba Group somewhat resented progressing in the other direction as he accumulated years of experience in China. "Even though we live in Suzhou, which is a golden cage for expats," he explained to me, "we are very integrated in local life. We do

---

[12] F. N. Pieke. November 2019. "How Immigration Is Shaping Chinese Society," *MERICS*. https://merics.org/en/report/how-immigration-shaping-chinese-society.

[13] Z. Qian and S. Elsinga. January 2015. "Nali Lai de?—An Overview of Expat Demographics in China," *China Briefing*. www.china-briefing.com/news/nali-lai-de-overview-expats-china/.

[14] "How Many Foreigners in China? 7th Population Census Tells." n.d. *Expat Focus*. https://mp.weixin.qq.com/s/z41mALLcni3Ei9rV_15o7g (accessed July 12, 2022).

not even live in a compound for foreigners. I don't want to spend my weekend complaining how warm my sparkling water is." Such scorn for China's foreigner hubs is understandable from seasoned expats with countrywide experience and networks, and perhaps proficiency in Mandarin. Their sentiment also intrigues newcomers, who cannot wait to experience *the real China*. But the nation's expat hubs have persisted for centuries for good reasons, shrinking and expanding with the ebb and flow of foreigners in the country. Without them, China would be a much less hospitable place for long-term immigrants, business travelers, and even tourists.

One reliable indicator of a nation's openness to the world is the percentage of non-natives among its population. That the Vatican tops the list with all its citizens born abroad is an abundant source of jokes among researchers, but the rest of the list reveals profound comparisons. At some popular expat destinations, a third or more of the population is foreign-born, including, Australia, New Zealand, Singapore, Switzerland, and the United Arab Emirates. About a fifth to tenth of people in the major economies of North America and Europe are immigrants, and the ranking continues down to the relatively unexposed lower single-digit range. Although the United Nations (UN) survey in question generously rounded up the number of foreigners to a million, China still featured at the bottom of the list with Myanmar, Cuba, and Vietnam.[15] "This amounts to 0.07 percent of the population, the smallest share of migrants of any country in the world," a 2019 INSEAD publication warned. "New York City has more than thrice as many foreign-born residents."[16] For expats and their employers, these ratios are significant for several reasons.

Foreigners in culturally challenging countries enjoy living close to one another to absorb the culture shock and access services that locals do not use. "Foreign residents generate specific demands for education, housing

---

[15] "List of Sovereign States and Dependent Territories by Immigrant Population." n.d. *Wikipedia*. https://en.wikipedia.org/wiki/List_of_sovereign_states_and_dependent_territories_by_immigrant_population (accessed July 12, 2022).
[16] J.S. Black. September 2019. "Why Foreign Firms Struggle to Break Into China," *INSEAD*. https://knowledge.insead.edu/strategy/why-foreign-firms-struggle-to-break-into-china-12421.

and health care and are setting new patterns in entertainment, life-style trends and popular culture," the MERICS study continues. If foreigners in China were as scattered across its territory as they are in the United States or Australia, accessing nonindigenous groceries, foreign-language schools, agencies, and entertainment would be nearly impossible, not to mention finding friends without fluency in Mandarin. Moreover, multinational firms also rely on expat populations as consumers and employees: Coca-Cola, Volkswagen, Lufthansa, or Google crowd-surfed to success in China, thanks to foreign firms and residents. Without expat clubs and societies, China's cities would be unwelcoming for most foreign spouses and kids. In statistical terms, even top-tier cities fall short of cosmopolitan standards. If we can believe official data published in 2017, around 1 percent of Shanghai's population was foreign-born, a ratio on par with the UN figures for Albania, Pakistan, and Ethiopia.[17]

Storefronts on Foreigner Street

It is hard to believe that statistically speaking, China has hardly any foreigners at all. Over years of keynote speaking, it became my guilty pleasure to quote statistics on the number and concentration of foreigners in China, then scan the audience for the inevitable the body language of surprise and disbelief. Their reactions are understandable, especially if they spent the previous Sunday queueing for a popular Italian restaurant among other expats in one of the nation's expat hubs. The explanation, of course, is a combination of deliberate regulation and the fickle human desire to seek out like-minded people. Most expats not only live in a handful of cities but mostly populate a few preferred districts within, and several Chinese cities have entertainment areas called *laowaijie*, or *foreigner street*. A casual stroll in such an area on a sunny weekend feels as if you took the wrong turn and ended up in downtown Boston or Singapore. That impression is a good start to understanding how China's expat enclaves work. The main function of the foreign-branded

---

17 X. Yi. January 2019. "Shanghai Home to Largest Foreign Worker Population in China," *China Daily*. www.chinadaily.com.cn/a/201901/16/WS5c3e d0a9a3106c65c34e4d2a.html.

supermarkets, cafes and restaurants, retail stores, and banks is exactly to defy the national mainstream and act as cultural shock absorbers to the foreign visitors and immigrants who invest, enterprise, labor, and spend in China.

Expat surveys rank Mainland China high on work-related prospects and much lower on other dimensions of life quality, but that does not reflect truthfully on the nation's overall values. Those who have had the privilege to roam far and wide in the country know how serene and patient Chinese people can be. Those rankings do, however, accurately describe the spirit of urban middle-class China, especially in the largest cities. For foreigners and locals alike, highly concentrated population centers increase the efficiency of daily work: they shorten commutes, concentrate material, natural and human resources, fasten communication, decisions, and action, and promptly turn the output of one business into the input of another. For visitors from China's small towns, those cities are just as mad as their foreigners. In a country whose population traditionally valued familial ties, tranquility, and spirituality above all else, SEZs were created to enable the frantic activity needed for financial recovery. To say that SEZs have rules of their own is more than simple figure of speech: the zones do in fact operate as municipalities with the right to draft their own legislation.[18]

The very concept of specially designated economic zones was adopted from abroad to boost China's development at the beginning of the Reform and Opening period. The first SEZs, defined as "geographical areas that allow the integration of free-market principles to attract additional foreign investment," were established around 1980 in the vicinity of Guangzhou and Xiamen, two former concessions.[19] How history repeated itself was not lost on observers. "It would have been more accurate to describe them as experiments in reverse-engineering the much reviled system of treaty ports," Orville Schell and John Delury write in their book

[18] D.Z. Zeng. February 2015. "Global Experiences With Special Economic Zones: With a Focus on China and Africa." The World Bank.
[19] B. Crane, C. Albrecht, K.M. Duffin, and C. Albrecht. 2018. "China's Special Economic Zones: An Analysis of Policy to Reduce Regional Disparities," *Regional Studies, Regional Science* 5, no. 1, pp. 98–107.

on China's modernization. "This time around, however, Deng hoped to make a growing foreign presence in coastal trade enhance China's wealth and power without undermining its sovereignty."[20] In doing so, Beijing relied on successful examples of similar zones established from the 1960s onward in Taiwan, Singapore, South Korea, India, the Philippines and, around the same time with China, the United Arab Emirates.[21]

Each nation's experiment with SEZs aimed at constructing a sort of landing strip for global capital in an otherwise restrictive system. Limitations could be economic, political, ideological, or all of these at the same time: authoritarian governments in Taiwan, Korea, and the Philippines, zealous prohibitions in Singapore, corruption in India, Sharia law in the Emirates, and so forth. As for China, allegedly the oldest continuous tradition in the world, it has puzzled foreigners for millennia with a certain sense of pride over rules and traditions that foreigners would never understand. Simplifying them for outsiders was never a priority: in fact, China worked long and hard to be misunderstood. It lacked diplomats, forbade its subjects to travel and to teach foreigners Chinese until the late 19th century. It rid itself of foreigners and most noneconomic cooperation until the 1990s. Combined with an imported Marxist–Leninist political blueprint and its local mutations, early-2000s China was a hopeless maze for foreigners without extensive local experience, which very few people had. SEZs shielded new arrivals from the confusion beyond. Within their confines, multinational firms, foreign-invested enterprises, and carefully handpicked local businesses happily interbred with one another as suppliers, clients and service providers.

"The SEZs were deliberately located far from the center of political power in Beijing, minimizing potential risks should any problems or political effects be generated during their functioning," the authors of one study wrote. "More specifically, the original four zones were sited in coastal areas of Guangdong and Fujian that had a long history of contact

---

[20] O. Schell and J. Delury. 2013. *China's Long March to the Twenty-first Century* (London: Little, Brown).

[21] "World Investment Report 2019, Special Economic Zones." n.d. *UNCTAD*, Chap. iv, pp. 142–145. https://unctad.org/system/files/official-document/WIR 2019_CH4.pdf.

with the outside world through out-migration, and at the same time were near Hong Kong, Macao, and Taiwan."[22] In these oases of otherness, executives could live and work without Chinese language skills or even vague ideas about the PRC's legal and political system. Foreign entrepreneurs incorporated, financed, populated, and promoted companies through intermediaries, keeping a convenient distance from confusing local authorities. Legislation ensured strict separation between local and foreign-incorporated entities. An ecosystem of expat-friendly recruiting agencies, law firms, banks, freight-forwarders, consultancies, chambers, and networking clubs took care of business. International kindergartens, schools, clinics, up-market grocery stores, laundries, bakeries, and entertainment settled everything else, and encouraged a segregated life between the international and local populations. In compliance with local law, many religious congregations and membership organizations in expat hubs still exclude PRC passport holders.

Protection and privilege often come at the cost of frustrating confinement. From early concession ports to mushrooming foreign settlements, then SEZs, and the expat communities they spawned, many foreigners lamented their transitory nature, characteristic obsession with work over everything else, and their ignorance of the nation that surrounded them. Some admitted that expats were free to chase plentiful opportunities within the zones, but protested that Chinese jobs, firms, and careers seemed to elude them outside the specially designated areas. Such complaints became louder as some indigenous firms like Huawei, Alibaba, and Tencent bloomed into highly visible success stories. "For the most part, for foreigners looking to get a foot in the door, it remains particularly difficult to secure a job with a 100% Chinese-owned firm," the BBC wrote in 2014. "There are more job opportunities available with foreign companies operating in the country. Around 85% of expats work for these international firms, with the largest proportion in sales and marketing, followed by banking and financial services and engineering."[23]

---

[22] Y. Yeung, J. Lee, and G. Kee. May 15, 2013. "China's Special Economic Zones at 30," *Eurasian Geography and Economics*. www.tandfonline.com/doi/abs/10.2747/1539-7216.50.2.222.

[23] M. Durnin. February 2014. "China Is Still a Jobs Hotspot for Expats," *BBC*. www.bbc.com/worklife/article/20140212-get-hired-in-china.

Such intermittent complaints stand in sharp contrast with count-less satisfied patrons of SEZs on all sides: expats, authorities, and local employees, customers, suppliers, and more. The regime has been a piv-otal part of China's unprecedented economic success story often labeled a *miracle*. "It was estimated that in recent years, SEZs at national level accounted for about 22% of national GDP, 46% of foreign investment and 60% of exports and generated in excess of 30 million jobs," a 2015 World Bank study reported. "In some regions, industrial parks account for anywhere between 50% to 80-90% of growth in GDP. Up to date, China's overall technology commercialization rate is only about 10%, while industrial parks in China on average boast a commercialization rate of over 60%."[24] Even the briefest visits to a handful of towns and compa-nies in China reveals the obvious advantage of SEZs over the country in general in terms of infrastructure, public and private services, and even the fashion choices and leisure activities of local inhabitants. In small towns, locals still ridicule foreign joggers for their hilarious habit. In Tianjin or Shenzhen, they scrutinize the runner's equipment.

It Is a Family Business

Beyond business, the most helpful feature of China's expat hubs is that newcomers are immediately surrounded by more experienced foreign families who crave to share their wisdom. "The expat network is incred-ibly helpful once you get access to it," Briana recalled. "Even before I relocated, I met someone who had just returned from Shanghai. He connected me to his driver, who picked me up from the airport. Another colleague told me about being an expat in Shanghai and what I should do differently there." Even in top-tier cities, novices might need help with the simplest things. "On my second day in China, I created complete chaos in a Blue Frog restaurant because I confused the two local wait-ers," Attila Hilbert of Danone said. "I am still grateful for the French couple who intervened." Shaken by their similar misadventures, Nicola thought hard about his prospects as a dependent spouse without English

---

[24] D.Z. Zeng. February 2015. "Global Experiences With Special Economic Zones: With a Focus on China and Africa," The World Bank.

or Chinese skills. Fellow foreigners suggested courses in both languages, which utterly changed his experience of Shanghai. Lucky breaks can come from unexpected sources: one expat manager described how he got a job offer while watching the football World Cup with fellow Germans at one of those foreigner-street bars.[25]

Speaking of bars: singles, especially single men, are overrepresented all over the expat universe including China. "Female assignees represent only 20% of the international assignee population, although with a steady upward trend compared to 14% in 2017 and 11% in 2015," relocation firm Mercer wrote.[26] Reasons are multiple, including the predominance of men in management in general, and especially in sectors where a vast majority of multinational firms in China belong: machinery, automotive, technology, financial services, and so on. China's reputation as a cultur-ally challenging and fairly workaholic culture makes it more likely that employers prefer to send single men there. As far as I can tell from con-versations with female candidates and expats, China's public image as a male-dominated society, above all media appearances by its political lead-ers, probably perpetuates the imbalance. What such data imply, however, is subject to each prospective expat's individual judgment.

Others arrive with dependents, and even solitary assignments may become family adventures over time. Either way, the success of the mission hinges on how each member weathers the transition and how successfully they support (or irritate) one another. When families relocate, self-reflection is required from everyone, Bronwyn Bowery-Ireland reckons. "The family must be aligned. Expat assignments are especially likely to fail when the spouse is not fully on board." The lifestyles of expat families in new locations can be fundamentally different from previous routines. "If your partner doesn't have a purpose, then after a while it will get difficult," Hays's Richard Eardley said. "If they are stuck in a condo making lunches,

---

[25] S. Thaerigen. "Podcast #81 First China job—Better Job—Own Business," *China Flexpat* (Podcast). https://podcasts.apple.com/hk/podcast/china-flexpat/id1514659021?l=en&i=1000550923269 (accessed July 12, 2022).

[26] "Worldwide Survey of International Assignment Policies and Practices," Mercer, accessed on July 31, 2022. https://mobilityexchange.mercer.com/international-assignments-survey

they will end up unhappy." Managing a home for an overworked spouse in a foreign land is tough. Finding a job in an unknown city is hardly easier. Both can be challenging without the support of familiar communities in a place that uses an inaccessible language. Whether a spouse builds a nest or runs a quest, the choice must be voluntary.

It may take a few turbulent weeks for consenting adults to reach the necessary alignment, but the work is not done yet. Ignoring proper preparation and setting sail into the unknown can be liberating for the travelers but devastating for dependents such as children and elderly relatives. "You must look at it in a holistic way," Richard Eardley continued. "Expat assignments that do not work for the whole family are bound to fail, so you must ask yourself some tough questions. I have a grown-up son who was just about to start university. Wondering whether I would be okay being away from him was probably the hardest part of my decision to leave." It took him weeks of contemplation and hours of conversation to make up his mind. For people who decide to start a new life abroad, that time is well invested. Today's corporate adventurers do not run the 50 percent risk of being massacred by pirates or succumbing to swamp fever, but the person or family that returns will not be the same one that high-fived the news of an overseas assignment. Managing the inevitable changes is one secret to fulfilling expat careers. At least the manageable ones, that is, because however well a foreign family prepares for their sojourn in China, there will always be life-changing circumstances beyond their control.

The comfort and convenience of well-serviced, English-speaking surroundings can help expats across countless daily hurdles, but critical life experiences would be nearly unimaginable without them. About half of the foreign families featured in this book delivered babies or raised children in China. The tone of their recollections was almost always positive, for which the country's insular expat economy can take some of the credit. "I knew from a friend's experience that delivering a baby in a local hospital can be tough for foreigners," Fernanda Barth, HR Manager for a Brazilian industrial firm WEG, told me when I visited her in Nantong, a south-eastern port city. By the time of our 2019 interview, I had trained WEG China managers in leadership skills for five years, while she and her husband had worked for the firm in Nantong for a decade. "Most Chinese hospitals are crowded and their medical staff are overworked, so they cannot treat patients gently: they just want to get on with their jobs. My friend could not find an English-speaking doctor there, so she brought along a work colleague to translate, which created a very awkward atmosphere for everyone. I delivered my daughter in a top international hospital, and it was a dramatically positive experience."

As kids grow and expat families start considering their education, choices vary from international to local schools, and various combinations of the two. Predictably, Markus Baumgartner opted for early education in Mandarin for his son. "We were extremely anxious to send him to a Chinese kindergarten because he only spoke German. On the first day, we heard him repeat *'ting bu dong'* (I don't understand), the only thing he knew in Chinese. But then, he started playing toy cars with other children and they found a common ground. In half a year he picked up enough Chinese." When children grow out of kindergarten, however, choices get harder for many expat families. Local and international education is strictly segregated in the People's Republic: beyond primary level, students who started their education in one system find it nearly impossible to transition to the other. Therefore, foreign families must think a decade ahead, taking into consideration their children's interest, cost, and possible relocation down the road. The pressure is especially high as tuition fees at most international schools target well-paid top executives and entrepreneurs at a time when many multinationals cut their expat budgets.

"When she finishes kindergarten, I would like my daughter to study at the only international school in Nantong," Fernanda Barth continued. "The problem is the price. The Chinese kindergarten costs around eighteen thousand Chinese yuan a year. The international school would cost a hundred and fifty thousand a year, only part of which can be paid by the company." For most foreign families, facing the edges of expat existence and gradually being exposed to the *real China* creates much anxiety. "I know we are spoiled with the insurance packages we get here," Chris from the European luxury fashion firm admitted. "But we had to take my daughter to check-ups at local children's hospitals, and after the queueing and language confusion, we were glad to return to private clinics." Many expats admitted having equally overwhelmed health care and education systems in their home countries, but that seemed to be beside the point.

Certain standards of physical and emotional comfort were simply part of the package. To guarantee that was the firm's business, just as running the business was the expat's concern. And companies do their best to take care of everything. Everything, at least, that is within their control.

The Air Is Everywhere

The best things in life are supposed to be free. Or perhaps it is the other way around. Perhaps we draw so much comfort, joy, and inspiration from the plants, animals, heavenly bodies, and even the air around us because they are always there without asking anything in return. But relocation to exotic places can shake life to its very basics, and China is among the best examples for that. In contrast with its stellar career opportunities, curious culture, and the lasting advantages of having worn the *Dragon Suit,* expat life in China also comes with considerable annoyances. Before the COVID-19 pandemic, topping the reasons why many talented foreigners either refused to relocate to China or prematurely terminated their assignments there were polluted air and restricted Internet connectivity. For over a decade, surveys by the American, European Union, German, Benelux, and other Chambers of Commerce consistently found these two irritations to interfere with the talent pool of foreign firms in China, and anecdotal evidence from my interviews supports their findings. It seems that the otherwise freely available joys of life like a refreshing walk in nature or the soothing voice of a friend can easily become hard-earned luxuries for expats in China.

"Living here does have its drawbacks," warns an HSBC country guide. "Air pollution is particularly bad—so you'll probably spend a lot of time indoors."[27] On the one hand, China was always infamous for its unhealthy air among most expats, even those who never went there. On the other, few newcomers realized the full extent of the problem before they directly experienced it. That is not a coincidence. A 2014 study reported Beijing's air pollution level since 2008 about six times the U.S.

---

[27] "Living in mainland China: Your guide to expat life in mainland China," HSBC, accessed on July 15, 2022. https://www.expat.hsbc.com/expat-explorer/expat-guides/mainland-china/living-in-mainland-china/

Environmental Protection Agency's limit but also a consistent reluctance from Chinese authorities to report the problem.[28] "For us, Shanghai was a city without outdoors," Chris, the luxury fashion CFO, told me years after he had moved his family to Hong Kong. Beyond obvious health hazards, the annoyances of confining work and play, evenings and weekends inside, filtering the air and ventilating rooms in rotation gradually overwhelmed nerves too. Over time, something akin to cabin fever could undermine the morale of individuals as well as the life of entire families.

Newcomers quickly developed the habit of compulsively checking their mobile phone's air quality apps. When they nervously consulted seasoned expats about readings that showed multiple times the recommended health limit, they often received a characteristically Chinese response: "You should have seen the pollution a few years ago!" Indeed, early 2000s expats were blissfully obvious of the fumes that they inhaled. China never published air quality data until the 2008 Beijing Olympic Games. That year, the U.S. Embassy in Beijing started sharing the readings of its rooftop monitor on Facebook and Twitter, then still accessible in China. State media hurriedly declared the initiative "not only confusing but also insulting."[29] After amusing attempts to choke monitoring equipment and data sharing, the government yielded to public uproar and broadcast air quality data since 2012. Many, however, still misjudged the severity of the problem. "I was in a long-distance cycling group for expats," Henrik König recalled. "I remember how upset I was when I received a text message that a fifty-kilometer bicycle tour had been cancelled because of an air quality index above 150. I often went for a run instead. It was not because I considered myself tougher than others—it simply was not an issue for me. I am not sure if that was stupid or lazy."

It was neither. The main reason why people remained so blasé about what they inhaled was the general lack of awareness. By then, advanced economies had long introduced restrictive measures for bad-air days.

---

[28] L. Kuo. April 10, 2014. "Six years of Beijing air pollution summed up in one scary chart," Quartz. https://qz.com/197786/six-years-of-bejing-air-pollution-summed-up-in-one-scary-chart/

[29] E.C. Economy. 2018. *The Third Revolution: Xi Jinping and the New Chinese State* (Oxford: Oxford University Press), p. 152.

By contrast, China seemed to go about its business regardless of pollution problems for several years after it had started monitoring the situation. During the 2013 *Airmageddon*, out of hundreds of major cities surveyed, only Haikou in China's southernmost Hainan Island, Lhasa in faraway Tibet, and Zhoushan in Zhejiang province passed Beijing's official air quality standards.[30] Flights were grounded and cars collided due to the all-engulfing purple haze, yet Chinese authorities contemplated and ultimately authorized fireworks for the upcoming Lunar New Year celebrations.[31] "We tended to dismiss it," luxury fashion CFO Chris said. "I remember how we played soccer on some of the most polluted days. It was so bad that we could hardly see each other in the purple clouds of smog. The air quality index was over 500 as opposed to the maximum 100 recommended for outdoor sports."

Managers who gained insight into the workings of the problem also realized that it was a complex systemic issue rather than an unfortunate side-effect of development that would solve itself over time. "The Chinese government allows industry to freely pollute the air, water and ground, which (combined with the low cost of labor) easily allows industry to undercut the prices charged by companies abiding by strict standards elsewhere in the world," the authors of an early 2000s study wrote. "However, the economic incentives offered to foreign capital to invest in China, including few controls over pollution and worker health and safety violations, have created an ecological nightmare."[32] Expats reacted accordingly. "I kept asking myself whether I was crazy to have brought my kids to this country," Attila Hilbert said. "Then I reminded myself that in critical situations, one must research, plan and prepare without panicking. I checked the seals on all doors and windows—this remains my primary criterion for choosing a flat in China whether I otherwise like it or not. I started

[30] Z. Yuchen. April 2014. "Expats seek breath of fresh air outside big, smoggy cities," China Daily USA. http://usa.chinadaily.com.cn/china/2014-04/11/content_17425595.htm.

[31] D. Grammaticas. January 2013. "'Airmageddon': China smog raises modernisation doubts," BBC. https://www.bbc.com/news/world-asia-china-21272328.

[32] L. King et al. 2009. *Environmental Sociology, From Analysis to Action* (Maryland: Rowman & Littlefield), p. 184.

investing in equipment: I have spent about twelve thousand euros on internal and external air quality monitors, air purifiers, sealing material, and masks."

Playing soccer with invisible friends and finding fearful refuge behind perfectly sealed doors and windows represent opposing attitudes to living with pollution. Both excesses can be harmful, although in different ways. "I had a colleague who was a passionate cycler," Attila Hilbert told me. "He cycled like a maniac, covering the 180-kilometre distance from Shanghai to Hangzhou and back, sometimes several times a week. In a few years, he was taken to surgery with heart problems. I use his story as a cautionary tale for new expats. We are not talking about imminent death, but you have to take the problem seriously." The vigorous outdoor exercise routine of his pedal-happy friend only accelerated otherwise common long-term health effects. The consequences of swinging the pendulum toward voluntary confinement may be less dramatic or China-specific but just as harmful. Spending entire weekends binge-watching TV shows and blaming Asian cuisine for the resulting extra pounds is comically stereotypical among China expats. Beyond obvious health effects, breathing contaminated air undermines cognitive performance as well. Microparticles like PM2.5 find their way into the bloodstream and cause harm wherever their chemical content is deposited, including the brain.[33]

Managers in China must also monitor air quality for the sake of their businesses. Bad-air days disrupt outdoor photography and filming, promotional events, sports games, concerts, exhibitions, and fairs. Mindful customers stay away from open-air restaurants, cafes, and swimming pools. Pollutants necessitate additional precaution in transporting and storing meat, fruits and vegetables, impact businesses that grow or breed anything, deface buildings and works of art. Companies track pollution-related productivity losses such as additional sick-days and medical cost, including spouses and children. Damage to people and businesses adds up. According to some calculations, each extra percentage of pollution measurement costs China nearly 0.01 percent of annual GDP,

---

[33] L. Sha. April 2018. "The Real Cost of Air Pollution in China," CKGSB Knowledge. https://knowledge.ckgsb.edu.cn/2018/04/13/environment/economic-effects-of-pollution-china/.

approaching two billion U.S. dollars a year.[34] "Our health and safety regulations demand that we provide adequate filtering when the air quality
index exceeds 200, I think, otherwise people can refuse to work," the
South China General Manager of a European electronics manufacturing firm told me during my visit. "If we complied, we would either lose
several working weeks every year, or spend millions on equipment. Fortunately, Chinese workers care more about cash than cancer. This is our
Band-Aid." The butt of his joke was a portable air purifier, humming
diligently near an open window.

Whether pollution amused or annoyed, foreigners in China during
the smog-clad 2000s and 2010s depended on their circumstances. Parents
of young children worried the most. "On days when you felt like you
could chew the air," said Shaun Rein of China Market Research, "even
me, who loves China and does reasonably well financially here, thought
about moving out of the country. We could not let my son play outdoor
soccer—we signed him up for basketball instead. We would not let him
walk or take a bike to school, instead we made him wear a face-mask
and drove him to classes every day." Those who never experienced vicious
circles of confinement and frustration in cities where yards, gardens, and
balconies are rare privileges cannot imagine how quickly family life turns
into incessant quarrel. "Expatriates based there are starting to ask their
employers to revert to 1980s and 1990s based hardship packages for pollution," a Bloomberg article wrote in 2014. "Multinationals are having
to work hard to retain them with some expats leaving their families at
home and starting often strenuous monthly or bi-weekly commutes to
see them."[35]

It is fair to assume, as employers and recruitment agencies typically
did, that behind the documented departures of expats due to pollution,
there were just as many people who refused postings to China due to

---

[34] L. Sha. April 2018. "The Real Cost of Air Pollution in China," CKGSB
Knowledge. https://knowledge.ckgsb.edu.cn/2018/04/13/environment/economic-
effects-of-pollution-china/.

[35] "China's Smog Causes Some Expat Families to Live Apart" n.d. Bloomberg
News. www.expatinfodesk.com/news/2014/04/10/chinas-smog-causes-some-
expat-families-to-live-apart/ (accessed on July 12, 2022).

the bad reputation of its air quality. Among those who stayed on, many admitted the problem but tried to see it in perspective, like Richard Eardley of Hays. "Sure, you must get used to living with poor air quality in China, but so is the case in many other, otherwise attractive expat destinations." Fernanda Barth of WEG Nantong made a more specific comparison. "Sure, the air is much better in Brazil. But life there has many negative aspects we do not have in China, like worrying about crime in the streets. Overall, the positives far outweigh the problems for us." Neither did pollution work identically on everyone. "Ironically, while Nicola suffered from breathing issues that got progressively worse with time, Shanghai's air cured me of my chronic asthma," Renata Santos told me, visibly amused.

In subsequent years, China both managed to improve its overall air quality and openly celebrated relative milestones like Beijing's removal from a list of the world's 200 most polluted cities.[36] Nevertheless, its air remains one of the world's worst alongside India and a handful of countries in the former Soviet Union, Middle East, and North Africa. As of mid-2022, three of the 10 most polluted cities in the world, and nine out the top 50, were in the PRC.[37] Thus, while pollution has graduated from debilitating disaster to irritating inconvenience, it remains a central theme to China's expat reality. "Today, expats are not going to get the blue skies they see in France and you won't be able to hike as you can on the West Coast of the United States, but pollution is not the deal-breaker that it once was," Shaun Rein said. "There is still a lack of natural beauty and the ability to go away for the weekend, like the Hamptons from New York City or the Alps from Paris. But this is also getting better with the high-speed train network: we are now able to reach locations that were inaccessible even just four years ago."

---

[36] H. Gu and D. Stanway. September 2019. "Beijing Set to Exit List of World's Top 200 Most-Polluted Cities," *Reuters*. www.reuters.com/article/us-china-pollution-beijing/beijing-set-to-exit-list-of-worlds-top-200-most-polluted-cities-data-idUSKCN1VX05Z.

[37] "Air Quality and Pollution City Ranking." n.d. IQAir. www.iqair.com/world-air-quality-ranking (accessed on July 12, 2022).

China's Intermittent Internet

Even before the recent COVID-19 pandemic, people all over the world found themselves grounded for various reasons: extreme heat or cold, sandstorms, wars, discrimination, crowds, crime, curfews, and pollution. When they did, they sought entertainment and encouragement online. But foreign families stuck with hazy top-floor views and whizzing air purifiers in the PRC had to contend with the added annoyance of restricted Internet connectivity since the mid-2000s. For predominantly political reasons, authorities block access to most global community sites and messaging apps, including Facebook, Twitter, LinkedIn, Instagram, Snapchat, WhatsApp, Viber, Signal, Reddit, Pinterest, and Flickr. Also unavailable are content-sharing tools like Dropbox, Tumblr, Picasa, Google Books, Docs, Drive, and Scholar, search engines like Yahoo and streaming (and parenting) platforms like YouTube, Netflix, Amazon, and Apple TV. Videoconferencing applications are selectively available: Skype and a few others freely, Zoom and Microsoft Teams with convoluted restriction protocols, some not at all. As consolation, expats in China become masters of the technology known as virtual private networks or VPNs.

"In China, there's nothing more annoying than the Internet," Whitney Shindelar, then Director of Operational Excellence for Starwood Hotels and Resorts, expressed a documented universal sentiment in a 2016 article.[38] Many expats initially approach Internet restrictions with cultural curiosity—testing limits, learning circumvention methods, and observing the collective psychology of digital isolation. "Cyberdetox really does improve your self-esteem," quipped the author of a 2018 expat memoir. "My sudden introspection had a lot to do with the fact that when I first arrived in China (without a VPN), I was pretty much cut off. For the first time in four years I felt disconnected from the unbridled access of modernity."[39] Recollections of such plunges into China's digital darkness

---

[38] W. Shindelar. May 2016. "6 Myths vs Realities of Living in China, written by an American expat," Matador Network. https://matadornetwork.com/abroad/6-myths-vs-realities-living-china-written-american-expat/.

[39] E. Korczynska. 2018. *Made in China: Confessions of an expat* (Amazon LLC), p. 28.

make excellent stories. My favorite is from a young expat researcher at a prestigious Hong Kong university, who took a short trip to Shenzhen just to test the network. "I wasn't particularly interested in the place, but I wanted to see for myself if connectivity was really so bad, or it was just Western propaganda." The experiment backfired: unable to contact him and seeing him vanish from all social media and tracking apps for days, his family reported him missing with the Hong Kong police.

Expats learn to live with, and sometimes even love exotic aspects of China, including the food, the climate, and curious rules of social interaction. But like pollution, shock and frustration over Internet restrictions do not abate over time and can even increase with each poorly connected hour, day, week, or in pandemic times, month or year. The saga starts with the disturbing realization that roughly half of the World Wide Web's content goes blank in the PRC. It continues with gradually noticing some method in the madness of blockages. Unavailable content tends to contradict the legitimacy or narrative of the Communist Party or fall in the categories of foreign news and social media, unchecked user-generated matter, anything deemed vulgar, pornographic, obscene, violent, or in competition with state-favored domestic tech services, one specialist publication summarized.[40] Then comes the equally unnerving discovery that experimenting with the limits of China's half-Internet may further worsen connectivity. "The most accurate test of censorship is conducted inside the censoring country, but doing so comes with a variety of risks," one 2015 article warned. "Continual attempts to visit blocked sites are detectable by the local authorities, and can therefore be dangerous political activity."[41]

A recurring theme among foreigners in China is the emotional trauma of isolation, helplessness, and sadness beyond the practical inconvenience. "It can be a lonely experience," Fernanda expressed her reactions, "being cut off from a large part of what is happening at home." Other disconnected expats fear for their business or children's education. "China is

---

[40] "Test if a site is blocked in China." n.d. Comparitech. www.comparitech.com/privacy-security-tools/blockedinchina/ (accessed on July 12, 2022).
[41] S. Wei. December 2014. "Inside the Firewall: Tracking the News That China Blocks," ProPublica. https://projects.propublica.org/firewall/.

Horrible for Digital Nomads," reads the farewell rant of a five-year resident. "I'm sick and tired of just not being able to get on Instagram, or having to drain my 4G to load a Snap. Wouldn't it be nice if the Internet just worked? I've almost forgotten what that's like."[42] Shaun Rein called attention to the damage done to expat children's education. "It is bothersome to lose access to Instagram, but the biggest issue for executives is the impact on education," he said. "Without VPNs, children at international schools are unable to access one-third to half of the websites that the school wants them to use. Kids can't get access to apps to improve typing skills, they can't get access to math courses, and that is a deep frustration that makes a lot of expats who might like China get extremely critical, depressed and angry."

VPNs can partially circumvent restrictions. "Initially, my children and I made active efforts to learn to live without the banned sites," said Marie, senior HR management executive at a world-leading pharmaceutical multinational. "Then, I joined a group of expat parents for playing cards, and I was surprised how much they knew about what was trending on YouTube." China's vibrant internal digital ecosystem complies with government censorship but works mostly in Mandarin and has little to do with life outside the PRC. Without VPN applications, most expats would be isolated from both global and local online communities. "Expats in China worship Virtual Private Networks (VPNs) because they allow access to websites that we'd be able to see if we were anywhere else in the world," one memoire explained. "As the VPN connection spikes up and down in bright blue and red, it mimics a heart monitor—except that it often falls flat for no particular reason. VPN access is even blocked when important political meetings are taking place in Beijing, or when China is in the global news, or whenever the hell the Chinese government wants to block it."[43] Emilia Korczynska says it best in her memoire: "I don't

---

[42] Richelle. October 2017. "After FIVE Years in China, I'm Finally Moving On," Adventures Around Asia. www.adventuresaroundasia.com/leaving-china/.

[43] W. Shindelar. May 3, 2016. "6 Myths Vs Realities of Living in China, Written by an American Expat," Matador Network. https://matadornetwork.com/abroad/6-myths-vs-realities-living-china-written-american-expat/.

have stronger feelings for anyone on Earth than my VPN. I think I would marry it if it wasn't so flaky."[44]

My interviews revealed similar tactical varieties toward pollution and Internet restrictions: some proudly prepared, some silently suffered, and a serene minority simply dismissed the problem. "Our intercultural trainer in Brazil taught us how to install a VPN before we entered the country, and how to use it," said Nicola Santos. "But even with it, the Internet is unstable. We had to get used to constantly changing servers." Once again, families with young children had a tougher time. "My son was already a teenager when we moved here, so he had done his research and seemed to be okay," Attila Hilbert recalled. "But my daughter basically cried through the first three months. Before we had a VPN, she could not call any of her friends or our family. When we installed one, she had to learn which content not to search, because visiting banned sights slowed down our connection incredibly." Finally, individual reactions also depend on how badly someone wants to stay connected while in China. "I grew up in a world without social media," Chris, the luxury fashion CFO admitted. "When I arrived in China, even Facebook did not exist, not to mention WeChat. I lived without them before, and I can live without them now."

For expat managers in China, social media troubles are just the beginning. Multinational corporations store, process, and share reports, inventories, employee profiles, balance sheets, and legal documents in global databases and cloud storages. Smart networks remotely operate buildings, factories, vehicles, equipment, warehouses, purchases, and teams. China's deliberately selective data flow creates fractures and bottlenecks that burden data-intensive work with daily headaches. "The Internet is incredibly unreliable and slow," wrote Kristina Kinder, an architect. "Sometimes it takes one hour to e-mail my portfolio, or the process stops in the middle and I have to start all over again. How spoiled we are at home!" Attila Hilbert coached many expats through the shock of losing access to essential applications like search engines, Google Maps, and databases. "Expats face an information shortage that is not only infinitely frustrating but can also be dangerous," he said. "At home, these apps are part of normal life,

---

[44] E. Korczynska. 2018. *Made in China: Confessions of an expat* (Amazon LLC), p. 70.

and many expats feel imprisoned here when they realize their absence. The only solution is to know and accept what you cannot access in China."

Acceptance often resembles the problem more than the solution. "The worst part was that our team kept losing time and data, but nobody knew exactly how," said Marie. "There was no official guidance on the restrictions. There were even look-alike front pages to Google and other inaccessible sites. What frustrated us the most was the disruption of a data base called Taleo, where the Human Resources Department uploaded and processed resumés for the entire organization. When we compared the speed and ease of the process to other countries, we found that in China we lost a few seconds on every single transaction. When you work with large volumes of data, those extra seconds add up and cause measurable damage." A 2019 EU Chamber China paper estimated that loss of document exchanges with headquarters, partners, and customers, office productivity, and essential research amount to 6 percent of the annual revenue of member firms.[45] "It's a disturbing situation," Fernanda Barth admitted. "Broadband connections appear fast in China, but somehow the data transfer is still slow. Without a VPN, it is virtually impossible to do research or even finish routine tasks. We are a Brazilian company, but lots of websites hosted in Brazil are blocked. To access those, managers must go home and use a VPN."

China to the World, Unplugged

The so-called Great Firewall, a gargantuan information technology project that enables control over the Internet, is surprisingly little-known outside of China. Those who are aware of its existence often believe that it is the remnant of darker times before recent reforms. In reality, it is better understood as pushback against initial online enthusiasm that proved too much for Beijing's taste. "When it formally arrived in 1994, it was relatively free and seen as an extension of the Open Door policy of tapping Western knowledge to reform the economy," a 2018 Bloomberg article explained the Internet's early spread in China. "From

---

[45] European Union Chamber of Commerce in China. June 2019. "European Business in China Business Confidence Survey 2019," p. 34.

2000, the foundations of the Great Firewall were laid with the introduction of the Golden Shield Project, a database-driven surveillance system capable of accessing every citizen's record and connecting China's security organizations."[46] Restrictions steadily accelerated in the early 2010s with a new State Internet Information Office (SIIO), later renamed Cyberspace Administration of China (CAC) now headed directly by President Xi Jinping. A State Administration of Press, Publications, Radio, Film, and Television (SAPPRFT) was created to coordinate censorship across diverse media.

While it did benefit local technology firms, the PRC's half-Internet is a fundamentally political project. In 2017, in preparation for the 19th National Congress of the Chinese Communist Party, new regulations required personal identification from owners of websites and URL addresses and allowed the close monitoring of chat messages. Scrutiny was later extended to unlikely forums such as the text chats of Mainland users in online video games.[47] "I think I know what they are trying to do," Shaun Rein told me. "I generally believe in free speech and oppose censorship, but you have seen the disinformation that's being spread about China in the Western world. There would be much more elegant solutions to this problem, but I understand the intentions." Meanwhile, he admitted the futility of the methods used: according to surveys conducted by his firm China Market Research Group, nearly four-fifth of Chinese in their 20s used VPNs to surf the net in major cities. Not only that, he added. "Internet policies in China need a rethink also because Chinese people support their government, including those who can access foreign sites. The restrictions only make people frustrated."

Beyond annoying locals and expats alike, restrictions face foreign firms with impossible choices. The legalities of China's peculiar online ecosystem are blurred at best. "The first step in censorship is you can't talk about the censorship," CNN quoted Eric Liu of China Digital Times

---

[46] Bloomberg UK. n.d. "The Great Firewall of China." www.bloomberg.com/quicktake/great-firewall-of-china (updated November 6, 2018).

[47] A. Rautela. April 2020. "China to Ban Online Gaming, Chatting With Foreigners," TalkEsport. www.talkesport.com/news/china-to-ban-online-gaming-chatting-with-foreigners.

in 2021.[48] Most managers are unsure, for instance, whether their firms commit legal violations by unblocking restricted content with software downloaded abroad or through existing VPN connections. Granting access to Chinese employees is especially risky because the country's labor and national security laws enable authorities to hold companies accountable for violations by employees. "As far as I know," Fernanda said, "WEG does not install VPN solutions at least partly because they don't want Chinese employees to have full access at work." Many companies purchase circumvention software from the same state-owned Internet service providers that enforce the restrictions, but that option is expensive, partial, and allows the monitoring of user traffic.[49] Creative solutions abound. "Our communication goes through Hong Kong, so people can access most, but not all content. That includes our local colleagues," Attila Hilbert explained Danone's practice.

As universal connectivity became essential for business in most sectors, China's reputation and attractiveness among talented expats suffered. Widely referenced surveys routinely ranked China last in Internet freedom, with laggards like Iran, Saudi Arabia, and Cuba receiving double its score.[50] Despite its global ambitions as a technological powerhouse, the PRC increasingly found itself in terrible company. When the Solomon Islands contemplated blocking foreign sites, Freedom House reminded it that "if the government goes ahead with its plan to totally ban Facebook, it would be joining just three other countries which currently do so: China, North Korea and Iran." A 2021 censorship survey

[48] N. Gan and S. George. December 15, 2021. "The Communist Party Thinks China's Prolific Censors Are Not Censoring Enough," CNN Business. https://edition.cnn.com/2021/12/15/tech/china-weibo-censorship-fine-mic-intl-hnk/index.html.

[49] S. Denyer. January 2018. "Command and Control: China's Communist Party Extends Reach Into Foreign Companies," The Washington Post. www.washingtonpost.com/world/asia_pacific/command-and-control-chinas-communist-party-extends-reach-into-foreign-companies/2018/01/28/cd49ffa6-fc57-11e7-9b5d-bbf0da31214d_story.html.

[50] A. Shahbaz and A. Funk. 2019. "Freedom on the Net 2019," Freedom House, p. 25. https://freedomhouse.org/report/freedom-net.

unceremoniously grouped the PRC together with North Korea.[51] While China exports high-speed Internet equipment, its autonomous territories Taiwan and Hong Kong noticeably outpace the motherland in Internet freedom, speed, and competitiveness.[52] Departing expats give vocal testimony to statistics. "I also won't miss China's slow and restricted access to the Internet," serial entrepreneur Marc van der Chijs wrote in a CNN opinion piece. "When the government also started to block VPNs, I realized that the situation was not likely to improve anytime soon."[53]

As opposed to pollution, Internet restrictions keep showing worrying signs of deterioration. "The Chinese government asked Google's services to take down 2,290 items in the first half of last year, according to the company's statistics," a 2018 article reported. "That was more than triple the number it requested in the second half of 2016, which itself had set a record."[54] Foreigners nervously eye the digital horizon. Periodic news of a complete ban on VPN services add to their anxiety even when the rumors turn out to be incorrect. "There's only one remaining way to get unfiltered access to the outside world in China—and Beijing just banned it," announced one article entitled *China Is Trying to Give the Internet a Death Blow*.[55] "The whole situation is very symbolic of China's relationship with the outside world," explained Judith, a German industrial conglomerate's Shanghai-based senior manager for renewable energy investments I coached in intercultural leadership. "It is neither entirely closed, nor

---

[51] P. Bischoff. January 2022. "Internet Censorship 2022: A Global Map of Internet Restrictions," Comparitech. www.comparitech.com/blog/vpn-privacy/internet-censorship-map/.

[52] A. Bris and C. Cabolis. 2020. "IMD World Digital Competitiveness Ranking 2020," *IMD World Competitiveness Center*, p. 24.

[53] M. van der Chijs. March 2013. "Why I'm leaving China," CNN Business. https://money.cnn.com/2013/03/26/news/economy/china-business-pollution/index.html.

[54] "China Presses Its Internet Censorship Efforts Across the Globe." n.d. *The New York Times* www.nytimes.com/2018/03/02/technology/china-technology-censorship-borders-expansion.html (updated March 2, 2018).

[55] J. Palmer. August 2017. "China Is Trying to Give the Internet a Death Blow," *Foreign Policy*. https://foreignpolicy.com/2017/08/25/china-is-trying-to-give-the-internet-a-death-blow-vpn-technology/.

fully open. At work we use the censored internet in compliance with local law, but if commercial VPNs disappeared, it would undermine our whole existence here. You could not get even the most basic things done."

Tellingly, foreigners who ultimately moved away from China often rediscovered the blessings of Internet connectivity, including managers I coached after their relocations to South-East Asia, the Middle East, or Eastern Europe. "I then surprised myself after realizing how productive and seamless working remotely was these days," one former PRC resident wrote in his 2020 blog post. "In Bali there's (relatively) high-speed Internet access and, as a bonus, no need to leap over/through/around the Great Firewall of China with a VPN."[56] From their foreign enclaves, the Dragon Suits who stay witness the country's inner workings like neither locals nor outsiders could. They see it both for what it is and what it is becoming, often with sobering clarity. "Looking out of the window in our office in Lujiazui, you don't see hedge fund managers and Wall Street types walk around here," Shaun Rein told me in late 2019 as he pointed at Shanghai's busy commercial district below. "China is a comfortable place for state-owned banks and a few commercial banks, but with restrictions that hurt businesses on a daily basis, they cannot compete with places like Singapore. It is a real frustration, and that's why I think unless China rethinks its Internet policies, its cities cannot become financial centers."

Bracing for Culture Shock

Clients often ask me how they can spot the best expat candidates for China's frantic, crowded, and yet secluded environment. Bosses want to send their best people to China as advised by consultants, but best in which way? People tend to defy categories—foreigners in China, like any demographic group, show an amazing diversity of motives, choices, and lifestyles. Moreover, few managers who assign expats to China have the full picture necessary to make sufficiently clear decisions. HR specialists at headquarters typically know little about China, and those in China lack

---

[56] R. Robinson. December 2020. "2020 Year in Review. Beijing to Bali to Beijing and Back—or—Hindsight Is 2020," LinkedIn. www.linkedin.com/pulse/2020-year-review-beijing-bali-back-rich-robinson/.

complete insight into the available candidate pool. Most success stories that came out of my interviews were trial and error at the beginning, then a serendipitous combination of persistent self-improvement and accidental opportunity. As the subjects themselves often admitted, they found themselves at the right place at the right time, then worked very hard to do the right thing. Meanwhile, decision makers are aware how much of the process is up to luck, especially as their firms bet increasing amounts of money on the China market.

As coach Bronwyn Bowery-Ireland observed, almost anyone can be reasonably productive almost anywhere, including China. Still, decision makers who pair expats with jobs try hard to understand what separates thriving expats from the ones who simply get by. Why is it that two managers with very similar resumés approach their expat assignments completely differently, with dramatically diverse results? The key to the riddle, I tell my clients, is the difference between constants and variables within the complex formula of relocating someone: what will change and what will stay the same after the dramatic move of settling in another continent. Most multinational firms consult the performance records of applicants under the assumption that people who did well in one country would also succeed in another. In fact, little will remain of that record after relocation. Performance largely depends on surroundings: why would someone remain equally productive after moving to a place where everything, from colleagues to the climate and the job itself, is unfamiliar? Meanwhile, decision makers devote too little attention to what remains the same regardless of location: the candidate's character and personal history.

It seems that corporate hiring and promotion practices confuse the order of two essential elements of succeeding as an expat. They assume that if they successfully match a job with the right professional experience, the appointee's life in the new location will form spontaneously around work. In fact, it is the other way around: only expats with a favorable chemistry toward their new surroundings can do a better than average job. In order to establish that chemistry in advance, HR managers must learn to push resumés to the side for a minute, and consider subtleties such as the temperament, personal background, and recent life experience of possible candidates. Will they have the flexibility to adapt to an entirely different pace, the tranquility to accept China's cultural, environmental, and digital eccentricities, and the diligence to overcome them, personally as well as professionally? Are they alone, and are they likely to get lonely? Have they experienced subtropical summers, endless crowds, straight-faced bureaucrats in an autocratic regime, overtime hours, being the only non-native at a 100-person banquet?

As later chapters explain, such holistic personal profiles are not as hard to prepare as it may sound. However, to make good use of them, decision makers must avoid another frequent shortcoming of overseas appointments: to try and match them with stereotypical generalizations of conditions in China as a whole. In fact, I often advise companies to forget about *China* as a destination. What they must find is the best match with a specific job, in a specific place, at a specific time. Individual candidates will never have to adapt to what intercultural experts call macrocultures, in this case China, but to the specific subcultures and microcultures of the city, local community, workplace, surrounding colleagues, and fellow expats. The initial experience, and consequently the process of acclimatization, can be entirely different depending on whether newcomers live in the center or the green suburbs, work with local or foreign colleagues and how many times they had to relocate in recent years. Once the firm hired one project director at a business unit in China, the second one's requirements might be entirely different: talking to someone who has recently gone through the same experience is invaluable in stressful situations.

When we discuss the secrets of successful expatriate careers in China, personal experience is often the first thing that seasoned foreign executives mention. "To start with, China is not for first-time expats," Attila Hilbert of Danone echoed the opinion of several experienced HR specialists. "The culture shock is too big here, the risk of making cultural mistakes too high." The People's Republic stands apart from most expat destinations in terms of legal, financial, and commercial practices, political system, and administrative procedures. Regulations on routine business transactions, from the employment contracts through wire transfers to corporate mergers and acquisitions, are obscure combinations of a Soviet-style operating system, recent additions of market elements, and remnants of previous regimes. Policies can change overnight, and Chinese colleagues are so used to their fickleness that they gracefully comply without further notice. Many foreigners he met, Hilbert told me, lacked the mental agility required in such an environment, even after previous assignments in locations such as Hong Kong, Japan, or Singapore.

At Danone China, Hilbert preferred candidates with experience in challenging places like Africa, he said. They adapted much faster, which is essential even for seasoned expats. "In Pune, foreign families lived close by," Angelo Puglisi from Benteler Automotive recalled one of India's top expat hubs before his five years in China as Asia Pacific Head of HR and Marketing. "When we moved to Shanghai, it took time to get used to our foreign friends living an hour's drive away." A few years in a place with China's size and complexity can alter someone's mentality in many ways. One peculiarity of long-term Dragon Suits is how they dismiss contradictions between opposing beliefs. I witnessed this phenomenon every time someone described China as a diverse and cosmopolitan place, then proudly claimed to be the only foreigner around. "In the rest of China, foreigners are sprinkled and often scarce," someone commented to a discussion on online forum Quora in 2017. "One of my friends was the only foreigner in a small town (small by Chinese standards—it had a population of 2 million people). Even in the 'foreigner friendly areas', you can go for a few kilometers without seeing a foreigner."[57]

Most expats who adapted to life in China have similarly mixed feelings about challenges like pollution, restricted Internet, and other annoyances, including cultural misunderstandings, crowds, the lack of nature in and around large cities, confusing expectations at work, and the country's often anachronistic political environment. Whether they are annoyed or entertained by these peculiarities, and consequently how aptly they reap the considerable rewards of expat life in China, depends on their distinctive nature, culture, and circumstances. Single male executives with *work hard, play hard* philosophies fare better in Eastern Chinese metropolises than Briana's colleague on her tormented quest to find a life partner. Briana herself, however, another lone female executive, was one of my most fulfilled interview subjects. Renata and Nicola, a young couple from South America, found a rewarding niche after their initial difficulties. "Socializing with colleagues was not part of our culture anyway, so we

---

[57] Quora. n.d. "How Many Foreigners Are Living in China?" www.quora.com/How-many-foreigners-are-living-in-China (accessed July 12, 2022).

didn't expect it here. We started making friends once we signed up for an EMBA course and met local people."

In a few months, some foreigners may choose to blend neatly into the culture of their immediate surroundings, others remain obvious (and oblivious) outsiders. China's largest cities offer enough variety for all preferences. I often nurtured the secret hope that I would be able to play *China in One Word* again with the same group, a few years into their stay in China, but so far that has never happened. I am convinced that impressions would be more nuanced, perhaps to the point of making it impossible to summarize them in one carefully chosen word. Even though I cannot track entire teams, I often meet individual expats years after an introductory coaching or training program they attended as new arrivals in China. Some spend their weekends rubbing shoulders with local friends in alleyway noodle shops, some over champagne brunches at five-star hotels. Some become surprisingly fluent in Mandarin, others average a new vocabulary item each year. Still, most of them share one important characteristic. While many popular expat destinations teem with backpackers, digital nomads, academics on sabbaticals, wandering artists, and affluent retirees, most foreigners in China are in the country to work. To know their lives, we must enter their offices.

CHAPTER 3

Gearing Up

First Days at Work

Chinese people love inaugurations. When a new shop opens in your street in a Chinese city, you cannot miss the piling floral arrangements and loud rehearsals a week in advance. Welcoming ceremonies for incoming expats are great excuses to celebrate too, often complete with red banners and prepared speeches. Yet, most foreigners I asked were pleasantly surprised that after the somewhat overwhelming welcomes, the local teams and fellow managers who greeted them turned out to be straightforward urbanites, more Wall Street than Great Wall. "At the beginning, the lack of contrast puzzled me," Richard Eardley described his first impression of Hays Shanghai. "But then it occurred to me that the Chinese people surrounding me were pre-selected and pre-trained." He was right, and there was an even larger dynamic at play. Local employees at multinational companies are an adventurous minority on their own right. As they often admit at job interviews, they want work in foreign languages, meet foreign people, and eventually to travel or sometimes even relocate abroad. They want to be surrounded by things, ideas, news, and habits that mainstream China cannot offer.

This means that local colleagues serve as welcome committees to expats in many ways. "Without them, even the simplest tasks can cause daily frustration," Angelo Puglisi of Benteler explained. "You must trust your household to your housekeeper, and your and your kid's life to the driver, because most foreigners don't drive here." Judith fully agreed as she recalled her first weeks as an incoming senior manager. "I cannot imagine how people survived here before WeChat," she voiced her gratitude to a local social media app that links over a billion people, including foreign damsels in distress like herself. "One evening, there was a knock on my door and there were two uniformed men standing outside. Their English proficiency matched my Chinese: zero. To explain their purpose, they showed me a printed notice—in Chinese characters. Without instantaneous intervention from my colleagues through the messaging app, things could have gone messy before I realised that they came to match the name in my passport with the local police station's occupant register."

"Being an expat in China is not, psychologically speaking, an easy posting," warned a publication in 2014.[1] The nation's ageless cultural traditions influence a whole spectrum of daily habits, from tastes in tea to the way citizens should approach authorities. Camera-wielding new expats cheerfully notice that people breakfast differently, shop differently, ride bikes and buses differently. But as early exploration gives way to daily routine, the same differences can also obstruct and annoy: mistaking decoratively wrapped spicy beef jerky for candy, people crowding and jumping queues, a visa clerk's resentful expectation of a submissive approach. Local helpers are essential in that early stage of forming new routines: the right amount of intervention helps foreigners see mishaps as pleasurable learning opportunities with little downside. Professional service providers handle their essentials like accommodation, insurance, and police registration. For a few glorious days or weeks, newcomers have little more to do but show up for prearranged appointments (typically with a local aid) and learn to tell dried meat from confectionery.

I trained, coached, or advised hundreds of foreigners who had recently arrived in China convinced that a thorough understanding of the culture would ensure collaboration with local people. But their actual experience was more akin to Richard Eardley's pleasant surprise over the smooth sailing onto routine work. Understanding a culture, any culture, takes the number of years that most foreigners simply do not have in a given location. Therefore, the larger the cultural GAP between the home and destination countries, the wiser it is to operate through intercultural hubs: conferences, agencies, multinational corporations, and cosmopolitan

---

[1] C. Devonshire-Ellis. November 2014. "Hong Kong Murders and Expatriate Psychological Issues in China," *China Briefing*. www.china-briefing.com/ news/2014/11/04/can-recent-hong-kong-murders-teach-us-hr-issues-china .html.

cities in either or both territories. That makes it easier to work together but also less important to understand one another beyond superficial business transactions. Such cultural islands seldom result in profound changes in the perception and habits of people who work there, compared with more dramatic immersions such as marrying into a local family, or starting a small business far from visitor hubs. For most people who work at cultural islands, intercultural flexibility is a sort of behavioral dress code that they can freely ditch at the end of the working day.

Like Richard, most new China expats were surrounded by preselected colleagues accustomed to dealing with *laowai*—an endearingly discriminating Mandarin term for foreigners. That is a helpful arrangement: newcomers who plunge into the eye of a cultural hurricane (academics at local universities, agricultural experts, exchange students lodged with local families, and so forth) testify to the near-impossibility of normal routines for the first few weeks or even months. The culturally mixed workforce, procedures, and customs of multinational work environments at foreign firms allow relatively free experimentation without the danger of halting professional tasks with every misstep. "At the beginning, I tried to work with Chinese colleagues like I would with Germans, because they seemed to be open to a direct cultural style," Henrik König of Thyssen-Krupp recalled. "But their reactions were often the complete opposite of my expectations. At other times, I tried to use what I knew about traditional Chinese values, but the result was equally confusing. It felt as if they had a box where they could pack away their old Chinese ways, only to open it again when they wanted to."

Henrik instinctively spotted a scientifically proven fact: people respond to intercultural difficulties with a sort of face-changing routine. Acting differently to reduce the stress of working with foreigners is a rewarding experience. But second-guessing normal routines also requires extra attention and burns far more energy than just going about one's usual business. Eventually, the result is what psychologists call control fatigue: the claustrophobic feeling of constantly defying familiar habits, as if walking in undersized shoes. For many expats I asked, it all started with working without a common language. "Initially, I had no language problem with colleagues around me, who were all proficient in English," Judith told me. "But China was my first location where I also had team members with no shared language. For a while I communicated with them through local colleagues, but that is not the way I like to operate." At the time of writing, the English First English Proficiency Index ranked China at 49th place as a country of *moderate proficiency*, near Chile and Russia.[2] Urban hubs fare better than the country in general, but challenges of communicating with the wider local organization eventually limit many expat managers to their close circles of English-speaking collaborators.

The fatigue is often mutual. "Chinese people have two annoying habits when they work in English," explained Tony Shi of Benteler. "One is to start off in the team's shared language but constantly switch back to Chinese when the discussion becomes more complex. Another comes from a characteristic of the Chinese language: we understand each other by reading between the lines, even when we say very little. We do not have that efficiency in English, so local colleagues feel that they are wasting a lot of time when communicating with foreigners." Incoming expats know it would help to learn Mandarin, the official dialect of the PRC. Research published in Laurie Underwood's coauthored 2020 book *China CEO II* (a sequel to her previous *China CEO*) pointed at Mandarin proficiency as a differentiating factor of high-potential executives in China.[3] But that is understandably a tall order while working full-time. Angelo tried. "The bottom line is, you cannot do it alone," he said. "You need regular lessons or a tutor. It did help me after I reached a basic conversational level, but that took me six months of very hard work." Consequently, proficiency in Chinese did not become a requirement at most multinationals, who also struggle to hire locals with business-level proficiency in foreign languages.[4]

---

[2] Education First. n.d. "EF English Proficiency Index: The world's Largest Ranking of Countries and Regions by English Skills." www.ef.com/wwen/epi/ (accessed July 12, 2022).

[3] J.A. Fernandez and L. Underwood. 2020. *China CEO II: Voices of Experience From 25 Top Executives Leading MNCs in China* (Oxford: Wiley), p. 75.

[4] J. Huang. January 2013. "Developing Local Talent for Future Leadership," *China Business Review*. www.chinabusinessreview.com/developing-local-talent-for-future-leadership/.

Cultural challenges run deeper than language anyway, as one of my former consulting projects illustrates. In 2013, a Western European food conglomerate hired me to find out why their human resource practices clashed with Asian culture. One devil in the detail turned out to be— names. In the firm's traditional European markets, titles such as *Doctor* for PhDs and *Director* for certain seniority levels were so important that adding the proper prefixes to surnames was part of performance criteria for managers. Predictably, at Asian branches, the system imploded. China, Japan, Korea, Malaysia, and other countries in the region have fundamentally different naming traditions from both Europe and one another. People who live Chinese-speaking lives cannot be on first-name basis with each other, because surnames come first, and what follows is seldom used to informally address someone. If you ever meet Huawei founder Ren Zhengfei, bear in mind that his surname is *Ren*, and do not call him *Zhengfei* to break the ice. You may hear local colleagues call him by his family name with various suffixes, depending on their own seniority. The system makes locals proud, confuses foreign learners, and annoys those who hope for cultural shortcuts.

Studying Chinese naming traditions is good advice, but again, easier said than done. Conventions express intricate social assumptions and relationships, and mistakes carry alarmingly high reputational cost. To avoid offending others, cultural islands find creative ways to reduce the risk. In China, a characteristically nonconfrontational solution is what I call name swapping. Chinese people with international connections customarily chose foreign first names followed by their Mandarin family name. Scattered on my desk right now are business cards from Lily Le, Kevin Pan, Henry Zheng, Ben Zhong, and Kathy Lu. Creative first-name choices are part of the cultural fun: I recently met Apple, Rainbow, and Hawk, as well as Leonid, Hans, and Yuki. Meeting Lucy Liu or Jackie Chan is only a question of time in China—unless you insist on the real celebrities. "This 'borrowed identity' turns out to be very useful when communicating with old and new acquaintances alike," explained David C. S. Li from the Hong Kong Institute of Education. "It helps to speed up the process of getting acquainted—something that matters to a lot of people working in various professions, from business to public relations, from communications to international education. This is something that traditional Chinese practice does not encourage."[5]

In turn, foreigners take Chinese names, usually helped by local colleagues or Mandarin teachers. Like foreign first names for the Chinese, this habit also originates in former concession ports. Merchants there had a harder time than today's expats, having to multitask in French, English, Portuguese, Russian, Japanese, Hindi, Malay, and local dialects, including the then less widespread Mandarin but also Cantonese, Hokkien (from today's Fujian province), Hunanese, Yunnanese, Tibetan, Uyghur, and Mongolian. Adopted Chinese names helped interaction outside of foreign enclaves, and typically included, as they still do, a single-character surname and a double-character given name. Foreigners are advised to pick surnames from China's widely known list of a 100 common choices. Given names usually consist of two characters whose pronunciation imitates the bearer's given name. Chinese characters must be chosen carefully and with local help, because they reflect the bearer's own character and fate. Name swapping makes life easier primarily by reducing the chances of twisting someone's foreign-sounding name beyond recognition, a cultural mistake that few people accept with grace.

Being confused by all this is a sure sign of slowly understanding the cultural environment around foreigners in China. Expats do daily, sometimes hourly commutes between multiple cultures of families, firms, communities, districts, cities, and professional circles. Foreigners who momentarily forget where they are can easily upset those who hold the key to their success in the country. Navigating this cultural maze is hard and getting useful advice is even harder. Widely available materials on intercultural adaptation often echo superficial soundbites about China's collectivism, social harmony, and timelessly spiritual attitude to life, sending foreigners down the wrong adaptational path. Asking local colleagues or friends can be equally misleading. Most people are unable to describe their native cultures, and even if they do, their explanations reflect their personal circumstances at least as much as the surrounding culture.

---

[5] C. Chan. January 2016. "Why Some Chinese Speakers Also Use Western Names," *Deutsche Welle*. www.dw.com/en/why-some-chinese-speakers-also-use-western-names/a-18966907.

Expatriates, on the other hand, need to learn fast, and need widely applicable lessons. Above all, they must figure out the unspoken rules that guide their local colleagues, bosses, clients, and associates on whom their future success depends.

Cultures of Collaboration

It was one of those moments when a fleeting remark allowed a profound insight into the soul of millions. Since she uttered it in 2010, the casual admission of a Chinese dating show's participant that she would "rather cry in a BMW than laugh on a bicycle" has been endlessly quoted and examined.[6] Some paraded it as evidence for the erosion of China's societal values, others as a proof of its population's determination to come out ahead in a global race to economic domination. Some loved it, some hated it. But however people encountered the quote, in Mandarin, English, or other languages, wondering where China was located or after a decade in the country, few doubted that it was a noteworthy expression of something profound. It caught the world's imagination because in a few words, it revealed unresolved contradictions between traditional self-sacrifice and modern ambition, global aspirations, and national pride. It also sent a message to the world: China would prevail or die trying. Most likely, it would prevail. Characteristically urban, contemporary, and progressive, this mentality is an essential element of the environment that surrounds foreigners in the country.

With each passing year and new experience, foreigners start scratching the polished surface of social interaction in expat hubs and unveil ever deeper layers of local peculiarities. Based on my interviews, the most available source of such discoveries is how Chinese colleagues work among themselves, and the earliest challenge it reveals is a straightforward one: speed. How fast or slowly someone prefers to get things done is a highly intimate choice. An environment that dictates an unfamiliar

---

[6] R. Zavoretti. 2016. "Is It Better to Cry in a BMW or to Laugh on a Bicycle? Marriage, 'Financial Performance Anxiety', and the Production of Class in Nanjing (People's Republic of China)," *Modern Asian Studies* 50, no. 4, pp. 1190–1219.

pace can cause deep frustration, and the China where our expats arrived was extreme in this sense too. The country attracts and retains foreign talent with highly lucrative offers, but the pace is pitiless. Foreign firms that establish local branches must compete in one of Earth's most diligent societies. Chinese people are shrewd entrepreneurs in a hurry to make up for centuries of their nation's relative backwardness, and the nascent middle class of its largest cities insist on running Marathons at a sprinter's pace. Their ambition and enthusiasm are contagious. It takes a few months in Shanghai or Shenzhen to pull all-weekenders and answer work-related calls at night. It takes just a bit longer to sulk at newcomers who refuse to do so.

Chinese project teams work for velocity: faster manufacturing, speedier transportation and delivery, instant customer care. Foreign firms must stay competitive: *China CEO* names fast recruitment, training, and promotion as keys to retaining and motivating talented Chinese people.[7] Companies (local and foreign alike) dictate increasing speed not only to beat technological and fashion trends but also to outpace China's ubiquitous copycat competitors. Whether the product is cups of coffee or ocean liners, delivery times are fractions of the global average. "The first year was a shock, especially compared to my previous post in India," Angelo Puglisi admitted. "But then I managed to readjust my work style. I understood that Chinese people prioritise getting things done fast. Maybe not perfectly, but fast." Some love it, some hate it, some make the best of it. Eventually, Angelo not only adapted to the new pace but even started seeing his native culture in a different light. "Everybody was on board to do something big," he says. "Business in Europe can be too slow and organised. Managing people in India, my first overseas assignment, felt repetitive and stressful. Then I got transferred to China, and its speed, energy and dynamism swept me off my feet."

China's speed, like its climate, is either an irritation or inspiration depending on personal chemistry. Marie enjoyed the rush with her pharmaceutical team from the start. "Working with Chinese people is lots of fun," she told me. "Perhaps I enjoyed it so much because they are fast

---

[7] J.A. Fernandez and L. Underwood. 2011. *China CEO: Voices of Experience From 20 International Business Leaders* (New York, NY: John Wiley & Sons), p. 55.

learners, and I am good at delegating. Sometimes I felt like I was the one to put my feet on the gas pedal, and I had to remind myself to give people time to think and absorb." Christian Eh, Senior Vice President at Covestro China, disagreed. I coached Christian in China-specific leadership skills after he had spent years in various Asian countries. "I guess it all depends on individuals. For me personally, China was exhausting. The pace, the volume, the crowds—they burn energy like Christmas shopping in Cologne." Coping strategies vary wildly according to temperament. Some of the most successful foreign executives I met in China adopted the local work style so thoroughly that superiors at headquarters told me they seemed *too Chinese* for their taste. Others learned to tactically mimic but not internalize indigenous practices. Still others surrounded themselves with a trusted circle of like-minded colleagues.

Understandably, there are just as many locals fed up with China's fast-forward work culture as foreigners. As they burn the candle at both ends in the nation's most competitive industries, they are aware of the physical, mental, and spiritual damage it causes to them and their families. Even the Chinese government, seldom an advocate of moderation, repeatedly restricts abusive corporate practices like the so-called 9-9-6 regime: 12 straight work hours from nine in the morning to nine in the evening, six days a week. But pathological competition forces market participants, from individual employees to entire firms, to creatively evade regulations, for instance by logging overtime as voluntary, or not logging it at all.[8] Foreigners with mindful work habits risk losing corporate battles, wars, and their most ambitious people as well. "Local employees assume that multinational firms send their best managers to China, so there are high expectations on us foreigners," Renata Santos told me. Expats must deliver world-class performance without pushing their teams to exhaustion. Then, those with a successful survival strategy soon face an even subtler challenge: the relationship between individuals and the collective in Chinese society.

---

[8] M. Cyrill. April 2016. "The 996 Work Culture That's Causing a Burnout in China's Tech World," *China Briefing*. www.china-briefing.com/news/996-work-culture-china-tech-sector-burnout/.

The Culture of Closeness

"Chinese people are friendly and welcoming, so don't be surprised if someone asks you out for lunch or dinner," the *HSBC Expat Explorer Survey* wrote. "Equally, don't be offended if a stranger asks about your age, marital status or parents' jobs. These topics aren't considered private and are common points of discussion."[9] Westerners accustomed to intensive but skin-deep professional interactions and a six o'clock separation between work and private life often collide with local habits. "Chinese employees quarrel like families," Christian Eh told me, echoing a frequent observation. For better or worse, Chinese workplaces are emotional gatherings that can shock foreigners with little privacy, lots of intimacy, and endless compromises. A firm that feels like home sounds wonderful, but Asian families are more demanding than European or North American ones. Chinese people often choose their studies and first jobs according to dynastic aspirations, consult their elders on bonuses, promotions, international postings, and conflicts with superiors. Parents accompany young applicants to job interviews. At one firm I ran as a General Manager, the Chinese owner suggested I fix the performance issues of a local manager by phoning her husband.

Expats seldom manage to observe this dynamic from a safe distance. Locals give them temporary leeway to adjust, but sooner or later, expectations to treat Chinese colleagues, clients, and suppliers with due intimacy catch up with them. "Here, you cannot just say 'no' to customers if their request conflicts with company policy: you must work for compromises," Tony Shi of Benteler explained. "If you cannot find one, you must try harder. Compromises keep the customer happy, keep the team happy, which means the manager himself is happy. More importantly, everyone learns in the process: expats and local managers, even the client." Of course, compromises have drawbacks too. At many firms I advised, colleagues dutifully clocked in for absent friends, and managers had to infiltrate the loyal ranks to curb the practice. Foreigners with a tough and

---

[9] HSBC. n.d. "Living in Mainland China: Your Guide to Expat Life in Mainland China." www.expat.hsbc.com/expat-explorer/expat-guides/mainland-china/living-in-mainland-china/.

straightforward temperament resent such near-spiritual level of interdependence. Others begin to see its advantages over their home cultures. "In Germany, people who were left out of a meeting will torpedo the decision later," said Christian Eh. "In China, those who are in the room speak for everyone, and you can rest assured they will deliver collectively."

Accommodating to China's team culture is a steeper and more emotional learning curve than picking up its work speed. Some obviously take the wrong start. "My work style is task orientated," Renata admitted. "I get straight down to business without social niceties. Local employees disastrously misunderstood my intentions. They thought I was there to fire them. I made some of them cry." Others were unaware of their incompatibility until a few episodes, however mundane, revealed a gaping cultural canyon. "Chinese hospitality overwhelms me," architect Kristina Kinder's expat memoire described a series of business trips in the country. "I wonder if this kind of hospitality is expected by Chinese people when they visit us in the West. If that's the case, then the office I worked for, including myself, have been incredibly rude to Chinese friends and clients in the past."[10] Experimentation and even eventual success can be utterly confusing. "One day, a local colleague looked a bit sad," Renata told me. "It turned out that her parents were unwell in hospital. I felt helpless and wanted to comfort her in the Brazilian way, so I asked if she needed a hug. She flatly refused. But in a few days, she reappeared. 'Do you remember the hug you wanted to give me?' she said. 'I need it now.'"

The key to success with China's collective culture, my interview subjects almost invariably said, was to accept its differences without trying too hard to assimilate. "The Chinese speed is based on the way the Chinese economy works, and the Western speed is based on the pace of Europe or the US—there is a strong disconnect between these two," explained Rachel, China Director at a world-leading corporate think-tank, over black tea in the café of her Beijing gated community in early 2020. Taking sides and forcing that pace on the company seldom works across cultural divisions. A soberly balanced attitude enables foreigners to contemplate the advantages and disadvantages of local habits and manage

---

[10] K. Kinder. 2015. *Wonderlanded: Life as an Expat in China* (Amazon LLC), p. 35.

their work accordingly. "The pace can be fast and focused," Briana told me. "Once a decision is made, getting to the end-product happens very quickly. But at the beginning it also baffled me how late in the day they started working and the long lunchbreaks they took. In North America you can walk around in the office at five-thirty in the afternoon and hear a pin drop, because people dash off to pick up kids and run errands. Here, people are still at work at seven in the evening."

Ultimately, the way to reduce pressure is not cultural imitation but a clever combination of imported and indigenous work styles to match personal temperament with performance goals. Communication between newcomers and experienced Dragon Suits is essential. "My expat manager told me to focus on results instead of hours," Briana recalled. "He told me I would get messages day and night. That working from home on Fridays would not function here because I had to be physically present. But he also said, 'Just because you are in China, it doesn't mean you have to completely adapt.' He said a lot of those extra hours would be filled with activity, not outcome." Annoyances aside, most expats I talked to were delighted to play an important part in China's thrilling saga of economic success story. Research on global corporate culture revealed China as one of the most optimistic societies on Earth.[11] Their enthusiasm can be contagious. "The Chinese were far from perfectionists, but they got things done quickly," Angelo said. "Everyone had a lot of positive energy, at work and afterwards." Thrill, however, can also be tiring. This leads us to another danger of expat life in China: exhaustion.

Work, Life, Balance

Workdays in China's metropolises, like their bustling streets and blinking neon signs, can swipe anyone off their feet. Long and strenuous hours breed collaboration, camaraderie, and performance beyond expectations. Personal chauffeurs, secretaries, and housekeepers boost self-confidence and allow foreign families to work, learn, and socialize without worrying

---

[11] OC Tanner Institute. n.d. "2018 Global Culture Report," p. 24. www.octanner.com/content/dam/oc-tanner/documents/white-papers/2018/2018_Global_Culture_Report.pdf.

about distracting duties. For a few decades, expatriates inhabited a sweet triangle of generous performance-based remuneration, a soaring economy, and local prices that compared well with richer countries. With incomes matching those in the United States and top European destinations, residences, rides, home trips, medical care, and children's education paid by employers, they could save for rainy days. Singles could hit the night with fellow foreigners from all over the world. Families trusted their kids to nannies and the multiethnic faculties of international schools. Nor did they have to worry about driving to incessant soccer practices and parent–teacher meetings: international schools in China occupied kids with the spartan routines set by affluent local families.

Expats themselves adopted the local work ethic. Many Dragon Suits felt that in China, everything aligned for doing great things, perhaps the first time in their lives. "A year or two here, and many European managers secretly dread the time when they eventually return home," Christian Eh told me. "There, you must be genuinely rich to have this lifestyle." But work psychologists classify money as a so-called hygienic motivator, whose lack stimulates more directly than its abundance. Once the family repaid debts, bought a home or two, and saved enough for their children's education, few managers celebrated monthly paychecks anymore. Their focus shifted to less tangible goals like learning new skills and plotting promotions. China was the perfect place for such ambitions, but after a year or two, the thrill could wear off, and incessant challenges could wear anyone down. "During my first year I did little else than work, and that was very hard," Judith recalled her transition from a previous job in Manila. "Of course, we worked hard in the Philippines too, but that made me much happier there. Filipinos are straightforward and cheerful. China makes it much harder and lengthier to establish relationships."

It is easy to see why expatriates get lonely in China's megacities. "Companies sponsor a highly desirable lifestyle and expect nearly superhuman performance in return," explained to me Dr. George Hu, Chief of Mental Health at Shanghai's United Family Pudong Hospital, in early 2019. "As busy managers see it, their employers provide the family's house, cars, cleaning staff and schooling so that they can focus on work. It is easy to lose sight of healthy boundaries." The result is what Dr. Hu called a weakened sense of agency—busy expats dutifully toil away without asking too many questions. Once caught up in that robotic mindset heroically called *firefighting* in business circles, regaining control is problematic. Alerts, reminders, appointments, tasks, and chores cast their victims into vicious downward spirals of stress, fatigue, and ceaseless activity. Eventually, the shock of abandoning familiar places and loved ones, relocation, adjustment to new places, jobs, cultures, colleagues, and homes often accumulate into a cartoon raincloud that casts a shadow on every commute, meeting, and meal, regardless of stellar careers and swelling bank accounts.

Earning the privilege of an enviable lifestyle is the defining mindset among many expat communities, and China is no exception. While a family could earn, spend, and show off like never before, they often neglect rest, intimacy, and spirituality. Managers, spouses, kids, and even household pets frantically follow precision routines, and their surroundings reinforce unhealthy habits. China made astonishing leaps in economic welfare, but life quality, mental and physical health stumble behind of feeble feet. Urban citizens of the PRC long suffered from varieties of conditions related to the scarcity of nature and nurture, from cardiovascular to reproductive and mental ills.[12] Secret weapons of economic triumph like the 9-9-6 regime tragically fired in both directions, damaging individuals, families, and communities. In 2021, in the midst of debates about China's waning population, academic Zeng Diyang rang a widely heeded alarm bell when he wrote that "being forced to work outside regular hours and not getting compensated is a powerful restraint against people from engaging in activities related to reproduction"— simply put, they were too busy for sex.[13]

"It's kind of a workaholic culture," Rachel explained. "It starts with school and then it goes up to professional life." But expats must know where duty ends and dysfunctions begin, and chronic workaholism in Chinese cities has long fallen in the latter category. In a 2010

---

[12] G. Filippelli and P. Gong. May 2018. "Aspiring Toward Healthy Cities in China," *Eos*. https://eos.org/editors-vox/aspiring-toward-healthy-cities-in-china.

[13] G. James. September 2021. "Too Much Work and Not Enough Sex Threatens China's New Population Plans," *Society & Culture*. https://supchina.com/2021/09/23/too-much-work-and-not-enough-sex-threatens-chinas-new-population-plans/.

Gallup Global Wellbeing study, China unflatteringly ranked between Afghanistan and Nepal.[14] The forced transition from poverty to economic miracle took its human toll, and expats received their share of damages as well as benefits. To make things worse, habitual means of stress relief are absent from the futuristic, skyscraper-pierced landscape. Simple remedies like a walk in the crisp morning air, an idle day in nature or the closeness of a trusted friend are rare and dear for expats enclosed by physical and digital walls. Emotional isolation follows almost inevitably. Depressed people feel lonely even in the thickest crowd. Helpline operators bear daily witness to the grotesque evolutionary instinct to fig-leaf our wounds with false confidence when we are most vulnerable, and expats are a proud lot. Unwilling to offload their insecurities on their bosses, colleagues, and clients for one reason, their family and friends for another, outwardly successful professionals often wither emotionally.

Modern urbanism was a brainchild of the industrial revolution. One of its side-effects was the stress relief we call sports today. Engines became faster and stronger but also louder, dirtier, and uglier than traditional transportation. Nostalgic middle-class urbanites turned boating, horse-riding, running, and cycling into ways to release steam after long working weeks. Engines widened the outreach of empires, and Western colonizers enthusiastically carried their pastimes around the globe, coaching reluctant locals in the useless skills of golfing, tennis, cricket, and going nowhere in outdated vehicles. Initial resistance gradually subsided, and wherever modernization went, the folly followed: today, perspiring Tokyo bankers run around the Imperial Palace on weekends. Chinese cities were not designed with such pastimes in mind. Traditional medicine shunned rigorous exercise and recommended a restful lifestyle instead. Legend has it that when 19th-century British officials invited Qing counterparts for tennis, the Mandarins sent their servants to run such bothersome errands. Up to the present day, sports were periodically labeled by nationalist movements as tools of Western domination alien from local traditions.[15]

---

[14] Gallup. 2010. "Gallup Global Wellbeing the Behavioral Economics of GDP Growth." https://news.gallup.com/poll/126965/gallup-global-wellbeing.aspx.

[15] Y. Yufei. February 2022. "When Beijing's Skating Rinks Were Battlefields," *Sixth Tone*. www.sixthtone.com/news/1009514/when-beijings-skating-rinks-were-battlefields.

In the early 2000s when I arrived in China, most people I saw exercising in cities were senior citizens following the ancient Taoist practices of forearm-slapping and reverse-walking. Those who ran were usually armed forces, athletes, or in a hurry. A renewed interest in modernity brought football pitches, jogging lanes, and badminton parlors but often at the expense of remaining green patches. In most public parks, flowers are neatly rank-and-filed, lawns are off-limits, and climbing trees is prohibited. Industry dominated suburbs and beaches until developers recently started converting them into exclusive resorts. Superhighways, skyscrapers, rapid trains, and glitzy malls thoroughly impress foreigners at the beginning, but can gradually get bothersome. "In the long run, the lack of nature was difficult to bear," Henrik König explained. As a substitute to long-distance running or cycling, he took early walks along the Huangpu River promenade near Shanghai's Mercedes-Benz Arena, and watched the crowds grow. "Soon it felt like a railway station: thousands of people cramming together with cheap music blasting from mounted speakers and mobile phones. Eventually, it was so annoying that I stopped going there."

Most expats live and work in commercial and residential centers enclosed by 30 stories of concrete, in turn surrounded by more concrete. When families are fed up with confinement, where do they go? Dinners, parties, barbecues, and spa resorts. Those places can easily overdo the job of making people forget the pressures of daily life. The problem, Dr. Hu explained, was that busy expats often reach for the hair of the dog that bit them, seeking relief in intense activity rather than rest. Asked to name the most harmful example, he joined the chorus of other health experts I interviewed: alcohol! On average, Chinese people are moderate drinkers.[16] Although boozy dinners are quintessential status symbols among rich businesspeople and party cadres, Chinese tradition stigmatizes public drunkenness and discourages women from drinking at all. Expats, on the other hand, freely go with the flow. Networking events serve free-flowing wine from the afternoon onward and urban restaurants take pride in their imported and local liquor selections. "When I first arrived, I was at bars

---

[16] American Addiction Centers. n.d. "Global Drinking Demographics." www.alcohol.org/guides/global-drinking-demographics/ (accessed July 12, 2022).

four or five nights a week," Henrik König recalled. "It was not about the drinking: it was just fun to hang out with Germans from all the big companies, expats from all over the world, Filipino cover bands and random people of all kinds and nationalities."

Eventually, expat families must finish their drinks, return to normalcy, and face another risk of self-healing. Expat jobs in China attract ambitious people, and selection criteria are strict. But the temperament that spurs applicants to high performance at work can backfire when it is time to rest. "As the years went by," Henrik König continued, "bar-hopping gave way to badminton with friends over the weekend, or trips to Dalian and Qingdao. I joined a gym nearby, the largest I have ever seen." But some expats fail to notice how persistently they focus on performance targets even in their pastimes: strenuous fitness routines, Marathons, dramatic yoga positions, or competing for attention at charities, dinners, networking events, and on social media. Gigantic gyms, indoor badminton courts, and networking lack the natural cleansing power of beaches, mountains, and peaceful parks. Self-improvement and socializing may be enviable, but they add further items to the already-busy schedule of expat families, and China's metropolises offer little alternative. "When I advised managers to get away from their phones and relax," Dr. Hu said, "many downloaded fitness and meditation apps. I had to remind them to fight the temptation and put the gadget away in a drawer."

Employers of China-based expats should pay close attention to such seemingly mundane issues. Regaining control in unfamiliar surroundings is an uphill struggle. Those who fail often leave: turnover rates at Chinese branches of global firms are consistently a quarter higher than the global average, reaching 40 percent in some industries.[17] Premature departures are seldom due to dissatisfaction with performance. One paramount problem, one 2020 study found, is inability to adjust to the new location. Another, the same paper showed, is the family's unhappiness

---

[17] G. Wilson. 23 February, 2017. "How to prepare employees for international assignment success," *ECA International*. www.eca-international.com/insights/articles/february-2017/how-to-prepare-employees-for-assignment-success.

with the host country.[18] "Family considerations are often the main reason to accept assignments in China," Kurt Yu, Regional President at Voith Group, a German industrial conglomerate told me in 2020. I trained one after another of Kurt's leadership teams over two years and witnessed how he mentored incoming expats through adjustment to his native China's challenges. "Parents hope that their children can learn foreign languages and receive good international education, while the company pays for all that. But then, the husband typically goes to work and travels frequently, while taking care of the kids is left to the wife. Spouses and kids do not have their own networks in China, so they can feel lost."

That does not mean that dependents are exempt from the competitive lifestyle of China-based expats. The pressure on students in international schools can be especially high. Their teachers are excellent, their curricula demanding, if for no other reason than to attract the brightest domestic students from affluent families. That, however, also raises the performance bar from a very early age. "Expats must understand that schools here work differently," Attila Hilbert of Danone explained. "Their children must study seven days a week. Otherwise, they might be excluded by classmates as underachievers or deviants. Children should be aware of the one-child policy and the fact that in a thousand years, the only way for Chinese people to elevate the family was education." Based on his clinical practice, Dr. Hu agreed. "China's expat circles do not meet the needs of many otherwise healthy young foreigners, even if they live in villas with private swimming pools. Busy managers who juggle projects and business trips can do little for their kids. Just the opposite: it often happens that the working expat and spouse come to my clinic for help during the day, their kids after school hours."

A final challenge for foreign families is that even a lighter daily routine would not necessarily make them happier. China offers lots of fulfillment from work, study, and activities related to status (shopping, social gatherings, and so forth), but in the long run, little else. In fact, Dr. Hu advised against staying idle. "Spouses without jobs are much more exposed than

---

[18] Mercer. n.d. "Worldwide Survey of International Assignment Policies and Practices." https://mobilityexchange.mercer.com/international-assignments-survey (accessed July 31, 2022).

their working partners," he explained. "They feel the lack of friends and support groups much more severely, and consequently put pressure on the spousal relationship itself." China's laws add to the pressure on foreign families, a 2019 report by European think-tank MERICS suggested. "The immigration regime," the paper explained, "draws clear discrete lines between visa categories: if you came to work, then work on a working visa; if you came on a family visa, then sit at home and look after children; if you came to study, study and don't work." The same laws make it very complicated for expat kids to remain in the country after they reach legal age, making their time in China a high-risk, high-yield but short-term investment for most foreign families.

Of course, a feeling of impermanence can also help expat families weather through the difficulties. With the right amount of flexibility and a constructive mindset, even the most worrying features of life in China prove soluble. "However dramatic the pollution situation is in Chinese cities, it is possible to plan around the missed outdoor time and stay physically and mentally healthy," Dr. George Hu suggested. Following an understandable adjustment period in reaction to the culture shock, he continued, new arrivals could find the balance between typical extremes: ignoring problems on one hand, paranoid worries and self-imposed isolation on the other. Attila Hilbert's frantic home-sealing project was an eloquent example of reasonable coping. Briana shared a similarly agile attitude toward Internet connectivity problems. "It's part of the fun to learn living like a local," she said. "Instead of fussing that I cannot access Amazon, I learned how to shop on Taobao. On the other hand, I still enjoy walking into an Apple store and buying something that is exactly like in America. Instead of Mandarin apps, I order food on ones for foreigners, and I probably overpay."

Culture-Mapping Matches and Mismatches

Cultural adaptation is a complex and frequently underrated process, especially in the early stages of expat assignments. In the honeymoon phase of the first months, it appears deceptively easy to follow a simplistic strategy that everyone remembers from their first days at school: observe, understand, and try to blend in. If you cannot understand them, imitate their rituals. When in Rome, do as Romans do. When in Shanghai—the rest is common sense. The numerous intellectual descendants of the *when in Rome* school, like the business culture guidebook *Kiss, Bow or Shake Hands* by a team of American business advisors, are loose collections of curious facts about how people meet, greet, dress, negotiate, agree, or disagree, instruct, implement, and entertain in various national cultures.[19] They imply that understanding the underlying rules of an exotic culture guarantees successful collaboration with people there, often leading to adorably pointless advice. "Familiarize yourself with all aspects of China before you arrive," the authors of *Kiss, Bow or Shake Hands* suggest. Those who fail to *learn China* the week before they arrive should supposedly blame themselves and indemnify the authors.

Trying to observe and tactically imitate another culture's behaviors is ineffective even if the expectations sound clear. "Be patient, expect delays, show little emotion, and do not talk about your deadlines," the book's authors recommend, based on their evaluation of Chinese cultural norms. Such mimicry might be one way to achieve skin-deep acclimatization, especially while every little curiosity of the surrounding culture is new and exciting. But business travelers want more than merely avoid culturally awkward situations, and they soon realize that imitation leads to fatigue and futility. The list of an unfamiliar culture's peculiar practices is endless and lacks cohesion. Knowing how Chinese people dress for meetings, enter a conference room, greet junior and senior colleagues, exchange business cards, and decide seating arrangements will not guarantee a clear understanding of who speaks first, whether the meeting should start with pleasantries or presentations and what happens afterward. Even if it did, what if different Chinese people represent different values? What if they follow the same cultural adaptation strategy, imitate you, and thus become less predictably Chinese? Generations of businesspeople learned of such hurdles the hard way, and systematic cultural comparisons emerged only recently.

East and West have been in an increasingly direct contact for millennia. Wandering merchants tried hard to get their bearings not only

[19] T. Morrison. 2006. *Kiss, Bow, or Shake Hands: The Bestselling Guide to Doing Business in More Than 60 Countries* (UK: Adams Media), p. 95.

at sea but also among the countless cultural reefs that could shipwreck potentially lucrative ventures. Around 500 B.C., traveling philosopher Herodotus recorded the curious peoples, beliefs, and habits of the world he knew, meticulously but fully assured of Greek superiority. A few centuries later, Chinese Court official Jia Yi provided a frighteningly pragmatic example of faking cultural adaptation for self-interest, called *three standards and five baits*. "The 'standards' were to deal with barbarians in good faith," author Michael Schuman wrote in his book *Superpower Interrupted*, "pretend to enjoy their strange appearance, and take interest in their stranger habits; the 'baits' were to clothe the barbarians in silks and feed them delicious food; entertain them with music, dancing, and women; give them mansions with slaves; and shower them with attention. In sum, spoil them rotten to win their compliance."[20] The means of indulgence have changed, but *tolerance* still too often means pretending to accept others in order to squeeze out of them what we want.

Ancient explorers drifted between continents without clear points of reference, in both the navigational and cultural sense. Without maps and clear orientation, they followed the coastline and hoped that friendly currents would take them to their destination. When their life and livelihood depended on people of incomprehensible languages and habits, they worked hard to decipher and pilot cultural currents as best they could. It took over a millennium to discover the application of latitudes and longitudes in navigation, a revolution in intercontinental travel and exploration. Scientific cartography enabled not only easier journeys to places that people knew but also anticipating the location of yet unvisited ones. Meanwhile, navigating across cultural distances blindly followed coastlines and currents for centuries longer, until similarly reliable intercultural mapping could emerge. Even in the age of jet engines and fiberoptic communication, basic fallacies persist and undermine international negotiations, teamwork, and leadership.

Most known early cultures, from Hammurabi's courtiers to Native American chiefdoms, imagined themselves at the navel of the universe. World maps printed in the Americas, Europe, and Asia still illustrate

---

[20] M. Schuman. 2020. *Superpower Interrupted: The Chinese History of the World* (New York, NY: PublicAffairs), p. 68.

this bias, placing their respective continents in the center. As in topography, so in anthropology. Early Chinese descriptions of people outside the Heavenly Kingdom, the sort that Jia Yi wrote, were treatises on how and why foreigners lacked civilization—contemporary Indian, Persian, or European writings were equally biased. Prejudice followed us into modernity. All nations claim to be the greatest, down to Ecuador, wrote British philosopher Bertrand Russell in *The Problem of China* in 1922.[21] Twentieth-century intercultural experts like Edward T. Hall, an advisor to U.S. governments, armed forces, and firms, essentially instructed leaders on ways to do business with the Native Americans, Japanese, Arabs, South Americans, and other curious natives. The established assumption that the West was ahead of the East on a linear developmental curve yielded wildly inaccurate and often disastrous predictions on the forthcoming conduct of the people of the Soviet Union, China, Japan, Korea, Vietnam, and elsewhere.

The inherently judgmental comparison of cultures explains why national, regional, and local traditions make such awkward conversations. "Speaking about a person's culture often provokes the same type of reaction as speaking about his mother," writes INSEAD Professor Erin Meyer. "Most of us have a deep protective instinct for the culture we consider our own, and, though we may criticize it bitterly ourselves, we may become easily incensed if someone from outside the culture dares to do so."[22] In a modern world where mundane objects and even our meals increasingly depend on collaboration between distant places, this inability to transcend cultural comfort zones became a tangible liability. Rich and successful nations rely on countries whose values they cannot accept: think of the love–hate relationship between the United States and Saudi Arabia. Supply followed demand, and academics like Dutch social scientist Gert Hofstede developed cultural classification systems that borrowed behavioral criteria from psychology. Like individuals, they claimed, families, communities, and entire nations can be classified into courageous or

---

[21] B. Russell. 1922. *The Problem of China* (Abingdon-on-Thames: Routledge), p. 52.
[22] E. Meyer. 2016. *The Culture Map* (New York, NY: Public Affairs), p. 36.

cautious, stubborn or flexible, social or solitary, caring or selfish, pedantic or spontaneous ones.

The first system of cultural comparisons that entered the management mainstream was Hofstede's six cultural dimensions: power distance, individualism, uncertainty avoidance, masculinity, time orientation and indulgence. The resulting charts were insightful and scientific, showing how selected countries compared against each of the six criteria. But charts showing all six comparisons for even two countries were hard to remember, and including three or four countries looked as convoluted as wiring panels in contemporary television sets. Politicians, diplomats, and managers were routinely pressed for prompt decisions based on limited data. They needed dashboards, not circuit boards. The solution was the emergence of so-called culture maps after academic Erin Meyer arranged intercultural research data into a matrix resembling the personality chart known as DISC.[23] Emotionally expressive cultures were on top, reserved ones at the bottom. Confrontational ones on the left and nonconfrontational ones on the right. The resulting two-by-two layout of culture maps replaced Hofstede's spaghetti bowl of interlocking curves with four visually memorable cultural quadrants.

The Culture Map's four-fold visualization of behavioral styles is nearly idiot-proof, mainly because humanity has intuitively used them for millennia. The four DISC styles called direction (top-left, expressive, and confrontational), inspiration (top-right, expressive but nonconfrontational), service (bottom-left, reserved, and nonconfrontational), and competence (bottom-right, reserved but confrontational) borrowed from the work of psychologists Carl Gustav Jung, Gordon Allport, and others. In turn, those pioneers of behavioral research had drawn inspiration from ancient classifications of human qualities like the four essences of fire, air, water, and earth, and their applications to early forms of medicine, engineering, and governance. Thanks to their efforts, today's map-like charts translate temperamental differences into clear and memorable visual representations: once someone places their own or another country,

---

[23] E. Meyer. December 2015. "Getting to Si, Ja, Oui, Hai, and Da," *Harvard Business Review*. https://hbr.org/2015/12/getting-to-si-ja-oui-hai-and-da.

corporate culture, or personal work style in a specific quadrant of a culture map, it is practically impossible to forget where it was.

Culture maps also allow easier comparisons between traditions, the same way as maps replaced the myth of infinite oceans with coordinates to enable orientation. The farther away two societies (in Meyer's map, countries) are from each other, the bigger the differences, suggesting a fiercer culture shock when someone commutes or collaborates between them. The placement of societies instantly reveals the remarkable fact that cultural differences have little to do with geographical distance. In Meyer's map, the United Kingdom and Sweden share the emotionally reserved and nonconfrontational service-style quadrant with Korea and Japan, while Germany and France are in respectively different corners. At my training courses, I encourage participants to imagine culture shock as rubber bands stretched out between countries in the map. The tighter the band, the greater the pressure of understanding and adopting local life-styles. Like rubber bands, people may simply snap when they are expected to bridge excessive distances between cultures.

Poor matches between personal temperament and the local culture can ruin projects and careers, not to mention the mood of families, colleagues, and clients. Experienced overseas workers can spot such mismatches in a few weeks, if not days, of working together. As Bronwyn Bowery-Ireland cautioned, not everyone is cut out to be an expat, and although nobody is unfit for a country, they can be poorly adjustable to the culture of a specific city or firm. But spotting expats just before they succumb to acute culture shock is too late: reversing overseas assignments is costly and harmful. At headquarters, someone mistakenly promoted to the executive floor can be demoted again at the cost of some extra cardboard boxes, awkward negotiation, and some compensation. Failed expat assignments, on the other hand, squander thousands of air miles, relocation, rental and agency fees, unnecessarily disrupt teams, and uproot families. They also undermine relations with clients, suppliers, and government agencies, and cause reputational damage to the company.

One serious hurdle is that someone's birthplace is a poor predictor of adaptability to China or any other place in the world—individual differences within countries are simply too big. One advantage of culture maps is that since their terminology originally described individual character, they allow straightforward scientific comparisons between individuals and societies. Research reveals that the determining factors of people's behavior are evenly split between nature and culture, in other words, that character is half inherited and half imprinted by society. That also implies that babies have a roughly even chance of being born in a culture that aligns or conflicts with their natural temperament. There are as many genetically fun-loving, curious, and whimsical (emotionally expressive and nonconfrontational) children born in Rio as in Tokyo, but they experience dramatically different treatment as they grow up. As humans instinctively try to reduce conflict, life is about finding like-minded companions and communities—friends, teachers, peers, professions, spouses, clubs, and so forth. Those who are born into a natural mismatch with their immediate surroundings feel a stronger urge to explore. Leaving one's native land is one of the most symbolic ways to wipe the cultural slate clean.

Strategies and Tactics of Cultural Adaptation

Culture mapping could prevent mistaken expat placements, but daily business practice is not that simple. Profiling one candidate with cutting-edge tools costs less than a wheely bag. The reason why many firms still deploy people without cultural scrutiny is that the reputation of inter-cultural behavior assessment has ridden a roller-coaster between hype and hatred in recent decades. A century ago, progressive intellectuals celebrated Carl Gustav Jung and his like minds as geniuses. Sadly, they also conflated psychology with Taoism, reincarnation, and other forms of magic and mystery, which repelled technocrats at corporations and government offices. (This was the time when authoritative figures also dismissed Keynesian economics as humbug.) When recession and war in the 1930s and 1940s demanded new solutions, intercultural studies crowded their way into war rooms and boardrooms along with other new sciences. Edward T. Hall had studied culturally diverse approaches to time, space, body language, agreements, disagreements, and hierarchies from the 1930s, but only became prominent when U.S. armed forces harnessed his research to *win hearts and minds* among both allied and hostile nations during the Second World War.

Meanwhile, statistical minds like Robert McNamara, former Price-Waterhouse accountant and future Ford Motors President, U.S. Secretary of Defense, and World Bank President, taught armed forces to efficiently poll their people and turn massive amounts of data into speedy solutions. Bomber pilots panicked under fire and used minor mechanical issues as excuses to prematurely return to base, McNamara explained to an interviewer in 2003: commanders had to understand individual temperaments and deploy people accordingly.[24] American armed forces and their European allies retrospectively analyzed data collected since the First World War, systematically conducted entry and exit polls for a wide range of deployments, and appointed military psychologists who occasionally followed troops into combat. One such combat psychologist unknowingly made a lasting impression on the U.S. Army Air Corps Gunnery Officer Arnold Daniels, and through him millions of future job seekers, workers, and managers. After the war, Daniels turned McNamara's methodology into Predictive Index, a widely used workforce analytics instrument based on the same behavioral principles as DISC.[25]

War widened the scope of American interest from the exotic eccentricities of Brits, Belgians, and Italians to farther shores. Most of the fascination went to Japan, whose spectacular economic rise and resilience as a wartime enemy inspired as much bewilderment as the cultural distinctiveness of Japanese immigrants in the United States. Of course, curiosity and scientific rigor aside, wartime intercultural researchers served the same ultimate purpose as chemists and meteorologists: military victory. If culture specialists helped win wars, governments did not return the favor. The United States emerged from the conflict as the only genuine winner militarily as well as economically and politically, and the triumph lessened collective curiosity about the cultural roots of the conflicts it tried to police in Korea, Vietnam, then the Middle East and elsewhere. Projecting American blueprints onto local terrains seemed a surer secret to success

---

[24] E. Morris. April 2004. "The Fog of War," Sony Pictures Classics, documentary.
[25] M. Zani. n.d. "Harnessing Clinical Science to Identify Talent: The Predictive Index," *The Silicon Review*. https://thesiliconreview.com/magazine/profile/harnessing-clinical-science-to-identify-talent-the-predictive-index (accessed July 12, 2022).

not only in Washington but gradually among power elites in allied and conquered nations as well. Once again, intercultural research appeared to become an academic oddity with little practical relevance.

But the aftermath of each war also became a heyday of multinational business as corporations eagerly picked up the pieces that generals and politicians left behind. Private firms suddenly found themselves in charge to rebuild a global network of transportation lanes and warehouses, and simultaneously employ the anxious men who had shed their uniforms. Soldiers returned from overseas and went into business with heads full of ideas and hearts full of hope, but hurdles were as numerous as opportunities. Understanding and properly approaching faraway populations was essential for investment, sales, marketing, and management. Identical assembly lines and rulebooks yielded dramatically different results in diverse locations like the United States, France, Germany, China, and Japan. The work styles that characterized different nations and ethnic groups seemed haphazard. What accounted for the differences, and was there a way to overcome them? It was not too long before some nosy war veterans, now in corner offices, remembered the silent tons of archived survey sheets that recorded the meticulously penciled-in hopes, fears, habits, achievements, and mischiefs of soldiers, officers, support staff, and dependents all over the world.

In a few decades, a virtual trade secret of the armed forces became industry standard in advanced economies. Researchers of statistical analysis, anthropology, economics, and social psychology found new careers as consultants: Edward T. Hall's 1987 book *Hidden Differences* came out with the subtitle "Doing Business with the Japanese." By then, the practice of assessing job applicants and leadership candidates with surveying tools surprised nobody at global corporations. Increasingly, aptitude tests became a standard requirement for the placement of sales representatives, machine operators, airline pilots, managers, and executives. True to the circular nature of human learning, police, firefighting, and armed forces adopted private-sector assessment tools once developed by army psychologists. Experts hopped between sectors and cross-pollinated business with medical and behavioral science. Anthropologist Helen Fisher worked as an academic researcher, Chief Technology Officer at a top online matchmaking provider and leadership consultant within the span of two decades. The assessment tool she developed, NeuroColor, was part of a proliferation of tools that found their way to countless firms in dozens of languages.

Apostles of this upheaval of applied sciences never tire of presenting the benefits of mapping and harnessing human diversity at organizations. Meredith Belbin's revolutionary work on *Alpha teams* demonstrated the importance of combining individual styles: a room full of natural leaders gets nowhere without followers.[26] Anyone can spot the same four fundamental behavioral styles in management inspired systems like Situational Leadership, an elaborate methodology for managing people according to each person's background, competence, and interest. Erin Meyer built on previous research about the nature of culture clashes and developed her Culture Map into a series of tools for human resources management, leadership, and more.[27] London-based Hungarian entrepreneur Csaba Toth creatively fused the DISC personal profiling system and research data on national cultures to create Global DISC, an intercultural assessment and coaching toolkit. Year after year, multinational firms with winning intercultural strategies, and their entourages of business students, academics and think-tanks published convincing best-practice cases along with their documented financial, operational, and reputational benefits. The evidence appeared irrefutable.

Lost and Found in Cultural Roadmaps

Consultants like myself spent countless hours of conversation with decision makers over an ocean of variously toxic beverages to calmy reflect on past placements and strategize about the best use of advanced assessment tools. But when the rubber hit the road and companies had to choose among candidates, usually fast and based on limited information, old habits returned with a false promise of efficiency. Assessment tools are simple but still take some training and adaptation. Successful managers

---

[26] R.M. Belbin. 1996. *Management Teams: Why They Succeed or Fail* (Oxford: Butterworth-Heinemann).

[27] E. Meyer. December 2015. "Getting to Si, Ja, Oui, Hai, and Da," *Harvard Business Review*. https://hbr.org/2015/12/getting-to-si-ja-oui-hai-and-da.

enjoy learning but hate the inevitable loss of self-confidence associated with new methods. They also tend to be busy and lack the foresight to experiment during calmer times between recruiting seasons. When they need to hire or promote someone, it is urgent. Under time pressure, most of them reach for the proverbial hammer of the human resource management toolbox, and make decisions based on a track record of past performance. But the only thing proven about such appointments is how often they fail. No wonder: when specialists and managers are transferred between countries and continents, they may retain their previous field of expertise, but everything else changes dramatically.

While often labeled *soft skills* as opposed to *hard skills* like finance, sales, engineering, and project management, cultural difficulties persistently bounce back, smack managers in the face, and bite them behind, especially those with a dismissive attitude. Early into expat assignments, people with insufficient cultural awareness sense that their personal effectiveness and trust with their teams are on shaky ground, but they justify that as a fair price for *getting things done.* Like an athlete with a neglected injury, they push through the pain and watch their performance ebb away in a vicious circle of discomfort, irritation, and conflict. The wider the GAP between the natural work styles of individuals and the cultural styles of their surroundings, the faster they race to the bottom of this destructive downward spiral. Like sports teams who run their players through medical check before the next game, cultural mapping methodologies help firms save time, money, effort, individual and collective dignity. Mapping behavioral matches and mismatches between candidates and target locations not only reveals how quickly the new arrival can roll up their sleeves and get to work, but also the kind of support they require in the longer run.

The thorough cultural orientation and VPN crash-course provided to Renata and Nicola is the exception rather than the rule. "I don't think we prepare our people for China very well," Attila Hilbert of Danone told me. "When we came here, we only took a short and unimpressive cultural introduction course. I refer my new expats to YouTube videos instead: they can learn more from those." Some decision makers complete intercultural assessment but then forget about it, or feel too much in a hurry to decipher it. Others have more understandable concerns, starting with the fear that another layer of selection would shrink their talent pool. The long-term benefit of better placements should compensate for that worry, but there are other, less obvious advantages. Behavioral mapping can actually widen talent pools, because people with the right talent can learn the necessary skills but missing talent cannot be acquired. Assessment enables cross-functional hiring and promotion: firms that regularly profile their candidates can more easily move candidates for expat vacancies between fields like production, sales, customer service, or project management.

Another widespread source of skepticism toward behavioral mapping is the belief that ultimately, technical experience tramps culture fit. It only takes a few months of experience in an exotic country like China to realize how mistaken that belief is. Cultural tension devastates the morale, clarity, and motivation of managers with a poor fit to local work styles. At the end of the initial adjustment period, it even wears down ones who have the potential to succeed in the long run. The resulting surge of negative energy makes affected expats see everything in darker colors for a while. A perfect illustration is a straightforward admission from Fernanda, perhaps the most upbeat among all my interviewees. "After two years, I felt stressed and isolated. It seemed that people were unreliable and unwilling to help. That they constantly made promises that they didn't keep. I had to ask myself 'What am I doing here?'" At such times, expats must return to the proverbial drawing board and contemplate fundamental questions about their presence and prospects in their chosen location.

"The question is what you want to be as an expat," Rachel told me. "Do you want to be a change agent, or do you want to fit in?" The choice may feel harsh to outsiders and newcomers, who often seek ways to synthesize the best of both options. But seasoned expats know how important it is to soberly assess matches and mismatches between their own expectations and the surrounding layers of work cultures: team, firm, city, and country. The data provided by intercultural assessment serves as an essential resource for such soul-searching, which successful expat managers tend to repeat every couple of years. They must start with the culture in the center: their own personality, values, and habits. Naturally sociable managers pick up the pace much faster than relative recluses. "I must have had about fifty introductory one-on-ones during my first weeks," Briana recalled. "I had never done that in previous jobs, but I'd learned that relationships were critically important to get anything done in China, so I saw that time as investment. I was surprised that the otherwise 'go-go-go' sort of Chinese managers had an hour to chat and how transparent they were. People don't do that in North America."

Expats with a temperamental preference for clear boundaries, consistency, and privacy adapt slower and with numerous reservations. But then again, in a culturally challenging business environment, fitting in is not always desirable. "The objective of the acquired understanding isn't to become like the people in that cultural group or to be able to play their games," authors David Livermore and Soon Ang wrote in *Leading with Cultural Intelligence*. "The goal is to understand and appreciate the rules behind their lives and society so that you can effectively lead."[28] In China's dynamic but capricious market, keen-eyed organizers and evaluators deliver just as much value as courageous explorers, especially if the two styles collaborate well. "Multinational business matured in China, and the local workforce matured with them," coach Bronwyn Bowery-Ireland explained. "Large international firms represent middle-class values, and the majority of expats are sent in to enforce compliance." Naturally calm and cautious leaders can also help foreigners under their guidance to avoid the reactive firefighting mentality mentioned earlier.

Initial self-reflection can naturally proceed to wider comparisons, for instance between an expat's native culture and local habits. "Frankly, coming from Italy helped me to pick up the pace in China," Angelo Puglisi of Benteler told me. "Italians are fast and flexible, just like Chinese people. They summon each other for last-minute meetings, and people actually show up. That style definitely doesn't work at our headquarters in Germany." Even if the temperament of individual foreign managers does not reflect the work style of their homelands, having been raised, educated, and employed there guarantees certain cultural survival tactics—otherwise they would have never been promoted to management. Mapping matches and mismatches between a manager's personal work style and surrounding cultures can make crucial decisions much easier, be they about career or private life. Whether an expat's preference is blending in

---

[28] D.A. Livermore. 2009. *Leading With Cultural Intelligence: The New Secret to Success* (New York, NY: Amacom), p. 70.

or inspiring change, obscure towns, or glamorous metropolises, culture mapping can replace some of the costly and painful experimentation with a simple analytical exercise.

High-stake promotions to senior positions often raise the question whether a candidate's personal characteristics, like the balance between confrontational and conciliatory tendencies, are genetically determined or caused by family and ethnic background, life experience, or even factors such as gender and age. That sounds like a relevant question, because social influences change over a lifetime of personal and professional experiences, while innate ones stubbornly remain. Did Attila Hilbert, native to the confrontational culture of Hungary, develop his empathy during a childhood spent between cultures, or was he born that way? Should Angelo Puglisi thank his genes, the chatty confidence of his native Italy or his managerial experience in India for his agility? Being from candid North America, are Briana's patient listening skills a personality trait or the fruit of trial-and-error learning? But as opposed to therapy, in a corporate environment, the distinction makes little difference. Expats are mature adults whose profiles stay relevant whether their drive, curiosity, empathy, or diligence come from their inherited genetic code or upbringing. As long as they show the potential to manage cultural ambiguity and deliver results, the underlying reason is of secondary importance.

Intercultural assessment can also clarify sensitive and deeply misunderstood topics like diversity. Managers are often aware that uniformity undermines performance, and try to add demonstrable but superficial varieties of minority ethnic, religious, gender, and generational backgrounds. But, as neuroleadership expert Hans W. Hagemann pointed out, "a team that looks like the UN may not be diverse. Teams succeed not because of the variety of their appearances or backgrounds, but because of the diversity of skills and personality types they possess."[29] Scientific assessment helps managers consider more sources of diversity than meets the eye, including personal temperament and influences from early childhood to recent professional postings. Remember how Angelo

---

[29] F. Fabritius and H.W. Hagemann. 2018. *The Leading Brain: Neuroscience Hacks to Work Smarter, Better, Happier: Powerful Science-Based Strategies for Achieving Peak Performance* (New York, NY: Tarcherperigee).

Puglisi's experience in India helped him in China. Or Attila Hilbert's preference for expats with experience in other developing nations, which has its root in his own childhood. "I remember how outraged I was at the condescension and arrogance of Europeans in Tunisia," he recalled his youthful experience as the son of a Hungarian expat. "When I saw the sons of Italian factory managers act like princes, I felt closer to the Arabs. I still cannot stand that attitude." Assessment profiles clearly reveal such mixtures of commitment and empathy.

The value of second-generation expats and so-called *third-culture kids* from ethnically mixed families, for instance, had been an open secret in diplomatic services and international commercial missions long before corporations realized it. Kids surrounded by multiple cultures playfully master lessons that adults must drill in through ossified biases and prejudices. Candidates from such backgrounds welcome the opportunity to work in culturally diverse and flexible environments. In the hands of smart managers, culture mapping reveals shortcuts across this otherwise problematic leadership area, and can benefit entire firms. "L'Oréal Paris builds product development teams around these managers, who, by virtue of their upbringing and experiences, have gained familiarity with the norms and behaviours of multiple cultures and can switch easily among them," one expert wrote in a 2016 *Harvard Business Review* article. "They are uniquely qualified to play several crucial roles: spotting new-product opportunities, facilitating communication across cultural boundaries, assimilating newcomers, and serving as a cultural buffer between executives and their direct reports and between subsidiaries and headquarters."[30]

A couple of hours with expats over dinner or drinks proves that scientific methods only confirm the wisdom of generations: exposure to diverse lifestyles is a good preparation for handling daily culture clashes. But even seasoned wanderers have a lot to learn in each new culture they encounter. Open-minded people, no matter how they acquired their mental agility, suffer less and make faster progress under cultural pressure. Their abilities are often so subtle that even they do not understand the

---

[30] H.-J. Hong and Y.L. Doz. June 2013. "L'Oréal Masters Multiculturalism," *Harvard Business Review Press*. https://hbr.org/2013/06/loreal-masters-multiculturalism.

secret of their successes. Were his achievements in China due to active effort or gradual socialization, I asked Henrik König. "Is there a difference, Gabor?" he countered. "It's hard for me to tell the difference." The enormous value of Dragon Suits for global firms lies exactly in the fact that the daily grind of busy jobs polishes their potential into the kind of minimalistic wisdom that is tried, true, and digestible. "The bottom line here is that they will respect you for respecting their culture," wrote a long-time foreign resident in 2017. "They won't respect you for ditching your own."[31] Such soundbites may be the best proof that someone is ready to ascend to the next level of responsibilities in China, and lead others along the same learning journey.

---

[31] R. McMunn. August 2014. "8 Tips for a Life In China," Huffpost. www .huffpost.com/entry/eight-tips-for-a-life-in-_b_5674838.

CHAPTER 4

Stepping Up

Leading Others as a Foreigner in China

Dragon Suits are corporate champions in their respective leagues. By the time I interviewed the expat mangers featured in this book, served as their executive coach, or trained their teams, they had overcome countless barriers and hurdles, both physical and mental. By personality, performance, and politics, they had been earmarked for international careers. Unlike most of their colleagues, they had been offered expat jobs. Unlike countless unsung heroes of family and patriotic duties, they had accepted. They had taken farewells, boarded, arrived, unpacked, logged in, rolled up their sleeves, solved problems, hired some, fired others, said goodbye to those who left willingly or otherwise, then passed one milestone after another: launches, fiascos, uncertain contract renewals, births in the family, first days at school, graduations, corporate mergers and restructuring, bothersome new bosses, divorces, illnesses, mid-life crises, triumphs, promotions, and the inevitable melancholy of too much experience, too many triumphs in China's monotonously changeable environment. Things happen fast in China: a single year packs enough anxiety and achievement for a decade at home. "They know that this is the most competitive labor market in the world," Attila Hilbert told me. "If you can beat the odds here, you can beat them anywhere."

Some managers who appear on these pages arrived in China as students, entrepreneurs or junior employees. Fernanda Barth of WEG had quit her previous job to study Chinese in the hope of new career opportunities. I met Chris, the luxury fashion CFO as a consultant to an EU firm that had recently hired him because of his entrepreneurial experience in the country. Some of my interview subjects were proficient in Mandarin when they landed their first management positions, others conversational.

But typical Dragon Suits entered the country on expat jobs, sometimes on their first visit to the country or even their first overseas assignment. There were those who brought years, occasionally decades of experience in other locations. In this country, it did not matter that much anyway. All of them had their leadership development clocks reset in China, starting again from mundane issues and gradually building up toward new strategic horizons. China's special position among possible destinations for ambitious managers, its size, economic volume, and potential, the responsibilities it offered, and the cultural challenges that complicated smooth performance gave them a true taste of genuine global leadership.

Multinationals send their best and brightest to China, and candidates know that. Ironically, that can make adjustment harder, especially for first-time expats. Being right too often can play tricks on one's mind, and newly appointed China expats often come from previous jobs that had earned them regular praise. They gradually learned to trust their instincts in addressing complex issues, which in turn added to their effectiveness and efficiency (simply put, impact and speed) as problem-solvers. They mastered the legal, logistical, social, and cultural frameworks that surrounded their projects. When they felt stuck, a trusted network of fellow managers and experts helped them get unstuck. Then they relocated to China, and everything changed. The familiar laws, facts, habits, and traditions that once supported their projects ceased to apply in the new environment. Guidance was absent or misleading. Previous mentors and advisors were of little help unless they were current or former Dragon Suits themselves. Business often took place in an unintelligible language under meaningless rules. Pride and politics stood in the way of openly asking for help.

The information vacuum that surrounds new expat managers in unfamiliar cultures can turn trusted instincts into risky guesswork, and downgrade self-confidence to the nervous self-doubt that psychologists call impostor syndrome. Overwhelmed managers maintain an appearance of assurance, while inside, they anxiously second-guess their own decisions. But panic is great news: false confidence does more harm. Faced with uncertainty, overconfident managers can fall victim to another misperception known as confirmation bias: the belief that if they were right before, they must also be right under the new circumstances, whatever their local colleagues, clients, and suppliers say. "Previous international experience is crucially important," Laurie Underwood, coauthor of *China CEO* told me. "Managers must approach the new environment with humility, because basically they don't know what they don't know. They must accept that there will be aspects of their work and life that they have to adapt to China." The required adjustments go far beyond familiarity with a different geography, language, etiquette, legal, and financial codes. New expats must expect to make nearly comical slips in aspects of work and life as simple as picking the right clothes for the day, greeting employees and clients, or picking the right chair in a conference room.

Human culture is a symbolic world where the meaning of someone's actions depends on the respective background of observers. A CEO who cycles to a meeting may impress clients in Amsterdam and intrigue them in New York but embarrass them in Beijing. Western superiors take central seats and lead discussions, while in China and several other Asian nations, real authority figures often prefer to quietly observe from the side or send their representatives instead. Personally engaging team members is a veritable cultural minefield. An Australian CEO I coached was eager to know his team better a few weeks after he arrived in Shanghai, but heavy workloads and language barriers made socializing hard. One evening, as he exited across the mostly vacant open office area, in a cubicle he spotted the lone figure of a sales representative with whom he had already met and chatted in English before. He grabbed the opportunity and invited the rep for a steak dinner and beers in at nearby barbeque restaurant. The next day, rumors started circulating that the salesperson would soon be promoted.

Borrowing the title of a 2007 DreamWorks animation film, at my leadership coaching and workshops, I explain the cultural cluelessness of newly appointed expat executives as the *Boss Baby* phase. I remind managers to brace for predictably awkward situations at work, and to accept the necessity to revisit basic life skills: walking, talking, eating with unfamiliar utensils, and figuring out furniture, and above all, the intricacies of adult communication, whether conventional or digital. "Initially, I was surprised how much work people do through WeChat," Briana recalled. "Doing that completely blurs the borderline between professional and personal issues." Unfamiliar names and faces, strange hierarchies, food, weather patterns, and loyalties: foreigners have to learn fast, and often remind themselves of the difference between China and the mature welfare states where many of them enjoyed a settled existence. "Austria is very conservative, and most people are unwilling to move abroad," Markus Baumgartner of Miba Group told me. "But I was ready for change, knowing that the new position would involve much more responsibility."

Theoretically, an upgrade in authority is exactly what attracts ambitious international managers to China. In practice, few measure up to the challenge of the initial months. When multinational firms invest in China, they limit the number of their business locations to a few of the country's top commercial hubs in order to minimize red tape, logistics, and cost. Consequently, in comparison to someone with the same job title in the UK or Germany, a Managing Director or CEO in China may shoulder 10 times as many people, projects, clients, and suppliers. "The all-consuming nature of leading in China takes an emotional and physical toll on most executives," the *Harvard Business Review* already quoted one CEO in 2010. "Here you have three months to accomplish what would take two years in most other places." Expats with great ambitions in China must develop laser-sharp priorities on the run, the article continued. "If you stop to think, decisions will pile up behind you."[1] A decade later, Marie experienced a similar pace. "Response time is really fast," she said. "You have to be able to respond to messages from six in the morning, twenty-four-seven."

The race is fast, the stakes are high. "In this society, people are constantly pressed for time and money, so checking the boxes is the best strategy," Briana explained. That is alright with expat managers, whose careers take giant leaps forward as long as they can keep up with China's sprint-paced Marathons. But as they check their own boxes and shoulder ever greater responsibilities, issues become not only larger in size but more complex in nature and ever more entangled in the PRC's unique economic, social, and political reality. They cannot be lone champions anymore: they must race entire organizations to finish lines. Understanding local cultures of intimacy and hierarchy is not enough: they must make

---

[1] L.S. Paine. June 2010. "The Globe: The China Rules," *Harvard Business School*. https://hbr.org/2010/06/the-globe-the-china-rules.

sure that people perform willingly and efficiently, without undue conflict. Pollution problems balloon into collective health hazards, Internet irritations into data leaks, awkward cultural missteps into costly political fiascos. Successful expat executives in China cannot simply overcome such challenges—they must be energized by them. In return, China's business hubs promise, and usually deliver, disproportionate financial rewards, visibility and opportunities. Few Dragon Suits I asked wondered whether it was worth the trouble.

Assuming Roles and Responsibilities

Corporate leaders I train or coach often raise a defiant question: Why should China differ from other places? Typical participants of my leadership programs have lived and worked in several countries, or at least traveled often and extensively. Many of them are proficient in multiple foreign languages. The younger they are, the likelier it is that their upbringing and education prepared them to work across multiple countries, continents, and industries. Why would China be exceptionally difficult to understand? Some argue that it is not, and they are not alone. "There is nothing mysterious or terribly difficult about Chinese companies or markets," the authors of *The 1 Hour China Book* insist. "In business, there is really nothing new under the sun. Consumers behave pretty much the same everywhere. Competition is pretty much the same everywhere. You just need to ignore the hype and hyperbole and stay focused on the basics."[2] If that were true, the outsized attention that global firms dedicate to Chinese consumers, whose per capita purchasing power does not exceed the world average, would be misplaced. So would the fortunes spent on customizing products, from burgers to Bentleys, to Chinese tastes. Huawei would conjure similar global sentiments as IBM, Motorola, or Samsung.

But China is different, and its uniqueness has roots in ancient traditions as well as recent developments. Not everyone takes notice. I meet

---

[2] T J. Towson and J. Woetzel. 2014. *The One Hour China Book: Two Peking University Professors Explain All of China Business in Six Short Stories: Volume 1* (Cayman Islands: Towson Group LLC), p. 5.

experts and executives who tell me how grateful they are to be specialists in accounting, law, engineering, chemistry, architecture, information
technology, or goose-feather pillows: they can dismiss fuzzy cultural issues
and stick to specifics. Eventual disappointment follows when they discover that culture is everywhere. Values and traditions dictate how strict
or casual people are with pennies, pounds, and compounds, and what
separates carelessness from corruption or capital crime. They explain why
laws allow us to enter, sit, stand, talk, work, invest, hire and fire, lead,
litigate, congregate, eat, drink, dress, undress, and mate in certain places
and not others. They define the features of our vehicles and traffic, food,
drink and medications, clothes, homes, offices and towns, software and
hardware, and yes, even the size, shape, firmness, and usage of feather
pillows. Culture maps demonstrate the possibility of wider or narrower
deviations between the cultural mainstreams of select societies. For
Europeans and North Americans, collaboration with Singaporeans or
Indians is measurably easier than working with Mainland China, regardless of geographical distance.

Most successful foreign managers in China accomplish their results
without ever using culture maps: they rely on instinct and experience.
Some of them are masters of intuition, the sort that allows fast decisions
in highly complex and risky situations. But even such instinctive geniuses
of intercultural leadership benefit from backing their insight with com-
parative data, if for no other reason than to convince others. As they
mature with their positions, the authority they accumulate in their organizations makes them appreciate the difference between getting things
done and making others perform, including their local team members.
Clarity about their own leadership style becomes even more valuable as
they find out, as every successful expat manager does, that mediation
between headquarters, their own branch, and various other locations is
an essential part of the job. In other words, those who want to succeed as
expat executives must learn to become cultural translators between various traditions and values, aligning conflicting opinions for the sake of
delivering the expected results.

One widely misunderstood nuance of Chinese society that can make
or break expat careers is hierarchy. Specifically, the difference between the
recent hierarchies exemplified by local state-owned and relatively conventional private firms on one hand, and traditional Chinese leadership

roles on another. Foreign managers often tell me about their encounters with what they describe as *typical Chinese companies*: undisputed bosses surrounded by nearly ceremonial auras, top-down decisions executed by obedient workers, no questions asked. The local firm in question may be a client, supplier, a newly acquired and rebranded entity, or joint venture partner. Expat managers often experience such hierarchical work cultures indirectly, when they hire local managers who continue to work according to a previous code of conduct even in their multinational environment. They do what they are told. They speak when they are asked. When unsure, they stop and wait or follow their best guess of the boss's intentions.

Expats often try to explain Chinese attitudes to hierarchy with familiar stereotypes of ancient philosophies. But gaps in that reasoning soon become evident. "Strategists who believe that current People's Republic of China (PRC) strategies can be constructed from reading Sun Zi or Meng Zi are certainly mistaken, just as their Chinese counterparts would be if they thought that US policies are derived from Thucydides or Xenophon," David Shambaugh wrote in *China and the World*.[3] A century ago, British philosopher Bertrand Russell witnessed a waning Confucian business culture as described in his 1920s book *The Problem of China*. The best followers were to become leaders and role models based on virtue, self-sacrifice, and stern patronizing toward followers, usually family or clan members. This system hinged on near-unconditional trust within organizations, which is why the Confucian business ideal is still a family firm rooted in a local community. Chinese diasporas in Taiwan, Hong Kong, and South-East Asia maintain this tradition to the present day, researchers explain. "Like the father in a Chinese family, the superior in a company is expected to provide guidance, protection, nurture, and care to the subordinate; like a dutiful son, the subordinate, in return, is normally required to be loyal and deferent to the superior."[4]

This philosophy survived and thrived for surprisingly long: what we call China today was among the world's top economies from Confucius's

---

[3] D. Shambaugh. 2020. *China and the World* (Oxford and New York, NY: Oxford University press), p. 26.

[4] C.-C. Chen, and Y.-T. Lee. 2008. *Leadership and Management in China: Philosophies, Theories, and Practices* (Cambridge: Cambridge University Press), p. 171.

time until Russell's. But then the world changed, and China transformed with it. Leaders of the People's Republic promoted social strife through class struggle and the meritocratic reorganization of authority—all alien to Confucian traditions. Within a century, China imported one ideology after another: revolution, industrialization, modernization, innovation, and globalization. Each one redefined who should be in charge and why: heroes, builders, scientists, visionaries, technocrats. State-owned firms owe their organizational structure, processes, and culture to the former Soviet Union that lent financial aid, experts and the Five-Year Plan system to the nascent People's Republic in the 1950s. Chinese corporate champions of the reform period like the founders of Huawei and Alibaba modeled their firms on overseas examples, typically American ones. Multinational firms imported their respective national and corporate cultures, and locals judged the worth of each culture by the success of the products or services it produced. From the Internationale to Intel, each paradigm imprinted its own ideals of leadership and hierarchy on China.

Demystifying characteristic Chinese leadership styles is much more than academic hair-splitting. Managers who approach their jobs with misleading expectations overcomplicate the daily tasks of delegating responsibilities, setting goals, evaluating performance, motivating, and resolving conflicts. Recall Henrik König's dilemma: Neither home-grown German habits nor his rendition of traditional Chinese leadership seemed to work—observation and empathy did. Conflating Confucian versus Communist or capitalist traditions can also lead foreigners to condescending stereotypes and undermine trust with their local teams. It is tempting, for instance, to attribute the Communist Party's patronizing omnipotence to traditional ideals of hierarchy, or to see President and Party Chief Xi Jinping's ambitions for life-long rule as a return to an Imperial past. American political scientist Rory Truex's research on successful Communist Party officials showed how simplistic that assumption is. "They tend to have a personality profile that's not dissimilar from what I would observe among an average Princeton student where I work," he explained in a 2022 podcast.[5]

---

[5] K. Kuo. January 2022. "The Psychology of Political Discontent in China," *SupChina*, podcast. https://supchina.com/2022/01/27/the-psychology-of-political-discontent-in-china/.

In Chinese people's minds, social hierarchy and institutional authority are separate forces. Contemporary China can pose one challenge without another. Young Chinese employees often puzzle foreigners with their nationalism and party loyalty without any sign of respect for traditional hierarchies. Middle-aged local employees at large profit-making organizations often adhere to traditional family and communal duties with little enthusiasm for the party. Chinese people of millennia have believed that dynasties come and go, but the rules of civility are eternal. The most pervasive of such underlying beliefs is that the family, a traditional refuge from a perilous outside world, is the only reliable community in human existence, and consequently that any sustainable community, including businesses, must function like a family. In a sense, most Chinese people see the firm as an extension of their household clan. Addressing colleagues as brothers and sisters is not uncommon. Calling female caretakers at the Mainland China branches of global firms *Ayi*, or *auntie*, is so widespread that more than one multinational office I saw labeled their resting area *Ayi room*.

The basic metaphor is easy to grasp. "Especially in places like Nantong, being part of the community is crucial for daily life," Fernanda Barth described her life in the south-eastern port city. "Even if, or perhaps especially if you are a foreigner, you must ask your colleagues about their children's health, remember their birthdays and so forth." Some implications can puzzle foreign managers. "Taking an interest in workers' families and personal lives may feel like an invasion of privacy to foreigners, but to most Chinese, it's just part of showing respect and being a good boss," a *Harvard Business Review* article explained.[6] In many countries, this would seem superficial, which often blinds expats to underlying differences. Local colleagues at multinational companies are misleadingly determined, straightforward, competitive, and often earn on par with their counterparts from advanced economies. But scratch the surface over a sincere chat, and half-buried Confucian foundations will reveal themselves through recent layers of individualism. China's health care and social security systems are improving but still patchy, especially for

---

[6] L.S. Paine. June 2010. "The Globe: The China Rules," *Harvard Business School.* https://hbr.org/2010/06/the-globe-the-china-rules.

nonurban, elderly, and chronically ill people. From costly education for kids to medical care for elderly relatives, extended families have clear expectations toward relatives with stable jobs.

"For many Western executives, time spent on soft issues like these is time lost on hard ones such as achieving performance targets and improving productivity," the *Harvard Business Review* article observed. Many foreigners chafe under unwanted quasi-parental responsibilities. By nature or culture, others are more comfortable with the arrangement. "As a Hungarian, I grew up in a multi-generation home, but for American and Dutch managers, self-sacrifice is an alien concept," Attila Hilbert said. "In China, the metaphor of the family is the perfect way to keep people in line and guide them in the same direction. The spirit of the family makes it easier to build or restore trust, to define relationships." Those with a strong social orientation can even thrive in their new tribe. "Leading a team can be a lot of fun," Marie said. "There is a higher emotional investment into coaching people, because they tend to know little, partly because they advance in their carriers so fast, but also because China is still an emerging market where the infrastructure of expertise and continuous improvement is not in place yet."

How Bossy Should a Boss Be?

It may happen resentfully or eagerly, but foreign managers must eventually accept and harness the filial character of professional relations in China. Otherwise, they may find themselves banging their heads against traditions as ancient and solid as the Great Wall. "The way I explain this to Westerners is that while their way is the minimum number of people doing maximum amount of work, the Chinese way is the maximum number of people doing a medium amount of work," Leigh explained. Foreigners must adjust to this mindset. "Chinese people are constantly comparing themselves to their classmates and friends, and it takes a lot to keep up," Laurie Underwood explains. "You need some creativity to satisfy them. For instance, global firms do not promote people as fast as local employees would hope, but you can print different titles on the English and Chinese sides of business cards—a kind of semi-promotion for employees with restless ambition." Expats eventually learn to harness a more collective mindset to delegate tasks, share feedback, and measure performance. Human resources directors discover ways to reward employees for attracting their friends to the firm, for instance. Encouraging them to share vacancies among their WeChat friends works particularly well, Shaun Rein added.

Leadership philosophies are deeply personal. Adjusting them to new circumstances can be emotionally draining. Multinational firms from advanced economies promote flatter hierarchies than what Chinese conventions dictate. Consequently, most new expats experience the pressure to become *bossier* superiors than they would prefer. "Be careful with mixing friendship and professional interactions," Judith advised. "Don't try to treat everyone the same way, like you do at home. If you're a supervisor, you will stand apart in your Chinese team's eyes." Marie agreed: "It is a question of who is the accountable decision maker. The kind of democracy you have in most multinationals can be exhausting to Chinese people, because they have to justify their numbers and decisions to superiors." Some expats are more comfortable with these expectations than others. Managers with a sufficiently dominant temperament naturally slide into the role, grateful for the obedience they seldom encountered at home. Others accept it as a dubious price for efficiency. "If bosses don't tell local teams about the ultimate goal, it's fine as long as things are accomplished quickly," Briana said.

The value of thorough cultural analysis becomes the clearest when managers with friendly and equitable collaboration styles suddenly find themselves in rigid hierarchies. Many such expats see China's top-down culture as backwardness, even if they are generally in favor of the country and its people. "My closest colleague on arrival was a Chinese boss with completely outdated ideas," Henrik König recalled. "He knew little about project details, and spent most of his time calling clients over everyone else's head. I recall that his glitzy executive office was full of photos with Chinese political leaders, and currently he was busy negotiating the engine size of his chauffeured Audi." Foreigners who feel uncomfortable working with lofty corporate figureheads are understandably alarmed when they are pressured to become such leaders themselves. "Then, I suddenly became the big boss that others can occasionally approach with questions," Henrik continued, "but otherwise, nobody talked to me.

There was no small talk or shared coffee breaks. As I saw it, basically I was supposed to just sit behind my desk."

Friction between the local and Western approaches to corporate hierarchy is both more frequent and more intensive in China than most other Asian investment destinations. The reason is the very system of separation between indigenous and foreign economies. Historically, China first attracted industrial firms to its market, then their suppliers and service providers in an increasingly intangible sequence. The most promising sectors of foreign investment, such as automotive, pharmaceuticals, chemicals, construction, and energy, as well as many of the sectors servicing them, including banking and insurance, remained dominated by state-owned firms via Beijing's infamous *Negative List*, an elaborate system of restrictions that mandates foreign businesses to operate through joint ventures with state-owned partners even within Special Economic Zones.[7] Multinationals accept such forced marriages as an inconvenient price to access China's restricted but lucrative markets. But they do so at the risk of, in think-tank Deloitte's words, possible governance deadlocks, battles for control, cultural clashes, risk of competition with parent companies, and misalignment of business objectives.[8] Foreign managers at such entities are often expected not only to accept but also to imitate rigorous and poorly balanced pecking orders.

"At state-owned firms and manufacturing companies in China, you have a very clear system where the top guy is always right," explained Tony Shi of Benteler. "Bosses ask their people if everything is okay, and their people either tell them that everything is okay or say nothing and solve the problem." That is the exact opposite of the way leaders, managers, and teams are instructed to collaborate at most multinationals. Typical managers at global automotive, chemical, or pharmaceutical firms are process-orientated technocrats reasonably committed to candid communication, transparent processes, meritocratic promotions, and

[7] Z. Zhang. December 2019. "China's 2019 Market Access Negative List: What Investors Need to Know," *China Briefing*. www.china-briefing.com/news/chinas-2019-market-access-negative-list-whats-new-attention-investors/.

[8] Deloitte. September 2020. "Sino-Foreign Joint Ventures After COVID-19 What to Expect?," p. 5.

mutually constructive criticism between organizational units and levels. Leadership manuals at most firms I have advised explicitly encourage *managing upward*—proactively pointing out shortcomings to superiors and suggesting solutions. For an expat manager with an engineering or science degree, over a decade of experience in Western-style hierarchies and perhaps a recent MBA course that focused on progressive management methods, facing the top-down attitude of Chinese counterparts can be shocking.

Renata's experience aptly illustrates the disorienting discovery of expectations toward managers and their teams in China. "This is a very hierarchical culture, so I had the impression that they expected to be told before they did anything. It was not a comfortable feeling." The resulting period of experimentation with the right level of control can be perilous, especially as it usually coincides with heavy workloads and ruthless expectations from higher management. Stress undermines self-awareness and empathy, and can turn assertiveness into aggression. Newcomers may unwillingly re-enact disturbing stereotypes of the clueless foreigner. "One very frequent misunderstanding is the role of yelling and using swear-words in discussions," Shaun Rein explained. "For American managers, raising their voice and using the f-word is a legitimate way to add emphasis. Steve Jobs, an American hero, was known to swear at someone, then take the same employee out for coffee or a beer. In China, that behavior burns bridges, especially if done in front of others. The foreigner may think he finally managed an honest, stern discussion with an employee, and be shocked to find that the employee quit the next day."

To avoid such damaging cultural fiascos, adjustment must start with awareness, which is best achieved by trespassing the limits of expat existence and learn from local colleagues, business partners, or acquaintances. "The most valuable lesson for me was doing an executive program at Tsinghua University and meeting local Chinese executives," Renata recalled. "I realized that they do everything differently. They do not concern themselves with details, only the big picture." Most foreign managers need not even leave their premises to find useful advice. Their local colleagues or superiors are more than happy to share their insight. "When foreigners ask 'Do you understand?', Chinese people usually nod in response," Kurt Yu, Regional President for the Voith Group, described to me a challenge for which he tries to prepare his expat managers. "Half of the time it means they really understand, but the other half doesn't, because people are too shy to speak up. Foreigners must candidly probe whether they are really understood. 'Face' and personal relationships are important, but the difference between 'yes' and 'no' is a much more fundamental difference between East and West."

Advice from local colleagues often makes expats realize that, at least initially, they overemphasized business processes and targets, and neglected trust-building with their teams. They discover that as foreigners, one of their core functions is to bridge respective cultures, including the traditions of the firm's home country and China, and the multiple corporate cultures involved. But building bridges is easier said than done: advice is either absent or contradictory. A list of *must-have qualities for foreign CEOs in China* in Laurie Underwood's 2020 book *China CEO II* aptly illustrates a frequent dilemma. It consists of humility, cultural sensitivity, respect for *face* and *guanxi* (a term for networking that we shall clarify soon), flexibility, firmness, long-term commitment, and language acumen.[9] In other words, be humble and assertive, implement long-term plans flexibly, in an unfamiliar culture, preferably through recently acquired fluency in Mandarin. For managers who contemplate their first leap in such leadership acrobatics, instructions can sound utterly confusing. "Empower local teams even if they are not used to being empowered," Laurie Underwood recommended at a 2021 webinar I hosted.[10]

Contradictions persist even when expats better understand the Chinese concept of hierarchy and their own place in it. That is because in addition to conflicting national and corporate cultures, foreign managers must also balance between China's two cultural paradigms: assertiveness on top, diligence and obedience below. Some of their advice is straightforward, in line with the Confucian interpretation of local business culture, and often includes the somewhat patronizing tone of the parental leader.

---

[9] J.A. Fernandez and L. Underwood. 2020. *China CEO II: Voices of Experience From 25 Top Executives Leading MNCs in China* (Oxford: Wiley), pp. 42–50.

[10] G. Holch. July 2021. "Five Essential Qualities for China CEOs by Dr Laurie Underwood (East-West Leadership webinar)," video. www.youtube.com/watch?v=VIf1qC4B7rU.

"Never put people in a corner," fashion CFO Chris cautioned. "Don't try to bring Chinese people on board the way you do Western teams," Judith recommended, echoing many Dragon Suits I asked. But much of their guidance reflects the dialectic ambiguity that surrounds them in China. "Don't try to master your local team," Markus Baumgartner advised. "Instead, share your experience but make assertive decisions." And some call attention to the temptations of traversing from one leadership culture to the other. "Be patient and humble," Fernanda Barth recommended. "Local teams can at times make you believe that bosses are superhuman beings. Do not believe that."

Leading across cultures is a bit like playing badminton in windy weather. Leaders must use their best powers of observation to assess the environment, keep their goal in sight but often reach it in roundabout ways. "When it comes to leadership, I am completely different person after a few years in China," Renata admitted. "I do things I never did before. I invite my team for tea in my home. We eat out together and I pick up the bill." That change of perspective might feel superficial at first, but expats soon realize that the resulting new habits improve both their business performance and personal life. It is only then that foreign managers realize how *soft* and *hard* issues reinforce one another, and the value of time invested in intimacy and care. Then, and only then, *The 1 Hour China Book*'s claim rings true, because once we know them well enough, people are people everywhere. At that point, expat leaders can look beyond cultures and master the basics. "Over time, I learned to delegate little by little, breaking everything into smaller tasks," Renata continued. "This helped me delegate more. Before I was micromanaging. Now I learned to let them do their job."

Networks and Kinships

"Let's get a drink," says a Chinese character in Kyle Hegarty's entrepreneurial memoire *The Accidental Business Nomad*. "We can do that *guanxi* you Westerners always talk about." The Mandarin word *guanxi*, literally *connection* or *relationship*, is a darling of cultural guidebooks and a celebrity with its own private library: there are over 200 English-language books with the word in their title. As they experience the first benefits of gradually becoming more intimate with their local teams and business networks, foreign managers in China often congratulate themselves for mastering the subtle art of *guanxi* themselves. But while trusted business networks are important everywhere, and indeed more so in China than in most major economies, *guanxi* is also a frequently misunderstood and misinterpreted cultural phenomenon. As expats develop an ever more profound understanding of the local business culture, they learn two essential lessons. The first is that a foreigner cannot willingly infiltrate a traditional trust-based society. The other is that keeping foreigners at arm's length while granting them an illusion of cultural immersion is perhaps the most ingenuous feature of Chinese society.

What Chinese people label as *guanxi* is in fact an extended family network that gradually includes newly added clan members such as classmates and colleagues. This arrangement is necessary in a society with ancient traditions and an unreliable social security system. "Let's say I am ill and need to see a doctor," Leigh explained. "Appointments in China are messy and waiting times are long, so I will try to circumvent the normal process. I will call friends and family to see if someone in my circles, or in their respective circles, knows a doctor who can give me the inside track. I will do the same when I need a good lawyer, or basically anything else." As they delegate practical issues to their local teams, foreign managers soon become entangled in similar networks, and consequently start experiencing China as a place where nothing is sure but everything is possible. Whether that sounds like heaven or hell depends on personal temperament, the magnitude of responsibility, and available resources.

"Imagine that a number of firms are bidding for a BMW project, but the procurement people in charge are hardly listening because they already know who the winner is," Leigh continued. "They have someone in mind: a number of people went to school together, and one of them became the marketing director of BMW. He will then tell the others: 'I have million dollars to spend on marketing.'" Faced with such commonplace situations in China, foreign executives face the intimidating obligation to balance the need for fast decisions with both legal and ethical risks. Chinese clocks tick fast, and conventional advice about successful leadership in China is fraught with the usual contradictions: plan carefully and be flexible, control and collaborate, move fast, and avoid mistakes. Newly appointed expats often feel tempted to make compromises on transparency or compliance, perhaps hoping to finally master the Confucian game of *guanxi* as promised to them in their introductory readings. They should not learn to play it too well. Cautionary tales are countless, the best-known probably being the nearly 300 million-dollar fine levied on JP Morgan China in 2016 for hiring Communist Party princelings in return for favorable contracts.[11]

Expats can only develop a working knowledge of Chinese-style social networking through experiencing its good, bad, and bizarre sides. Natural extroverts usually welcome social shortcuts and quick fixes. "A lot of what's really critical comes in a very offline, indirect discussion," six-year China resident consultant Kimberly Kirkendall told a 2021 podcast. "It's not while sitting in a conference room that you'll hear what's wrong. It's more sitting over lunch, or drinks or while talking about something else."[12] Task-focused introverts often resent such informality, and even seasoned expats struggle to disentangle the intricate exchange of information and resources in Chinese professional networks, seemingly for the sole purpose of trading favors. "For instance, we discovered that brand new Maserati engines we shipped to China had been run for a significant mileage by the time they reached through customs," Leigh recalled. "The same happened at Ducati. We also found that Chinese managers working for these firms were swapping their vehicles with friends who worked for other brands. Why they needed such a scam is a mystery: anyone can buy a Maserati car or Ducati motorbike and test the engine if they want to."

Confusing shady horse-trading with Confucian collectivism ignores a century of dramatic cultural changes. Mao's early Communist rule severed the very roots of social traditions. Families were forcibly separated and relocated to distant parts of the country. Young people were encouraged to refute *old superstitions* like ancestor worship, conventional holidays, traditional Chinese medicine, martial arts, and local dialects—glues that

---

[11] BBC. November 17, 2016. "JP Morgan Pays $264m to Settle China 'Bribery' Probe." www.bbc.com/news/business-38013723.

[12] A. Dicker. November 2021. "Western and Chinese Business Cultures," *The Ganbei Podcast*, podcast. www.ganbei.tv/blog/transcript-western-and-chinese-business-cultures?categoryId=247144.

had bound local communities together. The infamous one-child policy broke the dynastic lineages that families had revered for millennia. The party tried to harness Chinese people's deep-seated collectivism toward revolutionary ideals, but the economic failures of the People's Republic soon necessitated a reversal. "Propaganda messages from the early 1960s from figures like Lei Feng to 'serve the people' and give no regard to the self were replaced by a set of new, more permissive strictures which seemed to be totally opposed to what had been stated before, like 'getting rich is glorious,' a common 1980s slogan," historian Kerry Brown wrote in *China's Dream*, only to "openly and unapologetically return to an era which had existed before 1949 of building personal links, creating business associations, and constructing a world beyond the state."[13]

A time traveler from Confucius's era would doubtlessly fear for his life in the streets of today's China, but once safely indoors, he would recognize the familiar patterns that psychologists call in-groups and out-groups. Nearly unconditional trust within restricted social circles of interest and suspicion between them still defines the nation's business relations. Instead of a filial bloodline traced back over generations, modern Chinese people's loyalties rest mainly with the place of their birth or that of their parents, educational institutions, the family's stance in political loyalties and the party hierarchy. This persistent cultural feature explains behaviors that have puzzled foreigners for decades: mysterious hiring decisions, unexpected conspiracies, extreme displays of self-sacrifice, and the collective departure of entire teams when one member is fired. It also guides relations between local and foreign managers at multinationals. Expats can read about *guanxi* until their thumbs bleed, but ultimately, they must accept that unlike their local colleagues and newcomers of Mainland ancestry, they watch local loyalty circles from the outside.

Most expats and their ancestors were born in neither this or that Chinese province to grant them identities rooted in the cunning diligence of Zhejiang, the proud frontier spirit of Sichuan, the imperial vanity of Beijing, or the southern curiosity of Guangdong. Their parents were not Qing-dynasty literati stripped of their wealth and status, Republican-era

---

[13] K. Brown. 2018. *China's Dream: The Culture of Chinese Communism and the Secret Sources of its Power* (Cambridge: Polity), p. 75.

warlords or capitalists, exploited serfs, heroes of the Long March, resentful Cultural Revolution veterans, or *red aristocrats* knighted by the Communist Party. Most are not graduates of *Bei Da*, *Jiao Da*, or any other esteemed state university, or indeed know which institutions these Mandarin acronyms signify. "When you lead Chinese people, you must accept that they are a community with intricate relations with each other," said Leigh, whose Mainland ancestry and birth allows some authority over the matter. "There are regional and generational differences, but ultimately they believe that they are all connected together, as the proverb goes, like rivers and lakes. And who are you? You are an expat with a large salary package."

Consequently, most foreigners who claim to have mastered the Chinese art of *guanxi* actually engage in Western-style networking—transactional favors for mutual benefit, typically with fellow foreigners, local colleagues, and business contacts. When I ask them about acquaintances beyond that, housekeepers feature prominently. Ironically, *guanxi* among expats can still yield the expected results. The general manager of a European manufacturing firm in Beijing or Suzhou is most likely to find a new client, supplier, or fellow single-malt whisky collector at a foreign chamber of commerce, English-language fitness class, or an international school's parent summit. An expat family's health care, insurance, investment, travel, or catering needs are best served by China's parallel economy of expat clinics, overseas banks, insurers, wealth managers, and providers of English-language services to clients with foreign passports and preferences. Some separations are spontaneous: weekend branches and outdoor swimming pools typically cater to foreign tastes. Others are deliberate: most places of worship in the PRC admit local or foreign nationals separately for political reasons.

Knitting and Fitting the Right Network

Although they may fall short of the elusive *guanxi* of an amateur Orientalist's daydreams, a solid local network is essential for expat managers after all. Chinese people tend to think of management in terms of *managing whom* rather than *managing what*. Personal loyalties play an outsized role in the rise and fall of projects, teams, and entire firms. Their headquarters may entrust expat appointees with titles, budgets, and mandates, but they are in no position to delegate to them the crucial resource of personal relations. A brand-new start in an exotic country is cheerful news in many respects, but in the Boss Baby phase, expats are pressured to create the network without which nothing gets done in China. "In previous jobs, work usually caught up with me eventually," Briana explained the back-story to her dozens of personal meetings at the beginning of her tenure. "But this time I was on a special assignment, my salary and expenses came off the US payroll, and local stakeholders did not know what to expect from me." Foreign managers must roll up their sleeves, but also remember that today's networking is not as daunting as it would be if they had to infiltrate the genuine local trust circles of Bertrand Russell's time.

The bad news is that expat managers often feel abandoned until they establish their local networks. The lucky few arrive in communities of seasoned international bosses, colleagues, and business partners. But as multinational firms proudly localize their management in Mainland China, assigning formerly expat positions to native candidates, the remaining foreigners may find themselves surrounded by local colleagues who have little idea about the challenges of relocation, and foreign superiors and peers stationed abroad. "Places like Singapore are still considered developmental examples for China," Marie explained. "For that reason, a lot of regional headquarters are located there. Often, there is an isolated General Manager in the PRC who doesn't receive enough support." Keeping in mind the limited familiarity and data shortage over the workings of the PRC at global headquarters, the success or failure of entire strategies may hinge on how fast and confidently foreign managers can surround themselves with trusted allies and advisors. What can seasoned expats suggest to newcomers?

The first secret to successful business networking in China seems to be the ability to notice and accept the limitations inherent in a foreign manager's outsider status. "Especially when you meet authorities, at home you may have the impression that you are the most important person in the room," Renata told me. "But in China, it's not like that. This means I take my seat, act respectfully and often choose not to say what is on my mind." Foreigners should also bear in mind that while their local counterparts navigate the intricacies of a single business culture that they know as their own, expats must comply with frequently conflicting local and international practices, be they legal or ethical. Having to comply with both the legal requirements of their firm's domicile, typically more mature than Chinese law, and toughening local regulations, foreign managers must avoid the creative tactics of local counterparts. At the time of writing, for instance, government scrutiny over gifting *red envelopes* of cash to purchasing or tax officials created an upsurge in digital gift cards and coupons, purchased anonymously and practically impossible to track.

The good news to tip the balance away from such challenges is that Chinese-style networking is neither art nor science, but an easily improvable skillset of managing time and basic resources. Most acts of *guanxi* turn out to be small and intangible concessions to business partners. The Janus-faced business cards mentioned by Laurie Underwood are a great entry-level example: title matters a lot to Chinese employees. Henrik König shared a similar story with higher stakes. "According to my contract, I reported directly to the German Headquarters rather than to the Chinese boss," he explained. "The local boss prepared an organizational chart that featured me underneath him. I asked him to check my contract, even though I knew it was quite unfair: his superior should have told him that somebody would arrive from Germany and not report to him. In a few weeks, he made a new chart where I was beside him, only a couple of millimeters away. You could see how important the arrangement was for him. It took some time, but before long I was working with him in the same way I would with my German colleagues, communicating very frankly about everything including the mistakes I made."

Experienced expats agree that a bit of empathy and effort can untangle highly sensitive situations. At times, the secret is the medium rather than the message: finance executive and academic Joel Gallo advised in a 2021 podcast to contact investors on social media instead of conventional ways like e-mail or telephone. "It's a bit cheesy," he admitted, "but cheesy or not, you must do it."[14] At others, timing is key. The European General Manager of a global electronics brand told me how he had confronted

---

[14] Ganbei. December 5, 2021. "The Gold Rush of International Banks' Expansion in China," podcast. www.ganbei.tv/blog/ep-27-the-gold-rush-of-international-banks-expansion-in-china?categoryId=245717.

his Chinese supplier after discovering that the local firm infringed some of their valuable intellectual property. He intended his visit as a friendly warning before his headquarters would proceed to sue. "Sue us by all means," the supplier's Director said in an unexpectedly calm tone. "But could you do it in two months? You will win the lawsuit, but by that time the stolen patent will have been credited by the local government towards our innovation target." Thanks to China's inconsistent regulations and widespread pragmatism, the surface of successful collaboration between local and foreign managers is almost invariably propped up by exchanges that never see the light of day.

The fireside stories of seasoned Dragon Suits prove that the ability to deal with ambiguity is an essential ingredient to management success in China. Selected for their outstanding performance in more predictable and compliant markets, many managers arrive in China to *put things in order* and align local operations with global standards and practices. After a few years in the country, some of them sound as obscure as the market they are supposed to explain. "Don't contradict people directly," Markus Baumgartner said. "Don't say that something is 'wrong'. Try to be subtle." The problem is that by definition, subtlety lacks explicit guidelines, and clarity is essential while expat managers work with their Chinese colleagues. When probed on how they developed the ability to approach complex management issues with the appropriate amount of tact, most experienced Dragon Suits respond along the lines of Angelo Puglisi's answer: "Trial and error." That gracefully simple approach, however, complicates the selection of expat leaders: what guarantees that candidates with the required technical abilities, qualifications, and track record can produce the appropriate gut-level response to inevitable contradictions?

Foreign managers who face such tough choices replay a centuries-old dilemma: whether to impose proven methods onto unfamiliar communities, or encourage the organic emergence of locally digestible hybrid practices. Sixteenth-century Jesuit Matteo Ricci cleverly customized Catholic dogma to Confucian tastes for Chinese coverts, and duly got in trouble with his European superiors. Today's foreign executives are expected to make comparable choices faster, with higher stakes and considerably less local knowledge than previous generations. From 1800 until today, the value of global trade increased over 2,000 times,[15] and the global movement of goods created parallel currents of money and people. But while a 100 years ago, candidates for China-based jobs had months to prepare at home, and weeks of perfecting their language skills at monotonous sea voyages, many of today's expats tidy up their desks in one continent and settle into a new office thousands of miles away within a week or two. It is this mobility that makes it crucial for global firms to predict well in advance who will flourish and who will flop under the multifaceted pressures of living and working in China.

Intercultural assessment systems enable human resources professionals to spot the secrets of successful expats and appoint people with similar capabilities to comparable jobs—two equally important sides of a highly valuable coin. One such secret we often identify with my clients is an approximate balance between confrontational and conflict-avoiding tendencies, pictured, respectively, on the left and right side of DISC charts and Erin Meyer's culture map. European and North American countries typically appear on the relatively confrontational left side of Meyer's charts, while China and most East Asian countries rooted in Confucian traditions are on the nonconfrontational right.[16] Managers with balanced DISC profiles, due either to personality, upbringing, or experience, instinctively bridge gaps between Western values and their applications in Asian cultures like China. Unsurprisingly, several executives featured in this book show such balance. Briana, Angelo Puglisi, Attila Hilbert, and others are natives to countries with straightforward cultures (the United States, Italy, and Hungary) but personally prefer to handle sensitive issues diplomatically—a sign of the required balance between determination and empathy.

Theoretically, the most effective approach for multinational firms would be to screen management candidates for the necessary behavioral traits and select those who best suit specific countries and assignments. In practice, cultural compatibility remains the kind of low-priority requisite that creative corporate lingo often labels as a *nice-to-have* as opposed to

---

[15] Our World in Data. n.d. "The Value of Global Exports." https://ourworld indata.org/grapher/world-trade-exports-constant-prices (accessed July 12, 2022).

[16] E. Meyer. 2016. *The Culture Map* (New York, NY: Public Affairs), pp. 89–90.

the *must-haves'*. The reason is not a lack of expertise or available tools, but understandable fears regarding the introduction of additional, culture-related screening criteria for candidates. Decision makers typically pick from a limited pool of applicants that gets ever thinner with higher leadership positions. For them, the immediate pain of having to dismiss otherwise eligible candidates for cultural mismatches is much stronger than the promise of better long-term performance. Equally importantly, behavioral criteria like a balanced attitude to confrontation can seem to directly conflict with core job requirements. "Trial and error" is an unwelcome phrase at clinical trials, warehouse management, or the drafting of multimillion-dollar contracts. Do human resources professionals have no other option but to expose the most professional candidate to the inevitable culture shock and hope for the best?

Fortunately, cultural adaptation does not equal cultural imitation: managers who represent different temperaments simply orient themselves to China's socially dependent business culture in different ways. A naturally affable character makes initial trust-building smoother. Managers with a balanced natural temperament toward confrontation, third culture kids, and expats with decades of experience in diverse cultural environments gracefully combine straightforward and evasive attitudes. Managers with a direct and practical work style may be mystified by indirect communication and the ability to balance corporate, expat, and local viewpoints, but they can develop the motivation to learn them *as a second language* when they see their utility in complex situations. "Those who know how Chinese management culture works can get rid of a weak employee without firing him," Shaun Rein said. "All you have to do is publicly point out that he is doing a bad job. You can rest assured that he will quit soon." Renata's experience reveals the bright side of socially engaged leadership in China. "This country completely changed the way I relate to others. At the beginning, my team may have hated me. Now they ask me not to leave. Best of all," she added, "I have a Godson in China now."

The Politics of Leading Businesses in China

There is too little and too much of everything in human life. The Flow theory of legendary psychologist Michael Csikszentmihalyi famously demonstrated how anything can turn from blessing to curse if it far exceeds or falls below desirable levels: food, drink, work, rest, fun, sex, company, solitude, distraction, focus, freedom, and even money. Moreover, Csikszentmihalyi showed that the ideal sweet spots are highly subjective: one person's heaven is another one's hell. Unsurprisingly, the same applies to cultural adaptation. In a challenging environment like China, unfamiliar weather, pollution, crowds, or strange food can inspire self-inflicted isolation in one expat and enthusiastic cultural immersion in another. Wobbly Internet connection with the outside world makes some people turn their bedrooms into hacker's dungeons, while others discipline themselves to live with China's indigenous half-Internet. At bars, house parties, and conventions in major Chinese cities, animated expats advocate the benefits of *going local*. Think of the above-quoted praise of forced *cyberdetox* or Markus Baumgartner's preference for living away from foreigners. A successful executive told me how she resented foreigners shopping for European designer brands in China instead of buying Three Guns, her preferred local fashion chain.

But I have yet to meet the expatriate who enjoys one characteristic challenge of doing business in China: the pervasive presence of politics. From broad strategic goals to minute details, the Soviet-inspired system in the People's Republic manifests itself in goals, rules, instructions, and restrictions in all aspects of establishing, populating, running, and developing corporations. Contrary to the expectations of many strategic planners a decade or longer ago, political interference in business has intensified in recent years. "For international companies looking to do business in China, the rules were once simple," the New York Times wrote in 2019. "Don't talk about the 3 T's: Tibet, Taiwan and the Tiananmen Square crackdown. No longer. Fast-changing geopolitical tensions, growing nationalism and the rise of social media in China have made it increasingly difficult for multinationals to navigate commerce in the Communist country."[17] Nevertheless, while Beijing's resurging ideological commitment heightened walls and toughened rules, the volume and

---

[17] The New York Times. October 21, 2021. "China Is a Minefield, and Foreign Firms Keep Hitting New Tripwires." www.nytimes.com/2019/10/08/world/asia/china-nba-tweet.html.

profitability of foreign enterprise in China kept growing. Dragon Suits simply learned to manage political unpredictability like other risks associated with enterprising in the world's largest market.

Executives in the PRC must expect sudden blows from any direction, despite careful compliance with local laws. Some sweep across the entire nation. Beijing's drastic bans on importing and recycling scrap material in 2019 suddenly placed foreign firms under scrutiny ahead of Chinese competitors. The Swissotel chain was the first to pay fines in Shanghai for violating new standards: they were no worse than local hotels, but their higher transparency standards helped local governments meet compulsory punishment quotas.[18] Entertainment and gaming businesses repeatedly become collateral casualties to *Socialist morality* campaigns.[19] In 2021, falling birth rates revealed by the previous year's national census inspired a clampdown on evening and weekend classes. Wall Street English, probably the country's most popular foreign-language school chain with headquarters in Italy, went down in weeks along with many private training firms.[20] Other disruptions are more limited in geographic and ideological scope, like a sudden push for a more patriotic hospitality industry in Shanghai around 2012. Restaurants and bars were forced to change names, menus, and marketing material that included *French Concession*, the remnant of a century-old administrative label popular among locals and expats alike.[21] Sly swaps for *former French Concession* to avoid fines fooled censors only briefly.

---

[18] The Economist. July 6, 2019. "Cheerleaders and Police Usher in a New Era of Trash-Sorting." www.economist.com/china/2019/07/06/cheerleaders-and-police-usher-in-a-new-era-of-trash-sorting.

[19] Financial Times. August 11, 2021. "China Cracks Down on Post-Work Drinking and 'Harmful Karaoke'." https://amp-ft-com.cdn.ampproject.org/c/s/amp.ft.com/content/adc14a48-73ea-4baa-8638-9dec6138c758 and Bloomberg UK. August 18, 2018. "China Is Said to Freeze Game Approvals Amid Agency Shakeup." www.bloomberg.com/news/articles/2018-08-15/china-is-said-to-freeze-game-approvals-amid-agency-shakeup.

[20] Refer China. August 13, 2021. "What Leads to the Downfall of Wall Street English in China?." www.referchina.com/2021/08/What_Lead_to_the_Downfall_of__Wall_Street_English_in_China__43806.html.

[21] Financial Times. February 28, 2012. "Shanghai Netizens to Expats: Don't Mention the French Concession." www.ft.com/content/4378a9bf-6d5a-3c0a-a145-e73d7ab5a4f2.

The chaotic currents of China's politically inspired regulations puzzle newly appointed foreign managers in China. But those who stay vigilant and build basic expat networks can learn to accept and navigate them. They discover that as the old adage suggests, the only constant they can expect is change itself. In fact, a capricious regulatory environment surrounded the latest generation of foreign businesses in China from their inception. Knowingly or not, the *trial and error* philosophy of experienced expats imitates a similar approach from the PRC's paramount leaders. Deng Xiaoping's instructions for cadres to *seek solutions from the facts* (*shi shi qiu shi*) is so deeply ingrained in Communist political culture that it serves as the title of the party's internal policy bulletin: Qiu Shi.[22] Over two decades of *reform and opening* can be understood as a gargantuan experiment with Chinese characteristics, prematurely launching one initiative after another, then adjusting regulations as practical experience either confirmed or contradicted initial expectations. The outcome is a climate of alternating trends and countertrends that expat managers ignore at their own peril.

The core idea of *reform and opening* was to attract foreign enterprise into China's newly created Special Economic Zones. But a carefully crafted *negative list* excluded non-PRC investment in dozens of sectors that included defense, energy, telecom and Internet services, publishing, infrastructure, and key financial services, and restricted investment in many more, including banking, automotive, pharmaceuticals, and chemicals. Over time, a shortening list coincided with stricter regulations on the movement of people, money, and information as Beijing introduced new controls on visas, incoming and outgoing investment, and the Internet. Successive generations of foreign managers try and fail to explain new regulations with China's criminal code, data security needs, or economic aspirations. But once they learn to view them through political lenses, perplexing contradictions suddenly resolve themselves. Take, for instance, the salad bowl of items that users who connect their Tencent Alipay and Stripe payment applications must consent to avoid: "fetal gender determination, virtual private network tools (VPNs), crowd funding, religious websites, publications or accessories, gold investment, satellite

---

[22] J. McGregor. 2012. *No Ancient Wisdom, No Followers: The Challenges of Chinese Authoritarian Capitalism* (Prospecta Press), p. 42.

antennas, human organs, surrogacy services, real estate or charitable organizations."[23]

Foreign managers who understand the dialectics of tradition versus modernity, Confucian harmony versus Communist control in contemporary China can navigate an otherwise confusing environment. "From caveman to spaceman," Leigh explained, "the rules in China have always been made by a distant elite, and normal people could only get things done by violating them." Various levels of authority tactically switch sides between elevated elites and the self-asserting *masses*, the ideological core of all Leninist systems. Take laxity toward contractual obligations, which China-business manuals either abhor or celebrate as characteristically Confucian. It simultaneously benefited Chinese firms and undermined their dignity abroad. Until 2018, China ranked around 80th in the World Bank's annual *Ease of Doing Business Index*, near Oman and Panama. Ruthlessly effective government measures catapulted the PRC to 31st position by 2020, and its *enforcing contracts* subscore to an illustrious fifth in the world.[24] Unfortunately, the campaign itself had cut corners, triggering allegations of unfair influence to "push the data in a certain direction to accommodate geopolitical considerations."[25] The following year, the World Bank discontinued the index.[26]

The experience of preparing the necessary permits for relocation, landing in the country, settling in, getting to work, and establishing trusted professional and personal relationships often convinces new expats that going with China's rapid flow is the secret to success. In the short run of initial months, the formula seems clear: powerful local bureaucrats set

[23] Stripe. April 4, 2017. "Alipay Terms of Service." https://stripe.com/alipay/legal#prohibited-business-list.

[24] The World Bank. 2020. "Economy Profile China, Doing Business 2020," p. 4. https://www.doingbusiness.org/content/dam/doingBusiness/country/c/china/CHN.pdf.

[25] Al Jazeera. September 17, 2021. "Probe Finds World Bank Changed Data to Boost China Ranking." www.aljazeera.com/economy/2021/9/17/probe-finds-world-bank-changed-data-to-boost-china-ranking.

[26] S. Gold. September 2021. "World Bank Scraps Doing Business Rankings Due to Data Irregularities," *Devex*. www.devex.com/news/world-bank-scraps-doing-business-rankings-due-to-data-irregularities-101630.

all-encompassing goals, businesses mobilize resources, and the workforce delivers. The siren song of history's biggest economic boom keeps everyone in sync. Further down the road, as we already saw, expats discover the dangers of blindly goose-stepping with the mainstream and sacrificing physical and mental health, social life, and even long-term career prospects. Over time, foreigners must learn to self-manage in China's hectic environment, keeping and even setting the pace with a firm hand on the off switch when necessary. "The ability to make tough decisions," Laurie Underwood said, "is one of the key qualities for foreign executives in China."

The Politics of Coffee, Shirts, and Drop-Down Lists

While flexibility is one necessary quality for expat executives, another one is knowing when to stop being flexible. The country's vast, rapid, and politically perilous business environment narrows the room for errors and magnifies their consequences. The hierarchical leadership philosophy that characterizes China, combined with scarce institutional support, means that expat managers must maintain a high level of authority over all aspects of business. They must drive their busload of people (teams, customers, and investors) at top speed through a rough and shifting terrain. At times, they are blindfolded due to China's secretive political system, but they must bear all consequences. "Few executives have had formal training in dealing with government, and approaches picked up in the U.S. or Europe don't translate well to China," a 2010 *Harvard Business Review* article explained. "Successful CEOs ensure alignment between their strategies and the Chinese government's goals by deciphering the state's priorities and gaining insight into how the bureaucratic machinery works. Lining pockets, moreover, can be perilous, as recent settlements of bribery charges by companies like Lucent, Siemens, and Daimler underscore."[27]

Basic familiarity with local governance is necessary for any expat assignment's success, but China's political setting is more pervasive, more hazardous, and more complex than in most major markets. "If you decide

---

[27] L.S. Paine. June 2010. "The Globe: The China Rules," *Harvard Business School.* https://hbr.org/2010/06/the-globe-the-china-rules.

to move into China with a new idea," Amway Executive Vice President Eva Cheng said in a 2010 interview, "you must fully convince the government why what you propose is good for the nation, the economy, and the Chinese people. For the Chinese government, social stability overrides economic considerations. Politics come before economics."[28] Cultural commentator Zhu Dake hit viewers of the documentary *China: Power and Prosperity* with the unvarnished version of the same message: "All successful people must be on the same side as the government. If you're not on the same side, they will make you unsuccessful."[29] But how should foreign managers know where the government stands? For most countries, a handful of corporate lawyers, often in headquarters, turn new laws and regulations into unsophisticated white papers that businesspeople can apply in a prompt and straightforward way. There are many reasons why that approach is unwise in China.

The Communist Party governs the PRC through a combination of transparent legislation and elusive decrees, declarations, memos, and announcements from various levels of governance that are practically impossible to comprehend without some understanding of the country's Leninist-style state apparatus. Authorities often make new rules indefinitely retroactive. Few of them ever appear in foreign languages, and thanks to the thorough demarcations of the Great Firewall, even Mandarin speakers outside of China may struggle to find them. The lack of reliable information is not an excuse, however. From a single bank transfer through hiring to managing supply chains, politics rears its unwelcome head at multinational offices on a daily basis. Beyond heightened risks associated with every decision, this also means added pressure and workload for already overburdened managers. "Despite the opening of the economy to foreign companies over the past three decades, more than half the CEOs I spoke with spend 20% to 50% of their time coping with policy issues and dealing with the authorities in China," reads the quoted *Harvard Business Review* article.

---

[28] C. Knape. November 2010. "Amway China Chairwoman: Dancing With Dragon Requires Give and Take," *MLive*. https://www.mlive.com/business/west-michigan/2010/11/amway_china_chairwoman_dancing.html.

[29] PBS NewsHour. November 22, 2019. "China: Power and Prosperity," documentary. www.youtube.com/watch?v=oIF-ujSeQho.

Learning to deal with politically muddled issues starts with the most basic clerical tasks. Managers must circumvent demarcations between state-run and private firms, local and foreign businesses, and Chinese territories more or less hospitable to overseas practices. "It's not uncommon for a lot of accounts to be processed through Hong Kong," Rachel told me. "They process expenses to Hong Kong, then courier documents over there, which adds two weeks to a normal deadline. Therefore, high level officials are involved in mundane decisions: CFOs discuss the way the office gets coffee." The arrival of advanced information technology in China freed foreign firms from most surface mail, but Internet restrictions forced them onto digital detours via non-PRC servers. Human resources management is even more sensitive, because the employee welfare, inclusion, and human rights standards of global firms often clash with murky interpretations of changeable local laws. Attila Hilbert described how multinational companies vacillated between their nondiscrimination policies and obligations to report violators of China's one-child, later two-child policies. They often chose the former at the risk of small fines, he added.

China presents foreign executives with seemingly impossible choices, but Dragon Suits have proved to be fast learners. True to Leigh's advice on conflicting strata of authority and interest, barriers erected by one zealous government bureau can often be circumnavigated with the help of other officials pressured for economic growth. Factories locked down in polluted cities can quietly reopen when air quality indices drop below critical levels. The prospect of a multinational firm bringing competitive technology, investment, and labor to a certain province can turn local mayors and Party Secretaries into advocates for foreign business. Of course, that adds endless hours to the workload of expat executives, their local managers, Chambers of Commerce, and Consulates. "You need to maintain a very close contact with the government so they know you well, to speed up approval processes," Laurie Underwood quotes Airbus China President Guy McLeod in *China CEO*. "Whatever we are doing, there are a number of ministries that you need to lobby."[30] That, Rachel added to our interview, also requires a direct hotline to global decision makers. "I think you

---

[30] J.A. Fernandez and L. Underwood. 2020. *China CEO II: Voices of Experience From 25 Top Executives Leading MNCs in China* (Oxford: Wiley), p. 215.

need to have somebody in China, who is high-ranking enough to report to the CEO of the company. I can think of one Pharma company that has an EVP to bring all these issues to the CEO."

Most China-based expat executives are corporate athletes with an appetite for disciplined self-improvement. They raise at dawn to read expert books or learn Mandarin, take policy podcasts with breakfast and organize their working days around carefully prioritized tasks and meetings. They train themselves to mind their team members, customers, suppliers, and their families, to tolerate and respect local conventions. They can work long hours, outsource marriages and kids, socialize over unfamiliar dishes and booze. Nevertheless, despite all effort, control over their China business can still slip through their fingers. However many laws they learn and concessions they make, authorities have more surprises in store. European companies were "navigating in the dark," The European Union Chamber of Commerce in China concluded in 2021. "While some of that may be due to increasingly competitive local players, the bulk of the challenges facing European companies in China are the result of regulatory issues and the political economy established by China's state-planners."[31] Nearly half of the survey's respondent firms reported lost business opportunities due to shady regulations.

In China's ambiguous regulatory environment, foreign managers must be prepared to find Beijing's target on their firm's back despite their best efforts, and bear the consequences. The question is not whether they will make mistakes—it is how frequent and how severe those errors will be. China's political climate expects all authority figures, including corporate leaders, to bandwagon the ideological mainstream, "an act known to all Chinese as 'biaotai,' literally to 'express an attitude' or 'declare one's position,'" David Shambaugh explained in *China and the World*. "The problem is that it expects foreigners to also biaotai. Yet, most foreigners do not understand the propaganda slogans, much less wish to mindlessly parrot them back."[32] VPN connections and English-speaking colleagues keep most expats blissfully ignorant of the subtle ideological nuances

---

[31] European Union Chamber of Commerce in China. June 2021. "European Business in China Business Confidence Survey 2021," pp. 1, 17.
[32] D. Shambaugh. 2020. *China and the World* (Oxford and New York, NY: Oxford University press), p. 364.

that locals master out of sheer self-preservation. Even if local employees alarmed management to the ways corporations can inadvertently insult the brittle national pride of Chinese authorities, it is unlikely that expats would take their warnings seriously. And yet, a poorly made online commercial, shirt design, or even dropdown menu repeatedly crashed multimillion-dollar businesses in China.

In retrospect, some fiascos were more predictable than others. German camera maker Leica should have anticipated irritation from Mainland Chinese buyer of its camera-phone lenses Huawei over the iconic *Tank Man* of the 1989 Tiananmen Square uprising featured in a 2019 commercial. The word *Leica* and its Chinese equivalent was wiped from China's top microblogging website Sina Weibo, the *Financial Times* found.[33] American clothing conglomerate The GAP should have looked twice the previous year, before decorating millions of tee-shirts with China's map without Taiwan.[34] Pictures of the unfortunate item damaged GAP's already fragile local business beyond repair. The same year saw party mouthpiece *People's Daily* call German car maker Daimler "enemy of the people" after it quoted the Dalai Lama on Instagram.[35] Government officials still drove Mercedes and Maybach cars to work, as they did Audis after that firm was chastised for decorating its annual meeting with an also Taiwan-less map in 2017. In 2021–2022, several sports and fast-fashion brands, including Nike, Adidas and H&M, exposed themselves to sanctions when they refused to purchase cotton suspected of involving forced labor in the northern Xinjiang region.[36]

---

[33] Financial Times. April 18, 2019. "China Censors Ban Leica Name Over Tiananmen Square video." www.ft.com/content/7191da2c-6253-11e9-a27a-fdd51850994c.

[34] S. Denyer. May 2018. "Gap Apologizes to China Over Map on T-Shirt That Omits Taiwan, South China Sea," *The Washington Post*. www.washingtonpost.com/news/worldviews/wp/2018/05/15/u-s-retailer-gap-apologizes-to-china-over-map-on-t-shirt-that-omits-taiwan-south-china-sea/.

[35] The New York Times. March 2, 2018. "China Presses Its Internet Censorship Efforts Across the Globe. www.nytimes.com/2018/03/02/technology/china-technology-censorship-borders-expansion.html.

[36] L. He. January 2022. "China Is Still the Ultimate Prize That Western Banks Can't Resist," *CNN Business*. https://edition.cnn.com/2022/01/14/investing/china-western-banks-mic-intl-hnk/index.html.

Other mistakes were hard to avoid. A 2018 Dolce & Gabbana (D&G) commercial that featured a Chinese model struggle to eat Italian food with chopsticks, arguably in poor taste but intended as apolitical, invited an invisible hand other than market forces. D&G products vanished from online stores overnight, causing the firm to cancel most promotions in the country.[37] Some claimed that the fiasco exposed cultural ignorance, but the violent national backlash even surprised the video's Chinese model herself.[38] In a similarly unforeseen act the same year, censors unceremoniously blocked the Marriott hotel group's website for a week because an online form listed Tibet and Taiwan as countries.[39] Simultaneously and for the same reason, a number of American airlines received warnings to "follow Chinese law."[40] Sometimes, authorities display bizarre stretches of imagination. In 2021, Sony was fined a million yuan for releasing its latest camera on a date that coincided with a Japanese attack on China 84 years before.[41] The 2022 Disney film *Doctor Strange* was removed from Mainland circulation because in one action scene, a news kiosk that flashed across the screen stacked copies of a newspaper banned in the PRC—evidently a detail that superhero fans would notice.[42]

---

[37] BBC. November 23, 2018. "D&G: China Shopping Sites Pull Products in Ad Backlash." www.bbc.com/news/business-46312844.

[38] BBC. January 23, 2019. "'Racist' D&G Ad: Chinese Model Says Campaign Almost Ruined Career." www.bbc.com/news/world-asia-china-46968750.

[39] BBC. January 12, 2018. "China Shuts Marriott's Website Over Tibet and Taiwan Error." www.bbc.com/news/business-42658070.

[40] J. Palmer. April 2018. "China Threatens U.S. Airlines Over Taiwan References," *Foreign Policy*. https://foreignpolicy.com/2018/04/27/china-threatens-u-s-airlines-over-taiwan-references-united-american-flight-beijing/.

[41] J. Schneider. October 20, 202. "China Fines Sony ¥1M for Announcing a Camera on a Controversial Date," *PetaPixel*. https://petapixel.com/2021/10/20/china-fines-sony-%C2%A51m-for-announcing-a-camera-on-a-controversial-date/.

[42] J. Goldsmith. May 2022. "Disney CEO Bob Chapek on the "Difficulty" of Getting Films Released in China," *Deadline*. https://deadline.com/2022/05/disney-ceo-bob-chapek-china-dr-strange-1235021804/.

Masters of Apology

Finally, foreign business in China can become helpless collateral damage to geopolitical showdowns. Ask Honda, Carrefour, or almost any South Korean multinational. Honda repeatedly fell victim to Beijing's outbursts against Japan's wartime crimes. In 2005, near my Shanghai apartment, anti-Japan rioters damaged vehicles bearing Japanese brands, while police stood by. Frightened Chinese owners hurriedly decorated their locally made Hondas and Toyotas with patriotic "I love China" stickers. Angry mobs gathered outside Carrefour stores in several cities in 2008 to protest the behavior of pro-Tibet activists along the Beijing Olympic torch relay's Paris leg.[43] The list continues: Swedish businesses suffered sanctions after jailed activist Liu Xiaobo received the 2010 Nobel Peace Prize, Australian food importers when Canberra insisted to investigate the origins of the COVID-19 pandemic in 2020. For foreign executives, the game is no fun: the rules are elusive and changeable, winning has no reward, and losing can be fatal. Starting 2019, state-controlled media repeatedly raised the prospect of an *unreliable entities list*, naming specific firms.[44]

Nothing illustrates the helplessness of multinationals in China better than the fate of South Korean businesses in 2017. Seoul's decision to accommodate American defense systems known as Terminal High Altitude Area Defense or THAAD, cast their China operations into an accelerating vortex of threatening *public opinion* and plummeting sales. State-run publication *Global Times* demanded that "South Korea must face bitter pill over THAAD."[45] In an article subsequently removed from the Internet, state media quoted an online retail influencer with millions of followers who "did not know what THAAD was, but after reading more online, she felt it was a serious threat, telling the Global Times that

[43] France24. May 2008. "Anti-Carrefour Protests Hit China." www.france24.com/en/20080501-anti-carrefour-protests-hit-china-china-carrefour.

[44] L. Niewenhuis. May 2020. "Will Beijing Take Revenge on Qualcomm, Cisco, Apple, and Boeing?," *SupChina*. https://supchina.com/2020/05/18/will-beijing-take-revenge-on-qualcomm-cisco-apple-and-boeing-2/.

[45] B. Ide. March 2, 2017. "Chinese Media Call for Boycott of South Korean Goods," *Voice of America*. www.voanews.com/a/chinese-media-call-for-boycott-of-south-korean-goods/3746701.html.

she thinks South Korea's actions are a serious provocation." Her epiphany, the article continued, came "after Dai Xu, air force colonel and military commentator, called for netizens to treat online ideological debates as a serious 'war' and be especially aware of foreign infiltration."[46] Boycotts of Korean products coincided with inspections against Korean Airlines, cosmetics maker Lotte Group, and others. Businesses in Jeju Island in South Korea lost most of their clientele as Chinese package tours were summarily halted.[47] "A tourist outflow that has become a political tool in itself," David Shambaugh commented.[48]

"China has carefully designed retaliation against South Korea so that it does not violate international laws," Reuters quoted an Ewha Law School professor.[49] There was little that the sanctioned firms could do to avoid the ire of the political establishment and popular outrage it created: the sanctions had nothing to do with how the firms behaved. Even state-controlled media admitted that much. "Lotte outlet stores and even a multi-billion-dollar real estate project began receiving inspections from local fire safety departments, several being forced to shut—including the building site—after the authorities said they found 'safety hazards,'" the *Global Times* gleamed with no intended irony. "This was applauded by many on the Internet, who read it as a sign of local governments taking action against the firm in subtle ways."[50] The subtlety was questionable: Beijing banned Korean Airlines flights, grounded tourists, and imposed

---

[46] Global Times. n.d. "Boycotting Korean Firms, Products Over THAAD Triggers Ideological Conflict Online in China." www.globaltimes.cn/content/1036693 .shtml (removed in 2022).

[47] The Economist. October 19, 2017. "A Geopolitical Row With China Damages South Korean Business Further." www.economist.com/business/2017/10/19/ a-geopolitical-row-with-china-damages-south-korean-business-further.

[48] D. Shambaugh. 2020. *China and the World* (Oxford and New York, NY: Oxford University press).

[49] C. Kim and H. Jin. March 2017. "South Korea Struggles to Retaliate in Missile Spat With China," *Reuters*. www.reuters.com/article/us-southkorea-china-lotte-idUSKBN16G1FR.

[50] Global Times. n.d. "Boycotting Korean Firms, Products Over THAAD Triggers Ideological Conflict Online in China." www.globaltimes.cn/content/1036693 .shtml (removed in 2022).

sanctions that caused Samsung, Hyundai, KIA, LG, and other South Korean firms in China over eight billion U.S. dollars of loss according to the Korea Development Bank's calculations.[51]

As tact disappeared from the Chinese government's tactics, expat executives put their skills of cultural adaptation to good use. "You can be a great chess player, but they will beat you at Go (Chinese checkers), where the objective is to occupy territory and thus suffocate the opponent," came Attila Hilbert's enthusiastic explanation. "The larger you are, the bigger your gravity, and gravity is unavoidable. Belt-and-Road is about Go, Confucius Institutes, Chinese diasporas and Chinatowns in the world are also about Go." Dragon Suits accepted the challenge mainly because for their businesses, the suffocation metaphor could easily become literal. A 2022 British Chamber China paper showed that 40 percent of the polled firms considered the PRC their top investment destination, and another one-fifth as their second.[52] For them, an unpredictable China presented existential risk. The harsher the country's political climate became, the more sophisticated responses from global and China-based executives had to become.

Stonewalling worked at first. "I categorically deny the allegations made against us on these blogs about the support that we would have given to this or that political or religious cause," LVMH Chief Executive Bernard Arnault told journalists as attacks against Carrefour and other French firms unfolded before the 2008 Olympics.[53] The luxury firm managed to avoid sanctions. Publicly firing employees who broke no law but became associated with assumed lapses in socialist morality became a corporate tactic borrowed from China's own playbook. Marriott promised to fire employees who clicked *like* on social media posts related to Tibet

---

[51] The Economist. October 17, 2017. "A Geopolitical Row With China Damages South Korean Business Further." www.economist.com/business/2017/10/19/a-geopolitical-row-with-china-damages-south-korean-business-further.

[52] British Chamber. 2022. "British Business in China: Sentiment Survey 2021–2022." www.britishchamber.cn/en/business-sentiment-survey/ p. 13.

[53] Reuters. April 2008. "LVMH Denies Tibet Support, Sees No Chinese Boycott—Report." www.reuters.com/article/idINIndia-33081720080416.

even outside of the PRC.[54] Cathay Pacific Airways did fire executives and pilots who were suspected sympathizers of the prodemocracy movement in Hong Kong.[55] But in political systems that use public shaming and vocal loyalty as control mechanisms, actions never speak as loud as words. Mercedes-Benz learned this lesson the hard way after it quoted the Dalai Lama in one of the firm's motivational posts on Instagram, an unavailable medium in Mainland China. Even after the counterrevolutionary quote had been removed by its editors, government paper *People's Daily* declared the car maker "an enemy of the Chinese people."[56]

It was after a series of similar incidents that international executives armed themselves with a blunt tactical weapon of the one-party system: the regretful apology. "Even though we deleted the related information as soon as possible, we know this has hurt the feelings of people of this country," Mercedes-Benz declared in response to the *People's Daily* tirades. To be fair, they merely followed the flow, and learned from the best. The tone had been set in early 2018 by Zhang Yiming, CEO of Toutiao, confessing after some of the platform's content got blocked that the firm "placed excessive emphasis on the role of technology, and we have not acknowledged that technology must be led by the Socialist core value system."[57] In successive years, as multinational firms suffered from shaming campaigns and sanctions, foreign chief executives worked themselves into various states of frantic penitence to salvage their Mainland businesses. The tone of self-shaming varied from stonewalling to remorse, its delivery from perfunctory to groveling, and in most cases sufficient to appease authorities.

---

[54] Deutsche Welle. February 7, 2018. "Mercedes Bows to Chinese Pressure After Dalai Lama Instagram Post Prompts Outrage." www.dw.com/en/mercedes-bows-to-chinese-pressure-after-dalai-lama-instagram-post-prompts-outrage/a-42475537.

[55] The New York Times. n.d. "China Is a Minefield, and Foreign Firms Keep Hitting New Tripwires." www.nytimes.com/2019/10/08/world/asia/china-nba-tweet.html (accessed July 12, 2022).

[56] Deutsche Welle. February 7, 2018. "Mercedes Bows to Chinese Pressure After Dalai Lama Instagram Post Prompts Outrage." www.dw.com/en/mercedes-bows-to-chinese-pressure-after-dalai-lama-instagram-post-prompts-outrage/a-42475537.

[57] D. Bandurski. n.d. "Tech Shame in the New Era," *China Media Project*. http://chinamediaproject.org/2018/04/11/tech-shame-in-the-new-era/.

Marriott and other firms whose country lists were tainted by Taiwan issued simple apologies: employee dismissals spoke for themselves. GAP took the blame and thanked their persecutors: "We are grateful to customers, media, employees and government regulators for their attention and support. In the future, we are committed to a more rigorous review to prevent similar mistakes from happening again."[58] Leica rejected *tank man*: "Leica Camera AG must therefore distance itself from the content shown in the video and regrets any misunderstandings or false conclusions that may have been drawn."[59] Luxury fashion house Versace humiliatingly lined up with GAP to issue apologies for shirts that featured Taiwan as a country, followed by Coach and Zara for one assumed insult to the nation after another.[60] By late 2018, foreign executives had become masters of forced apologies, but no effort rivaled the imploring video of D&G after the spaghetti-splattered commercial. True to their creative reputation, founders Domenico Dolce and Stefano Gabbana confessed to "have thought long and hard about our mistakes" and "begged for forgiveness." Poor lighting, nearby vacant chairs to underscore their well-deserved exclusion, and the befitting wooden body language were brilliantly tailored for their intended audience.[61]

Going With the Flow, Turning With the Tide

Dragon Suits are the kind of managers whose eyes light up at yet another neck-breaking political swirl, logistical crisis, or nationwide overhaul. They acknowledge a bold move by the government the way tennis players

---

[58] C. Dwyer. May 2018. "The Gap Apologizes for Shirts Showing Map of China Without Disputed Territories," *NPR*. www.npr.org/sections/thetwo-way/2018/05/15/611278789/the-gap-apologizes-for-t-shirts-showing-map-of-china-without-disputed-territorie.

[59] Financial Times. April 18, 2019. "China Censors Ban Leica Name Over Tiananmen Square video." www.ft.com/content/7191da2c-6253-11e9-a27a-fdd51850994c.

[60] The New York Times. n.d. "Versace, Givenchy and Coach Apologize to China After T-Shirt Row." www.nytimes.com/2019/08/12/fashion/china-donatella-versace-t-shirt.html (accessed July 12, 2022).

[61] Dolce & Gabbana. November 23, 2018. "Dolce&Gabbana Apologizes," video. https://youtu.be/7Ih62lTKicg.

admire an undefendable curved ball. "The best and the worst thing about China is that it changes every eighteen months," technology analyst Dan Wang said in a 2021 podcast.[62] Since their adoption from the Soviet Union, Five-Year Plans served as blueprints not only for the nation's economy, but for all things large and small including its geography and demography. State planners appointed Shanghai, a coastal city with little space to spare, as the country's automotive center and Shenzhen, a new development without universities at the time, the headquarter of its high-technology industry. The chief challenge of that approach is that today's world changes faster than Beijing's five-year cycles, so plans, laws, and infrastructure either lag behind recent developments or leap forward to meet anticipated future needs. Foreign businesses must make sure that strategies minimize volatility while maximizing opportunity.

Multinational managers must align not only with legislation but also with erratic state aspirations often labeled *the China dream*. Laws are drafted, passed, announced, and then enforced (or not) according to their immediate utility. Different provinces implement new (or not so new) regulations according to their distance from Beijing, local interests, and the power of their party and government leaders. A 2011 law regulating the contribution of foreign employees to the PRC's social security system was fully enforced in Beijing by 2022, on a voluntary basis in Shanghai and in various ways elsewhere.[63] Foreign firms and individuals are informally exempt from a long list of local regulations, which, however, hang over their heads like proverbial suspended swords: restrictions on movement, family planning, self-expression, and Internet use, among others. "Authorities have tried to reassure companies they won't be affected, but if the rules in the China Telecom letter are enforced, they could hamper activity ranging from gathering information

---

[62] K. Kuo. January 2022. "Dan Wang on China in 2021," *SupChina*, podcast. https://supchina.com/podcast/dan-wang-on-china-in-2021-common-prosperity-cultural-stunting-and-shortcomings-of-the-modal-china-story/.

[63] Q. Zhou. August 2021. "Will Foreigners Be Subject to China Social Insurance in Shanghai?," *China Briefing*. www.china-briefing.com/news/will-foreigners-be-subject-to-china-social-insurance-in-shanghai/.

for business deals to employees working on business trips," CNBC commented the state Internet provider's January 2017 memo on possible VPN bans.[64]

A great illustration is *Made in China 2025*, a blueprint to facilitate the dominance of domestic firms in ten key technological sectors, including information technology, processors, new energy vehicles, aerospace, robots, and medical devices.[65] Initiated in 2015 through hundreds of convoluted projects and campaigns, it far exceeded the political insight and expertise of multinational executives.[66] If superficial observers initially missed its dramatic implications, they were soon illuminated by announcements of Beijing's intentions. Shortly after the policy's launch, the government revealed efforts to develop a domestic operating system to replace commercial products like Microsoft Windows, Android, and Apple's OS at public institutions.[67] But *Made in China 2025* clearly conflicted with China's market access commitments to the World Trade Organization. "This program in state-driven tech-industrial policy has already caused considerable controversy around the world (particularly the United States and EU)—which, as a result, has caused the Chinese government to stop referring to the program in public (although it no doubt continues)," David Shambaugh wrote in *China and the World*.[68]

Whether local firms gained market share from multinationals in key technological industries due to top-down government intervention or simply due to superior solutions for China is passionately debated. What

---

[64] CNBC. July 20, 2017. "China Clamping Down on Use of VPNs to Evade Great Firewall." www.cnbc.com/2017/07/20/china-clamping-down-on-use-of-vpns-to-evade-great-firewall.html.

[65] E.B. Kania. February 2019. "Made in China 2025, Explained," *The Diplomat.* https://thediplomat.com/2019/02/made-in-china-2025-explained/.

[66] J. Wübbeke, M. Meissner, M.J. Zenglein, J. Ives, and B. Conrad. December 2016. "Made in China 2025," *Mercator Institute for China Studies*, papers on China 2, no. 74.

[67] C. Cimpanu. December 2019. "Two of China's Largest Tech Firms Are Uniting to Create a New 'Domestic OS'," *ZDet.* www.zdnet.com/article/two-of-chinas-largest-tech-firms-are-uniting-to-create-a-new-domestic-os/.

[68] D. Shambaugh. 2020. *China and the World* (Oxford and New York, NY: Oxford University press), p. 346.

seems certain is that the *Made in China 2025* scare nudged foreign executives toward higher value-added strategies and better intellectual property protection. That seems to be the secret to surviving and thriving in China's unpredictably cyclical economy. State authorities control entire industries they are unable to sufficiently micromanage, leading to recurring rotations of planning and improvisation. If foreign firms approach them as they do storms and floods, their businesses can weather through them well. Take the example of the luxury retail industry under President Xi Jinping's countercorruption campaign. Draconian measures to discipline an entire economy of government graft ended practices previously considered fundamental to doing business the Chinese way. But life went on after the storm, foreign businesses adapted and regained their optimism about China as their core market.

Not long ago, the West recognized corruption as essential to Chinese business. "While often in violation of Chinese law, gift giving is widespread," *Kiss, Bow, or Shake Hands* advised before it recommended gifting expensive pens and liquors, stamps ("stamp collecting is popular in China") and cigarette lighters.[69] I recall early-2000s conferences where foreign corporate lawyers and executives explained that suspicion toward written contracts, and gifts as trust-building measures, represented the holistic philosophies of Confucianism, Taoism, or Buddhism, to be tolerated in the name of cultural empathy. But stamps seldom did the trick: government and party officials were at the forefront of China's luxury retail revolution, and they did not come cheap. Connections between party and luxury ran so deep that Premier Wen Jiabao's wife was one of the country's top diamond traders.[70] China was known as a notorious avoider of international reporting obligations of high-value luxury items.[71] But Xi Jinping assumed Presidency in 2012 on a strong anticorruption agenda, and the party was over. Officials were imposed

---

[69] T. Morrison. 2006. *Kiss, Bow, or Shake Hands: The Bestselling Guide to Doing Business in More Than 60 Countries* (UK: Adams Media), p. 98.

[70] The New York Times. n.d. "Billions in Hidden Riches for Family of Chinese Leader." www.nytimes.com/2012/10/26/business/global/family-of-wen-jiabao-holds-a-hidden-fortune-in-china.html (accessed July 12, 2022).

[71] M. Haywood. 2017. "Tainted Treasures: Money Laundering Risks in Luxury Markets," *Transparency International*, pp. 25–26.

limits on their cars, watches, and even the permissible number of meal courses: four dishes and one soup.[72]

"For business, the new President's anti-corruption measures were a disaster," Chris, the luxury fashion CFO, recalled. "Many of us felt that some discipline was long overdue, but we were shocked to see eighty percent of our Mainland, Hong Kong and Macau sales vanish overnight." His firm was not alone: the campaign hit markets for watches, jewelry, home decoration, electronics, cars, motorcycles and yachts, art, and liquor. Scotch imports nearly halved, "with total direct exports to the People's Republic slumping from £71 million in 2012 to £41m in 2015."[73] The official China dream did not include Rolexes and Bentleys anymore. A decade later, a similar campaign targeted the riches of China's information technology entrepreneurs, levying heavy fines on Alibaba Group in the name of wealth redistribution.[74] Virtual luxuries like multiplayer games and online tutoring had defined the rise of China's new middle class. "But Xi will want Chinese to live in the physical world to make babies, make steel, and make semiconductors," technology commentator Dan Wang wrote in 2021.[75] Yet the same year, the EU Chamber China's *Business Confidence Survey* featured retail and IT among the most optimistic sectors in China, with over half of the polled firms reporting growing revenues.[76] How did multinationals manage to steer the headwinds?

Inside Tracks and Winnable Battles

What is the secret of foreign executives who manage to free their business of the chokeholds of politics and often state-sanctioned local competition,

---

[72] China Economic Review. January 22, 2013. "Four Dishes and One Soup." https://chinaeconomicreview.com/four-dishes-one-soup/.

[73] I. Fraser. February 2022. "Riding the Tiger—Scotch in China," *Whisky News*. www.whiskyinvestdirect.com/whisky-news/scotch-in-china-110220221.

[74] Financial Times. n.d. "China's Xi Calls for Wealth Redistribution and Clampdown on High Incomes." https://amp-ft-com.cdn.ampproject.org/c/s/amp.ft.com/content/87c3aa02-f970-48c8-b795-82768c9f7634 (accessed July 12, 2022).

[75] D. Wang. January 2022. "2021 letter," *blog*. https://danwang.co/2021-letter/.

[76] European Union Chamber of Commerce in China. June 8, 2021. "European Business in China Confidence Survey 2021," p. 6.

and find new directions in the Chinese market? Apparently, it is once again a balance between flexibility and resilience, what author David Clive Price called *bamboo strong*.[77] They learn to accept the turbulent winds of Chinese politics as their operating environment, methodically mitigating it like any other risk. Meanwhile, they realize that due to their very lack of assimilation in that environment, multinationals can turn their insular character (islands of global business in a uniquely local market) into competitive advantage. The first is key to surviving in China. The second, to thriving. Starting with survival skills, as one should, already in 2011 Laurie Underwood recommended that foreign firms in China "pick winnable battles."[78] At the time, the most popular examples for unwinnable battles were price wars with local competitors and dominance in market segments like white goods. But recent years erected much tougher walls that foreign executives should not try to siege.

The involvement of the Communist Party in business has been one delayed but not forgotten condition of foreign firms operating in China. Local state-owned and larger private firms have dual management structures with corporate and party bosses making sure that both cash and Communism are covered on both strategic and operational levels. Foreign-invested firms other than joint ventures with state-owned partners were largely exempt from direct party control. But the Xi Jinping administration renewed demands for party involvement in the private sector, not only in strategic but also in hiring, human resources, and disciplinary decisions.[79] Amidst debates about the likelihood and consequences of extending obligations to all foreign firms, one thing was sure: nobody would ask the firms themselves. "Companies should be alert to pressures to form party organizations in their China subsidiaries," one business

---

[77] D.C. Price. 2016. *Bamboo Strong: Cultural Intelligence Secrets to Succeed in the New Global Economy* (London: DCP Global Limited).

[78] J.A. Fernandez and L. Underwood. 2011. *China CEO: Voices of Experience From 20 International Business Leaders* (New York, NY: John Wiley & Sons), p. 131.

[79] G. Magnus. August 2021. "Going After the Private Sector: Xi on a Mission," *SOAS China Institute.* https://blogs.soas.ac.uk/china-institute/2021/08/24/going-after-the-private-sector-xi-on-a-mission/.

publication warned in 2018, "but also aware of the legal framework and best practices that may limit the impact of such organizations on governance and management."[80] As a harbinger of bigger changes to come, in summer 2022, HSBC became the first foreign bank to install a Chinese Communist Party committee.[81]

But while foreign executives must carefully steer their firms to comply with local laws and follow political currents, they can benefit from the fact that multinationals attract smart Chinese customers, suppliers, and workforce. Responding to political smearing campaigns, many young shoppers publicly boycotted Adidas sneakers and H&M shirts. Government officials proved more reluctant to swap their Mercedes, BMW, and Audi office vehicles for Red Flag, Geely, or Haval models. In market segments where such values count, Western brands still stand for quality and prestige. Contemplating their *winnable battles*, foreign executives know that they cannot win price wars, beat state-backed competitors, or avoid campaigns like *Made in China 2025* and party infiltration of private firms. But Dragon Suits I asked were confident about the advantage of multinationals in quality, from raw materials through management processes to end product, after-sales service, brand recognition, and more. Perhaps most importantly from a leadership perspective, however, multinationals attract some of the nation's top talent.

Ever since they reappeared in China, multinationals stayed ahead of local rivals in terms of safety, compliance, transparency, sustainability, inclusion, and other corporate social responsibility criteria. Benefits went beyond the intangible. While in 2020 foreign firms employed about 7 percent of the country's workforce, they provided a fifth of national VAT revenues, a quarter of gross output value, and 40 percent of trade value, EU Chamber China President and BASF China Chief Representative Joerg Wuttke told me in 2022. Multinationals are also ahead of local

[80] J. Laband. May 2018. "Fact Sheet: Communist Party Groups in Foreign Companies in China," *USCBC*. www.chinabusinessreview.com/fact-sheet-communist-party-groups-in-foreign-companies-in-china/.

[81] S. Morris and T. Kinder. July 21, 2022. "HSBC Installs Communist Party Committee in Chinese Investment Bank," *Financial Times*. www.ft.com/content/eac99fd9-0c30-4141-821a-45348f61c113.

firms and foreign-invested small and medium-sized enterprises (SMEs) in compliance with Beijing's ambitions to reach net-zero carbon emissions by 2060.[82] For ambitious Chinese people, such headway adds to previously mentioned advantages like the chance to interact with expats, use foreign languages, and travel internationally. Over time, the technological GAP closes fast between foreign and top local firms, multinationals compare poorly with local star employers in terms of salaries and promotion speed, and backing a local employer can earn the job-switcher approval in China's intensifying political climate. But cash, titles, and patriotism were never the big attraction of foreign firms anyway. It was work culture.

Despite China's impressive progress in making and following consistent rules, pressure and unpredictability remain features, not bugs. "While in the United States, the government would require years of testing and develop reams of regulations, in China the government would encourage companies to forge ahead," economist Elizabeth C. Economy commented. "If there were a few accidents, that was okay. China would come out ahead."[83] Early expats recall shocking first-hand experiences. "More than once, we had to rush someone injured by boiling steel to a hospital in our private cars because we were unable to get an ambulance," Markus Baumgartner of Miba Group remembers the early 2000s. "When we arrived, doctors refused to touch him unless we paid for the treatment in cash first." Such ruthlessness is a remnant of China's Communist Revolutionary spirit. Though cashless burn victims may not be tossed out of hospitals anymore, teeth-clenching ideals characterize firms associated with the state. The *wolf spirit* of Huawei, founded by former People's Liberation Army engineers, promotes "extreme resilience in the face of failure, a strong tolerance for self-sacrifice, and a sharp predator instinct," The *One Hour China Book* quoted. "During Libya's civil war in 2012, Huawei was the only international company that did not pull its employees from the country."[84]

---

[82] British Chamber. 2022. "British Business in China: Sentiment Survey 2021-2022.," p. 38. www.britishchamber.cn/en/business-sentiment-survey/.

[83] E.C. Economy. 2018. *The Third Revolution: Xi Jinping and the New Chinese State* (Oxford: Oxford University Press).

[84] T J. Towson and J. Woetzel. 2014. *The One Hour China Book: Two Peking University Professors Explain All of China Business in Six Short Stories: Volume 1* (Cayman Islands: Towson Group LLC).

Multinationals attract motivated Chinese workforce by offering alternatives to the forced-march culture of local firms. "Chinese people like working for foreigners," Fernanda Barth of WEG told me. "Once you earn their trust, they will consult you on a wide range of professional and personal issues." That trust, most expats tell me, suddenly strengthens when local employees realize that foreign bosses expect mutual attention, honesty, and commitment rather than the hierarchical tipped balance of local firms. "Chinese bosses tend to give orders," Angelo Puglisi explained. "Western ones typically expect trust if they give it first, and that style works pretty well with local employees." Applying such leadership values in practice can be challenging. An automotive CEO explained to me the importance of being upfront with local management candidates about the slow promotion policies at his firm. But like all constructive cultures, trust-based leadership becomes contagious over time. "At the beginning, I was trying to always be a little bit dominating," University of Zürich researcher Yuan Qin quotes a Chinese executive at an international firm. "I found it's not working at all, and also maybe that's not the best way to lead a company."[85]

Expatriate executives often insist on a culture of engagement out of personal or institutional commitment without any evidence whether, and why, it would work in China. But considerate corporate cultures resonate well with local employees for many reasons. The authors of China CEO explain how training and further education like Executive MBA courses cater to the most profound ambitions of Chinese families.[86] Bronwyn Bowery-Ireland agrees. "Most foreign managers don't realize how fast Chinese people learn, and how eager they are to learn. For them, education is the path to freedom." In a vast country with a low level of international mobility, multinationals also provide portals of global openness for the nation's globetrotting minority. Returnees, including foreign-born Chinese and locals returning after many years of international work or studies, are generally considered vital for the inflow of

---

[85] Y. Chin. Manuscript in preparation. "The Emergence of Chinese Global Executives." (accessed July 2022).

[86] J.A. Fernandez and L. Underwood. 2020. *China CEO II: Voices of Experience From 25 Top Executives Leading MNCs in China* (Oxford: Wiley), p. 215.

international ideas, expertise, network, and even investment. But on return, they often experience a "reverse culture shock," Joel Gallo of NYU Shanghai explained in a 2021 podcast. "Multinational companies can help them re-adjust."[87]

In terms of providing equal opportunities regardless of gender, sexual orientation, and ethnicity, leadership practices at multinationals may offer glimpses into China's future. Human resource managers at foreign firms are obligated to introduce global ethical practices at PRC branches and, thanks to overall trends in the profession, are more often women than men. The resulting focus on gender as a leadership issue contrasts sharply with China's reality. Mao Zedong's claim that "women hold up half the sky" is often presented as an accomplishment—in fact, it is an unfulfilled ambition. The latest, 2012 Women's Economic Opportunity Index by The Economist Intelligence Unit ranked China along Russia and Venezuela.[88] A 2021 poll by fintech firm N26 placed it 75th among a 100 countries, between Azerbaijan and Botswana. Recent improvements in education and business are in sharp contrast with its political leadership which is, in *Little Red Podcast* host Louisa Lim's words, "row after row of identical men."[89]

Meanwhile, successes are often overshadowed by mounting challenges. Gender equality campaigns long clashed, both in the party's eyes and in people's heads, with the PRC's family planning policies and the virtual lack of female representation among top political leaders. Recent party propaganda to restore population growth by encouraging women to be child-bearers, and People's Liberation Army campaigns to "fight femininity among men," among others by censoring the online presence

---

[87] Ganbei. December 5, 2021. "The Gold Rush of International Banks ' Expansion in China'," podcast. www.ganbei.tv/blog/ep-27-the-gold-rush-of-international-banks-expansion-in-china?categoryId=245717.

[88] Our World in Data. n.d. "Women's Economic Opportunity Index, 2012." https://ourworldindata.org/grapher/womens-economic-opportunity-2012-index (accessed July 30, 2022).

[89] G. Smith and L. Lim. "Gimme, Gimme, Gimme a Han After Midnight: China's Masculinity Crisis," *The Little Red Podcast*. https://podcasts.apple.com/hk/podcast/the-little-red-podcast/id1136685378?l=en&i=1000560480404 (accessed July 12, 2022).

of allegedly girlish-looking male stars, made matters worse. China is one society where demands for equal opportunity poke at serious taboos. "The public of every low-income or lower-middle-income society included in the Values Surveys—without a single exception—places relatively strong emphasis on Pro-fertility norms," wrote World Values Survey founder Ronald F. Inglehart. "These norms encourage women to cede leadership roles to men and devote themselves to bearing and raising children."[90] Those who care see opportunity. "International companies seem to be more advanced in gender equality, but this is because they've been doing it for years and because this is a requirement for their local markets," Sup-China wrote in 2021 "They have become a point of reference and step by step even local businesses have to adopt the same policies."[91]

During the decades of China's *reform and opening*, designated development areas, and foreign firms within were islands where imported ideals could take root: capitalism, consumerism, diversity and inclusion, performance-based pay, caring for individual well-being and motivation, design, fashion, luxury, feminism, fun, and the freedom to challenge authority. This parallel universe attracted talented Chinese people who were tired of both Confucian and Communist ideologies, not the least with whacky creativity: vividly decorated offices, casual Fridays, team-building, in-house chat apps, Christmas and Halloween parties where foreign bosses mingled, as Chinese friends told me, *like normal people*. But below the playful surface loomed serious issues. Global firms exist for profit: those hand-painted murals, yoga classes and *townhall meetings* are carefully calibrated productivity tools. As China's markets matured, it also seemed that separation was bad for business. If they wanted to meet increasing demand, win over local competitors, and attract the best people, multinationals had to adapt. The surest way to achieve that, expat executives already told me in the early 2000s, was a new generation of local mangers to eventually take over Chinese operations from foreigners.

---

[90] R.F. Inglehart. 2018. *Cultural Evolution: People's Motivations Are Changing, and Reshaping the World* (Cambridge: Cambridge University Press), p. 40.

[91] G. James. December 2021. "Multinationals in 2021: The New Reality of Doing Business in China," *SupChina*. https://supchina.com/2021/12/15/multinationals-in-2021-the-new-reality-of-doing-business-in-china/.

CHAPTER 5

Moving On

Localizing Leadership

To grasp the collective cognitive dissonance of the country's exalted and exhausted expats, browse *Why do I leave China* blogs and admire their diversity. Some are soberly factual. "I have a family with two young kids, and found myself wondering about the health effects of long-term exposure to hazardous air," one wrote in 2013, "having been forced to run indoors on a treadmill for several years—even while training for marathons."[1] Others get hysterical. "China is incredible, but I need a freakin' break! I just need a break from the constant construction, crowds, pushing and shoving, oily food, pollution, and internet censorship."[2] Some even become poetical. "When we first met, it was great. You were a developing nation, on the cusp of greatness, full of opportunity, innocence and frankly batshit behavior. And now? Now, you're a bellicose superpower with a victimhood complex and a whole bunch of incipient, growing social problems."[3] Finally, some aim for balance. "We'd both had front row seats at the greatest show on earth," a farewell blog reads. "All good, but those all came at a price which was paid in compromised quality of life."[4]

---

[1] M. van der Chijs. March 2013. "Why I'm Leaving China," *CNN Business*. https://money.cnn.com/2013/03/26/news/economy/china-business-pollution/index.html.

[2] Richelle. October 2017. "After FIVE Years in China, I'm Finally Moving On," *Adventures Around Asia*. www.adventuresaroundasia.com/leaving-china/.

[3] China Daily Show. August 15, 2012. "Why I'm Leaving China." http://china-dailyshow.com/why-im-leaving-china/.

[4] R. Robinson. December 2020. "2020 Year in Review. Beijing to Bali to Beijing and Back—or—Hindsight Is 2020 ;-)," *LinkedIn*. www.linkedin.com/pulse/2020-year-review-beijing-bali-back-rich-robinson/.

I perused many such posts over the years, then dismissed them as irrelevant to the larger picture. Although complaints about waning foreigner-friendliness proliferated since the mid-2010s, the first explicit study I saw on China's shrinking expat population was the *Sino Benelux Business Survey Report* of 2019. "On average, the number of expatriates per firm has decreased from 2017 to 2018 by 6%," the paper stated, "which we see is in line with the general trend experienced with foreign companies in China." From then on, the *expat exodus* was breaking news. "Loving China, Leaving China," *The Economist* magazine jingled triumphantly later in 2019.[5] "Foreign worker numbers nosediving," The EU Chamber's 2021 *Business in China Confidence Survey* announced after over 40 percent of member firms reported their expat workforces decreasing or gone entirely.[6] Would all foreigners leave? Admittedly, they had been long cornered by the motley monsters of modernity by then: fast-learning locals, returnees with fancy Western degrees, computerized factories and administration, shiny new robots, *dark factories*, and intangible industries that required less supervision. The main culprit, however, had been the innocent-sounding word *localization*.

Management localization is the practice of gradually and systematically replacing expatriate managers with local talent, something that has featured in the China strategies of multinational firms since the early 2000s. Indigenous candidates had many advantages over foreigners from the start of China's reopening. Expats arrived with solid experience and loyalty to the firm, especially after promotions to promising positions in the world's most dynamic market. But they also required a hefty baggage of inflated salaries, benefits, and insurance costs, not to mention spacious homes and international education for their families. In 2004, I met a General Manager for a German industrial firm whose employer had just shipped his grand piano and wine collection to Shanghai. It was an unsustainable dreamland for the airdropped few, but firms already planned to

[5] The Economist. July 11, 2019. "Supply Chains for Different Industries Are Fragmenting in Different Ways." www.economist.com/special-report/2019/07/11/supply-chains-for-different-industries-are-fragmenting-in-different-ways.
[6] European Union Chamber of Commerce in China. June 8, 2021. "European Business in China Confidence Survey 2021," p. 40.

put their budgets to better use. "Business grew and we needed Chinese mangers, especially on the technical level," Fernanda Barth explained practices at her Brazilian employer WEG. "We sent the most promising talent to Brazil for four months to learn the way the company worked."

Two decades later, the consequences of management localization are tangible. Nobody sees that clearer than the promoted local managers themselves. "Our customers still install English speakers in their companies," said Tony Shi of Benteler, "but at meetings you can hear the discussion switching back to Mandarin all the time." The interim two decades saw an entire generation of local leaders mature. "This was one of the biggest differences between research findings for *China CEO* and *China CEO II*," Laurie Underwood explained. "In 2006, none of the twenty CEOs we interviewed were PRC nationals. In 2020, seven of the twenty-five were." If the goal was to transfer expat jobs to homegrown managers, localization has been a success. Polls show that most multinationals in China plan to further cut their already shrinking expat work force in coming years.[7] "Localization is everywhere," Angelo Puglisi said. "It was the plan when I arrived, and it still goes strong. Expatriates dropped from seventy percent of our management to half." In other words, once the first generations of localized Chinese managers are in place, they switch to higher gear to accelerate the process.

Foreigners have always come to China mainly in pursuit of opportunity. It is only natural that the localization of desirable jobs at large firms, combined with cooling economic growth, makes some of them pack up and leave. Reliable data is hard to access, because the number of foreigners in the PRC has always been a hazy research area. "In 2020, a government census estimated there were around 850,000 overseas nationals living on the mainland, but this data includes an unspecified number of former Chinese citizens who have taken another nationality," a *Sixth Tone* article claimed.[8] But the trend was clear to all who walked the streets

---

[7] Financial Times. July 17, 2022. "China's Zero-Covid Policy Has Had a Severe Impact on Its Stock of Global Talent." www.ft.com/content/fef5a71d-8a19-4f65-804e-42bfb02af083.

[8] D. Morgan and Z. Ruiying. January 19, 2022. "China's Foreign Firms Are Running Out of a Key Resource: Foreigners," *Sixth Tone*. www.sixthtone.com/news/1009408/chinas-foreign-firms-are-running-out-of-a-key-resource-foreigners.

of China's main cities or asked friends who serviced their expat-bubble economy. Restaurants catering to global tastes closed one after another. International schools downsized. Farewell party invitations proliferated. Asian Tigers, a leading relocation firm for multinationals, experienced a one-third drop in inward business but a huge surge in moving foreigners out, Country Manager Jason Will told me. In early 2022, EU Chamber China President and BASF China Chief Representative Joerg Wuttke estimated that half of European expats had already left.[9]

While most expats lamented, some claimed it was better that way. "Because of the pandemic, we have realized that we still operate well without foreign managers," *Sixth Tone* quoted a local human resources professional. "We don't seem to need them much."[10] Claims that China only needed foreign presence at an early stage of modernization suited both the government's Soviet-induced development narrative and the hopes of multinational firms. From an employer's perspective, the benefits of management localization had started with the basics. It had been evident from the early 2000s onward that the language, culture, vastness, and diversity of China would exceed the capacity of most foreign managers, not to mention labyrinthine political climate of the People's Republic. "It is, for example, our custom to give some discount as a token of good will: just a little bit," Kurt Yu explained. "But foreign managers find it hard to understand how much 'a little bit' is. For a hundred-million-euro deal, one percent is huge. Managers who make such decisions must be sensitive to local body language and etiquette, at which local managers definitely do a better job."

Many well-intentioned textbooks insist that China-based expatriate executives should simply learn the language and master the culture before they get down to business. Beyond the complexities of Mandarin and insular expat existence, there are other reasons to suspect such advice.

---

[9] Bloomberg UK. April 18, 2022. "China Meets With Foreign Chambers as Lockdowns Hit Business." www.bloomberg.com/news/articles/2022-04-18/china-meets-with-foreign-chambers-as-lockdowns-hit-business.

[10] Q. Junya. May 2022. "Eventually, China's Borders Will Reopen. Will Foreigners Return?," *Sixth Tone*. www.sixthtone.com/news/1010282/eventually%2C-chinas-borders-will-reopen.-will-foreigners-return.

"Expats usually arrive for three to five years," Kurt Yu said. "They lack long-term goals because they already know when they will leave. They want to prove themselves and get a quick win before they return to head-quarters." That is understandable: career acceleration is a top reason for accepting jobs in China at all. But as a consequence, foreign firms often operate in detached, alternate universes, which bothers both local and engaged expat managers. "ThyssenKrupp in China would make a great case study," Henrik König told me. "Our Shanghai organization belonged to a sub-organization of the Asia-Pacific headquarters in Singapore, the Industrial Solutions headquarters. We had a parallel China Regional Cluster in Beijing, which had a sub-cluster in Shanghai, which was sep-arate from the Asia-Pacific Industrial Solutions. They tried to control all this from Germany through convoluted meetings, presentations and deci-sions. I kept flying between China, Germany, Singapore, Malaysia and Vietnam, often in vain."

Localization seemed to simultaneously focus the organization on local demands and remove linguistic and cultural hurdles. "For jobs that require a second language, employers prefer Chinese candidates who have had overseas experience," BBC quoted a local HR consultant for Hudson Global already in 2014. "Foreign hires are expensive and, more import-ant, there are language and cultural barriers."[11] But there was more. "Look at our Singapore operations," Richard Eardley said. "Our entire manage-ment are expats. Locals wonder whether they have a future there." His remarks pointed at an infamous *glass ceiling* that stopped local candidates from ascending to top jobs. Shaun Rein shared similar views. "I visit For-tune 500 firms in China where the top-ten executives are all white, except maybe the head of HR or finance. Such glass ceilings make Chinese talent lose interest in working there." As localization progresses, one condition of its long-term success is shattering that barrier. "That is why at our firm, we have no restrictions on promoting PRC nationals," Briana said. "We have no rules against conducting meetings in Mandarin either. I think this also offers a more authentic China experience to expats."

---

[11] M. Durnin. February 2014. "China Is Still a Jobs Hotspot for Expats," *BBC*. www.bbc.com/worklife/article/20140212-get-hired-in-china.

Limits to Localization

The benefits of passing formerly expatriate jobs to talented locals seem endless. "Communication between our Chinese managers and German headquarters might be harder than with expats in place," Tony Shi added, "but localization shows that the company is serious about the local market. People will feel proud that local employees are recognized." Fernanda Barth agreed and went further. "For local colleagues, it's an honor to be a multinational manager. They are open to change, more willing to move between locations in China, socialize more with their workers and consequently have better cross-departmental relations." An overseas degree gradually replaces foreign nationality as a requirement, the *Sixth Tone* article's HR expert reckoned.[12] Has it been seamless success, then? Not really, experienced expats told me. Gaps remain in both competency and trust. "Expat jobs are passed on to Chinese men and women in their forties with graduate degrees and years of experience in the United States," Shaun Rein said. "They understand the American, European and Chinese cultures and can navigate between them, but they still need help."

When a multinational firm entrusts a formerly expatriate job to a local manager, what changes hands is much more than titles, desks, passwords, and authority over resources, tasks, and people. Global firms wish to see their corporate cultures and legacy take root in China, and those go back decades, sometimes generations. Only part of the trust required for such succession comes from measurable performance criteria. Much of it must come from the enigmatic gut-level faith that is especially hard to nurture across distant cultures. At times, the result is the perfunctory and half-hearted appointment of local managers, paired with reluctance to delegate genuine authority. "Germans have the expression 'Frühstücksdirektor', literally 'breakfast director', meaning someone whose authority is limited to what they serve at the factory canteen," Henrik König told me. "ThyssenKrupp nominated a local CEO, whose most noteworthy competence was that she spoke fluent German. She soon realized she was

---

[12] Q. Junya. May 2022. "Eventually, China's Borders Will Reopen. Will Foreigners Return?," *Sixth Tone*. www.sixthtone.com/news/1010282/eventually %2C-chinas-borders-will-reopen.-will-foreigners-return.

a 'Frühstücksdirektor', left the company and an expat CFO became CEO instead. The lesson is that firms must either give local executives independence or not localize at all."

Once again, experienced Dragon Suits suggest a balanced approach: expat and local management should bring different but equally necessary benefits to the table. "Language skills are still the key to multinational organizations," Kurt Yu told me. "Translators, interpreters and personal assistants with foreign-language fluency have an outsized influence. Local managers are obviously better at sharing information with the organization without language barriers, and they often claim that a *'laowai'* manager can never understand China. On the other hand, expats see them as outsiders. When a German company puts an Austrian in charge, they still considered him 'our person'." Markus Baumgartner helped illustrate the usefulness of identity demarcations. "A foreigner can never master the local language and network like a local can, but that isn't always necessary. Business with local companies can be complicated, but relationships don't matter that much when you bid for a project with BMW or Daimler China. I find it better to keep a few expats in place for their special expertise. For instance, it's better to have a foreigner in charge of finance because it is good to know where the money is."

China gradually produces obvious success stories for management localization. "I knew that the Chinese managers I interviewed had to be not only fluent in English but also bicultural," Laurie Underwood recalled. "They had to be at ease during meetings in Berlin or Barcelona, with top management, and not only language-wise but at weekend socializing as well. I must say that all seven CEOs I interviewed were impressively able to float between cultures." Such local talent, however, is as rare as expats with instinctive cultural agility. Until they find one such brilliant China CEO, foreign firms must polish countless rough diamonds, and ultimately accept that most will never make the final cut. Regulation and tradition can both create obstacles. "Our Chinese managers were excited to be sent to the Brazil headquarters and an assembly plant in Austria, but visa procedures often stood in the way," Fernanda recalled. "It took months to acquire their visas to Austria. We had to shorten a planned half-year training period in Brazil to four months because we simply couldn't get longer visas for our managers."

Sometimes, glass ceilings materialize from the invisible fabric of inter-woven values and vulnerabilities. "Many Chinese managers view interna-tional assignments as a risk, especially senior ones," Kurt Yu explained. "It is not for family reasons—they actually look forward to educating their kids abroad in foreign languages, especially if the company foots the bill. But they worry about their own language skills and whether their subordinates would accept them there. From a career perspective, this is highly risky, and so far, I haven't seen any local manager who was very successful in this respect." Rachel added a thought-provoking example of the way China's soaring middle-class determination, the very quality that elevates many local candidates into powerful positions at global firms, can backfire abroad. "Some Chinese mangers are sent abroad with fifteen to twenty years of successful domestic track record and even some expe-rience abroad. Then, for instance in a place like Singapore, they are often seen as too pushy, too tough. They run the risk of rotating back to China with a tarnished reputation. In contrast, they are absolutely perfect for managing the local market."

Without careful preparation, throwing expats and locals into a musi-cal-chairs game of manager localization can actually widen culture gaps and create conflict. "A British colleague turned up in my office and asked me whether not speaking Mandarin and keeping a distance from local culture would influence his success in China," Leigh recalled. "He wasn't the first one to raise this issue, and I always suggest they do 'the flip test'. Could a Chinese manager do a good job in London without speaking English or knowing how to behave among Brits?" Most expats in that situation would note that Shanghai and London have essentially dif-ferent stance and aspirations in the world, and although it might in a century, Mandarin still cannot match English in global business. Some might say it out loud, escalating an already awkward conversation. Either way, foreign decision makers in charge of localization (executives, human resources professionals, and so forth) must devise adequate strategies for such in-house culture clashes. China's growing economic clout inspires growing self-confidence in its citizens. The way foreign headquarters and local leaders imagine the company's future can diverge dramatically.

Successful global firms operate a carefully calibrated, interlocking system of headquarter-induced strategic goals, processes, checks and balances, values, performance and competency management systems, customized but deployed in unison in worldwide locations. Branches of Bayer or General Electric in distant continents can adapt to local circumstances and differ from one another. But, as I keep hearing from executives, the *Bayer-ness* or *GE-ness* that holds everything together must remain. The puzzle is that each success factor of manager localization poses a challenge to that unity. When local managers engage their workers in Mandarin, most expats are removed from the conversation. Chinese networkers who master the intricacies of *guanxi* leave their foreign bosses clueless about what exactly happens, why and where it leads. When one of them befriend government officials to secure an inside track, headquarters become anxious about transparency and legal compliance. "Localization is often a far from ideal solution—and could be difficult to reverse in the future," one article pointed out in early 2022. "Multinationals worry the trend may lead to a growing disconnect between their China businesses and operations overseas."[13]

As management localization progresses and intensifies, especially among senior strategic leaders, PRC branches may drift from the mother ship. "Sure enough, what we see is that the first generation of local managers are very sophisticated, probably studied overseas," Rachel explained. "But then, a lot of them are snatched up by Chinese companies. The ones who replace them typically grew up locally, come from a sales background and can turn out to be job-hoppers focused on short-term wins. They think they can operate through local joint ventures, but that way they can bankrupt the company." If that sounds like dystopian fiction from the faraway future, consider the story of Arm China, representing probably the world's most important semiconductor firm in the PRC. Its Chinese top executive not only piggybacked Arm's reputation to start his own business while still on the job, but "held an event at which they formally declared their independence," a 2021 article reported. "They proclaimed," the article continued, that the local firm "was born from Arm, but is an independently operated, Chinese owned company. While

---

[13] D. Morgan and Z. Ruiying. January 19, 2022. "China's Foreign Firms Are Running Out of a Key Resource: Foreigners," *Sixth Tone*. www.sixthtone.com/ news/1009408/chinas-foreign-firms-are-running-out-of-a-key-resource-foreigners.

Arm is the largest individual owner in this firm, they have no control or power over the operations." He allegedly backed his words with a personal security detail at Arm's expense.[14]

While most Dragon Suits should not fear palace coups by rogue CEOs with private bodyguards, they should remember that one way to bridge headquarters and China is to nurture both international and local managers. "Young Chinese people speak languages and have more knowledge about the world," Tony Shi said. "They can help us cooperate better. The international-local GAP will not disappear, but things will get better." Kurt agrees. "The Chinese put relationship first. Foreigners are more straightforward, so they can push for results more effectively. Some clients constantly test Chinese managers with unreasonable requests, but to a foreigner they present a fair proposal." Foreigners may have their uses after all, even to the very local managers who took over expat jobs. "We need to hire some foreign employees because they speak better English, are good at expressing themselves, and have a talent for self-promotion," *Sixth Tone* quotes a local manager. "They can say some awesome words and appear very powerful and confident. They're suited to communicating with foreign clients."[15]

The solution sounds simple but takes meticulous implementation: manage the risks, bridge the gaps. "It is probably better to localize whenever you can," Shaun Rein advised. "Companies should either hire expats with a five-to-ten-year track record of success in China, or they should hire and promote local Chinese managers." While pushing for localization, company decision makers should bear in mind that ultimately, they still run a multinational operation. "In some companies, the CFO will always be an expat," Angelo Puglisi said. "But that is normal: US companies in Europe also have American managers in every department."

[14] D. Patel. August 27, 2021. "The Semiconductor Heist of the Century," *Semianalysis.* https://semianalysis.com/the-semiconductor-heist-of-the-century-arm-china-has-gone-completely-rogue-operating-as-an-independent-company-with-their-own-ip/.

[15] D. Morgan and Z. Ruiying. January 19, 2022. "China's Foreign Firms Are Running Out of a Key Resource: Foreigners," *Sixth Tone.* www.sixthtone.com/news/1009408/chinas-foreign-firms-are-running-out-of-a-key-resource-foreigners.

Finally, headquarters, China-based expats, and local managers should all remember that like in any other quest, triumph is the exception, not the rule. Chinese managers who seamlessly facilitate the transition from expatriate to indigenous leadership will always be the select few, found and promoted to the right job at the right time. "Voith showed exceptional courage when they entrusted me with this position," Kurt Yu told me. "Just think about it: one single order can be worth a hundred-fifty million euros. I think they were very brave to appoint a local manager."

Foreign Business Beyond *Decoupling*

In February 2021, just as China prepared to stagger back to work after the week-long Lunar New Year festivities, The U.S. Chamber of Commerce in China published a voluminous report entitled *Understanding U.S.-China Decoupling: Macro Trends and Industry Impacts*. "The two countries have attempted to disentangle aspects of our economies in recent years," the paper claimed, and warned that mutually increased mobility restrictions on goods, people, and funds could lead to gargantuan losses for the U.S. economy in sectors such as trade (up to U.S.D 190 billion by 2025), investment (25 billion annually), tourism (up to 30 billion per year), aviation (50 billion a year), semiconductors (over 100 billion and 100,000 jobs), chemicals, medical devices, and so forth.[16] The curious keyword to the publication, *decoupling*, had been around for a while and had split opinions. Some saw the coming separation of China from a global circulation of investment, ideas and workforce as an inevitable continuation of a perceived *expat exodus*, toughening immigration laws, and Internet restrictions. Others dismissed it outright: China's integration into a global investment and supply chain network had passed the point of no return, they claimed.

Both sides of the argument had a point. Back in 2019, prestigious research establishments like the Mercator Institute estimated about a

---

[16] "Understanding U.S.-China Decoupling: Macro Trends and Industry Impacts." February 17, 2021. *China Center, U.S. Chamber of Commerce*, p. 3. www.uschamber.com/international/understanding-us-china-decoupling-macro-trends-and-industry-impacts.

million foreigners in China.[17] The 2020 national census refuted that as a vast exaggeration, either implying that the foreign population had never been that large or that it was rapidly shrinking. The data also explained why foreigners felt their world was collapsing. Shanghai, a top expat hub with a population twice the size of London's, hosted a 160,000 foreigners, a number on par with the population of the modest German city Leverkusen. Understandably, every departing family increased a sense of loss among that small community. On the other hand, the EU Chamber's 2021 *Business Confidence Survey* was launched at China-wide live networking events while most advanced economies were still grounded by the COVID-19 pandemic and showed "the lowest desire to leave the market on record" with less than 10 percent of polled firms divesting.[18] U.S. Chamber surveys showed similar results. The same year, a study by data analytics firms FactSet revealed that global firms like Rio Tinto, Richemont, Volkswagen, and BMW pulled over a third of their revenues from Mainland China.[19]

With that level of integration, decoupling sounded absurd. But it was a time of absurdities anyway. In an era defined by Brexit and Donald Trump's turbulent presidency, would the escalating erosion of China's *One Country, Two Systems* for the Hong Kong Special Administrative Region become yet another nightmare coming true? Could a crisis of that magnitude severe Mainland China from a globalized economic order?[20] Others challenged the narrative on different grounds. "The concept of 'decoupling' assumes previous 'coupling,'" EU Chamber President Joerg Wuttke said at the launch of the 2021 *Business Confidence Survey*, but China had never fully integrated into the global system. Available data could back his

[17] F.N. Pieke. November 2019. "How Immigration Is Shaping Chinese Society," *MERICS*. https://merics.org/en/report/how-immigration-shaping-chinese-society.

[18] European Union Chamber of Commerce in China. June 8, 2021. "European Business in China Confidence Survey 2021," p. 11.

[19] T. Dams and X. Martin. April 2022. "Investors Beware: Europe's Top Firms Are Highly Exposed to China," *Clingendael*. www.clingendael.org/sites/default/files/2022-04/Report_Are_Europes_top_firms_highly_exposed_to_China.pdf.

[20] W.H. Overholt. 2019. "Hong Kong: The Rise and Fall of the 'One Country, Two Systems.'," Harvard Kennedy School. www.overholtgroup.com/media/Articles-Hong-Kong/Rise-Fall-of-One-Country-Two-Systems.pdf.

opinion too. Since 2000, consulting giant McKinsey has tracked a global *exposure index* based on trade, technological, and investment metrics. It showed that while the world's exposure to China steadily rose until 2019, the PRC's international exposure grew until 2007, sank to the level of 2000 by 2010, then kept declining to unprecedented depths since the survey began.[21] China might be rethinking a fair-weather friendship with the world, the data suggested.

As the 2020s began, those who needed proof for China's flawed engagement with the outside world did not have to look too closely or wait too long. "During the pandemic, senior Communist Party officials conceived a new political slogan: *dōngshēng xījiàng,* meaning the rise of the east and the descent of the west," *Politico* wrote. "The reasoning behind it included China's belief that it has had 'systemic advantages' in tackling the coronavirus, as well as a long-held belief that the country's state-backed technological advancement will soon put it in a position to overturn the Western world order."[22] The condescension was unwelcome during a pandemic for which many blamed China itself: a widely publicized autumn 2020 Pew Research Center poll showed plummeting trust in the PRC and its government's COVID-19 responses, especially among top trading partners including the United States, EU, Japan, and Australia.[23] Joseph S. Nye, the American political scientist who had previously mentored the Chinese government's *soft power* efforts, publicly criticized Beijing's approach. "Because China has problems with so many of its neighbours, Japan, India, Vietnam, the Philippines and so forth, that makes it hard to generate a lot of soft power there."[24]

---

[21] J. Woetzel. July 2019. "China and the World: Inside the Dynamics of a Changing Relationship," *McKinsey Insights.* www.mckinsey.com/featured-insights/china/china-and-the-world-inside-the-dynamics-of-a-changing-relationship.

[22] S. Lau. "Russia Crisis Gives EU a Grim Sense of What's to Come With China," *Politico.* www.politico.eu/article/china-xi-jinping-has-europe-eu-summit-russia (accessed July 12, 2022).

[23] L. Silver, K. Devlin, and C. Huang. October 2020. "Unfavorable Views of China Reach Historic Highs in Many Countries," *Pew Research Center.* www.pewresearch.org/global/2020/10/06/unfavorable-views-of-china-reach-historic-highs-in-many-countries/.

[24] China Power. February 27, 2016. "Is China's Soft Power Strategy Working?." https://chinapower.csis.org/is-chinas-soft-power-strategy-working.

Initial gratitude for relatively open internal movement and markets turned into resentment among expats due to long isolation from business contacts, family, and recreation abroad. "China is much more bearable with the possibility of short trips to Korea, the Philippines or Singapore," Renata and Nicola said. "We didn't travel to neighboring countries from Brazil, but here it's one of the perks." Triumphant but poorly scripted state broadcast from Beijing could not balance the flood of English-language complaints from foreign firms and organizations. A late 2021 British Chamber report named COVID-19-related travel bans as the primary obstacle to doing business in China.[25] The majority of respondents in an early 2022 American Chamber poll complained about lockdowns, broken supply chains, workforce shortages, transportation delays, unnecessary quarantines, and the inability to fill vital expatriate positions.[26] Foreign firms rubbed Beijing's previous plans under the government's nose to challenge victorious narratives. In 2019, Shanghai's government had announced plans to double the city's foreign population in a few years.[27] Two years later, an Italian resident told CNN, "it really feels like we're going backwards in time instead of looking forward to the future."[28] Expat event organizer Frank Tsai was widely quoted when he called the situation "a perfect storm of face loss for the Chinese government."[29]

[25] Reuters. December 7, 2021. "Travel Curbs Are Biggest Challenge for British Firms in China—Survey." www.reuters.com/world/china/travel-curbs-are-biggest-challenge-british-firms-china-survey-2021-12-07/.

[26] AmCham China. April 1, 2022. "COVID-19: Joint Survey Reveals Business Impact of Latest Outbreak." www.amchamchina.org/covid-19-joint-survey-reveals-business-impact-of-latest-outbreak/.

[27] X. Yi. January 2019. "Shanghai Home to Largest Foreign Worker Population in China," *China Daily*. www.chinadaily.com.cn/a/201901/16/WS5c3e-d0a9a3106c65c34e4d2a.html.

[28] J. Yeung. n.d. "Hong Kong and Shanghai Lose Their International Luster as Covid Restrictions Bite," *CNN*. https://edition.cnn.com/2022/04/22/china/china-hubs-shanghai-hong-kong-covid-intl-hnk-mic/index.html.

[29] Bloomberg UK. March 24, 2022. "Experts See China Stuck in a Slowly Evolving Covid-Zero Loop." www.bloomberg.com/news/articles/2022-03-24/experts-see-china-stuck-in-a-slowly-evolving-covid-zero-loop.

Grounded Globetrotters

The pandemic escalated debates about the role of foreigners in the People's Republic, triggering controversy and conflict. It is worth remembering that according to data from the *HSBC Expat Explorer Survey* and other similar polls, foreigners had typically arrived and stayed in China for tangible opportunities. Career prospects, economic growth, and disposable income topped the list. Experiencing the local culture featured as an initial attraction, but eventual integration into local life was practically impossible for most expats. Health, fun, and life quality typically fell victim to ambition. Absorbing the spirit of *Socialism with Chinese characteristics* was not a chief reason why talented foreigners chose the PRC. Yet, over the years between 2020 and 2022, expatriates not only lost various opportunities and conveniences of their previously negotiated existence, but somehow found themselves being tested, and predictably failing, on their loyalty to the one-party system. In the eyes of the expat community, that unexpected reversal began to question one of 21st-century China's most admired characteristics: its shrewd pragmatism in all things commercial.

For a while, annoyances where frequent and serious, but mostly material and thus manageable. In early 2021, Beijing announced imminent new regulations for foreign firms that would have made expat benefits such as rent and schooling taxable, effectively rewriting the tax policies that regulated the entire multinational and foreign-invested SME sectors. As the year ended and specialists had invested countless hours into panic-stricken planning, the government unexpectedly reverted, leaving multimillion-dollar Damocles swords hanging over the Christmas and New Year festivities of foreign executives.[30] Meanwhile, travel bans approached the second full year, and exhaustion set in over separation from families, recreation, meetings, and conferences. The pain of missing loved ones toxically mixed with the fear of missing out. "As a CEO or as a purchasing manager, you can't just fly quickly to Shanghai or to Guangzhou,

---

[30] Z. Zhang and K. Huang. December 31, 2021. "Tax-Exempt Fringe Benefits for Expatriates in China Extended till End of 2023," *China Briefing*. www.china-briefing.com/news/tax-exempt-benefits-for-expatriates-in-china-extended-end-2023/.

but today you can easily get to Jakarta, Kuala Lumpur or Manila," Joerg Wuttke told *The Market* in early 2022. "With the current situation in China comes a huge loss of confidence, which will eventually lead to changes in supply chains."[31]

It soon got worse. In spring 2022, Shanghai and other major expat hubs experienced their worst lockdowns in memory, surpassing 2020 and even the 2002 SARS epidemic. Most foreigners were physically and mentally unprepared for so-called *zero-COVID* measures, not only because government bureaus had assured citizens that lockdowns could be avoided until they were imposed, but also because, unlike locals, they never intended to stay sedentary for long. Family visits, domestic and international business, or recreational trips were such essential elements of their lifestyle that most employment contracts guaranteed them. As they often lamented on social media, *the real China* suddenly hit foreigners right where it hurt the most. "People were used to live on higher levels of Maslow's hierarchy of needs," Dr. George Hu told *The Sinica Podcast*. "Now they were dragged down to worrying about clean water and food, which triggers fight or flight instincts and negative emotions."[32] Worse still was the prospect that *zero-COVID* might not be a passing crisis but what The Montaigne Institute called "Xi Jinping's overall philosophy: minimize the risks from a dependence on the outside world, and stay ready for the possibility of a major geopolitical or geoeconomic crisis."[33]

"If corporate headquarters heard what some of their China representatives say in public, they would be shocked," Rachel told me in early 2020. "But companies should never force local people to choose between their loyalty to the company and the Communist Party." That became harder as China's foreign relations started resembling Twitter rants. Responding

[31] M. Dittli. April 2022. "China's Leadership Is Prisoner of Its Own Narrative," *The Market*. https://themarket-ch.cdn.ampproject.org/c/s/themarket.ch/amp/interview/chinas-leadership-is-prisoner-of-its-own-narrative-ld.6545.

[32] K. Kuo. n.d. "Mental Health Under Lockdown: A Clinical Psychologist in Shanghai," *SupChina*, podcast. https://podcasts.apple.com/hk/podcast/sinica-podcast/id1121407665?l=en&i=1000565045048 (accessed July 12, 2022).

[33] F. Godement. February 2022. "Xi Jinping as an Ordoliberal: China's Margins for Growth in 2022," *Institut Montaigne*. www.institutmontaigne.org/en/publications/xi-jinping-ordoliberal-chinas-margins-growth-2022.

to forced labor accusations in Xinjiang by foreign firms and governments, Chinese Foreign Ministry spokesperson Hua Chunying was quick to "remind NATO that they still owe a debt of blood to the Chinese people."[34] When the United States sanctioned Huawei over spying allegations, Beijing threatened with an *unreliable entities list*, naming Apple and Boeing as prime suspects.[35] British Chamber of Commerce China Director Steven Lynch warned that *zero-COVID* undermined China's attractiveness for investment and talent, and demanded measures "directly proportionate to the risk posed."[36] "The economy is enfeebled and being made worse by government actions and by zero Covid policies," added George Magnus of Oxford University.[37] "Blinded by their bias toward China," *The Global Times* countered, "foreign businesses should play a responsible role in the current battle against the virus, instead of making fear-mongering remarks that help no one."[38]

Top officials of the Trump Presidency famously considered the U.S.'s disputes with China a manifestation of the *clash of civilizations* predicted decades earlier by academic Samuel Huntington.[39] Expat executives in China took little notice, but the controversy soon invaded their lives. The spirit and sustainability of the *Belt and Road Initiative*, an infrastructure and policy program of East–West connectivity and cooperation, was already

---

[34] Global Times. March 26, 2021. "US-Led NATO Still Owes Blood Debt to Chinese People: FM." www.globaltimes.cn/page/202103/1219540.shtml.

[35] Global Times. May 16, 2020. "China Readies Biggest Counterattack Against US." www.globaltimes.cn/content/1188493.shtml.

[36] Bloomberg Uk. April 19, 2022. "China Vows to Ease Supply Chain Woes in Foreign Chamber Meeting." www.bloomberg.com/news/articles/2022-04-19/china-vows-to-ease-supply-chain-woes-in-foreign-chamber-meeting.

[37] L. He. April 2022. "Foreign Investors Are Ditching China. Russia's War Is the Latest Trigger," *CNN Business*. https://edition.cnn.com/2022/04/25/investing/china-capital-outflows-covid-ukraine-war-intl-mic-hnk/index.html.

[38] Global Times. April 7, 2022. "GT Voice: Western Slander Won't Undercut Shanghai's Global Attractiveness." www.globaltimes.cn/page/202204/1258762.shtml.

[39] P. Musgrave. July 2018. "John Bolton Is Warning of a "Clash of Civilizations" With China. Here Are the Five Things You Need to Know," *The Washington Post*. www.washingtonpost.com/politics/2019/07/18/john-bolton-is-warning-clash-civilizations-with-china-here-are-five-things-you-need-know/.

questioned in 2019 when at an international summit Foreign Minister Wang Yi ordered member nations to "cooperate or stop criticising."[40] Foreign businesses found themselves in political crossfires they could neither escape nor influence. Contrary to state media claims, they did not respond to the nation's troubles with vindictive delight. "Global investors don't want to play regulatory guessing games or worry that tomorrow's news may deplete another otherwise attractive company or business model," the head of an investment firm summarized the public mood to CNN.[41] "Member companies are mostly concerned about the future, because they don't see a strategy that will end this kind of on-off economy," the head of the EU Chamber of Commerce in Shenyang told local journalists.[42]

As a supercharged version of the political helplessness that had long characterized foreign businesses in China, multinationals found themselves criticized and sanctioned regardless of their compliance or engagement with local authorities. Committed supporters of China's global integration felt the most perplexed, perhaps even betrayed. "The political risk is so high right now that it doesn't make sense to keep investing in China," the Washington Post quoted Shaun Rein, the firmest China advocate among all voices featured in this book, in late 2019. "If you're not already here, you have to think three, four, five times harder about whether it's worth coming."[43] During the pandemic, the situation deteriorated fast. A May 2022 EU Chamber China and Roland Berger joint

[40] D. Shambaugh. 2020. *China and the World* (Oxford and New York, NY: Oxford University press), p. 359.

[41] L. He. April 2022. "Foreign Investors Are Ditching China. Russia's War Is the Latest Trigger," *CNN Business*. https://edition.cnn.com/2022/04/25/investing/china-capital-outflows-covid-ukraine-war-intl-mic-hnk/index.html.

[42] F. Tang. April 2022. "China's European Firms Warn 'On-Off Economy', Covid Lockdowns Cloud Business Outlook," *China Macro Economy*. www.scmp.com/economy/china-economy/article/3173287/chinas-european-firms-warn-economy-covid-lockdowns-cloud.

[43] G. Shih. October 2019. "Response to NBA Executive's Hong Kong Tweet Shows the Rift Between China and U.S.," *The Washington Post*. www.washingtonpost.com/world/nba-rockets-face-backlash-from-chinese-fans-after-tweet-in-support-of-hong-kong-protesters/2019/10/07/68e9ad24-e902-11e9-bafb-da248f8d5734_story.html.

survey quoted three-quarters of polled firms "feel that China is a less attractive investment destination as a result of its more stringent COVID-19 restrictions," and the bigger half decreased their 2022 revenue forecasts.[44] A quarter of European firms considered moving operations abroad and half of American firms delayed investment to the country, *The Wall Street Journal* summarized EU and U.S. Chamber reports, quoting EU Chamber President Joerg Wuttke: "The world is not waiting for China."[45]

Waning Welcome

Anxious expat executives were torn between political pressure on one side and the impossibility of *decoupling* on the other. Foreign businesses had matured in a globalizing China, Center for Strategic and International Studies Senior Adviser Scott Kennedy told the China Power Podcast. "Companies are ready for day one of the crisis: are my workers safe, are my assets safe? They are not ready for day two and onward. They are not ready to fully revise their strategies and fundamentally take China out of the equation as a place for manufacturing, or as a large market, or as a place for research and development."[46] Nevertheless, the impossible started happening: multinationals with stellar track records in China withdrew or saw their local business undermined. LinkedIn, the last global social networking site still accessible from the PRC, owned by long-term China ally Microsoft, closed its local service in late 2021.[47] Yahoo, once accused

---

[44] European Chamber of Commerce in China. n.d. "China's Covid-19 Policy and Russia's War in Ukraine Cause Severe Disruptions to European Business in China." www.europeanchamber.com.cn/en/press-releases/3431.

[45] L. Wei and B. Spegele. May 2022. "China's Top Two Leaders Diverge in Messaging on Covid Impact," *The Wall Street Journal.* www-wsj-com.cdn.amp-project.org/c/s/www.wsj.com/amp/articles/chinas-top-two-leaders-diverge-in-messaging-on-covid-impact-11653486508.

[46] B. Lin. "China's Economic Woes: A Conversation With Scott Kennedy," *CSIS.* www.csis.org/node/65721 (accessed July 12, 2022).

[47] M. Shroff. October 2021. "China: Sunset of Localized Version of LinkedIn and Launch of New InJobs App Later This Year," *LinkedIn.* https://blog.linkedin.com/2021/october/14/china-sunset-of-localized-version-of-linkedin-and-launch-of-new-injobs-app.

of collaborating with Chinese censorship, followed suit in a month.[48] Apple, previously a success story in U.S.–China supply chain integration, started shopping for manufacturing elsewhere.[49] The Tesla Gigafactory, inaugurated in 2019 near Shanghai as the first wholly foreign-owned automotive firm in the PRC, stalled under ad hoc lockdowns.[50]

Worst of all, scarcity and frustration heightened emotions to the point of questioning the legitimacy of foreigners in China at all. Special treatment within the bubble economy had turned foreigners into a discriminated minority and privileged elite at the same time. In practice, they lived in a safer, kinder, more tolerant version of the PRC than locals. But their small numbers and exclusion from civic life had also created a defensive mindset that they found hard to discuss with anyone, except current or former fellow foreigners. "In many ways Russia is a harder place to live, but China wears you down because you're isolated," Rachel told me. "It's like carrying a huge bag behind you. Companies learn to live with it because the more revenue comes from China, the more reason to live with the drag." One isolating factor was that in return for exemptions from censorship, family planning, and other restrictions, foreigners in China had been barred from playing significant roles in politics and civil society—something the 2020 Migrant Integration Policy Index called *Immigration without Integration* when they placed the PRC near the bottom of their ranking.

Mainland China has allowed foreign residence primarily for economic benefit. Integration has always been a low priority. Noncitizens are banned from political parties and functions, as well as civil society institutions like labor unions, nongovernmental organizations, and the

---

[48] Z. Soo. November 2021. "Yahoo Pulls Out of China, Citing 'Challenging' Environment," *Yahoo news.* https://news.yahoo.com/yahoo-pulls-china-amid-challenging-110457049.html.

[49] J. Bursztynsky. June 2022. "Apple Will Reportedly Move Some iPad Capacity to Vietnam After China Lockdowns," *CNBC.* www.cnbc.com/2022/06/01/apple-will-reportedly-move-some-ipad-capacity-from-china-to-vietnam.html.

[50] B. Yan and Z. Goh. June 2022. "Tesla's China Output Decline Trending Deeper Than Musk Forecast, Data and Internal Memos Show," *Reuters.* www.reuters.com/business/autos-transportation/teslas-china-output-decline-trending-deeper-than-musk-forecast-data-internal-2022-06-09/.

clergy. They cannot get local medical, accounting, notary, journalistic, and a variety of other professional licenses. They are barred from the bar too, unable to act as licensed legal practitioners. Multigeneration immigrant families and naturalized passport holders are virtually nonexistent. The PRC has issued less than 10,000 permanent residence permits since its foundation in 1949.[51] Major economies like the United States annually grant multiple times as many *green cards* to Chinese citizens alone. Neither can foreigners govern themselves: there is no official political or civic representation for immigrants in the PRC. The 2020 Migrant Integration Policy Index ranked China as *Critically Unfavorable* for Political participation: "international migrants are fully denied the opportunity to participate in public life in China, as foreign citizens have no right to vote, support or consultation by policymakers."[52] For all legal and civic purposes, the expat bubble is airtight.

Meanwhile, a slowing economy, tougher regulations, scarcity during the pandemic, and few avenues to vent resentment in the PRC made the privileges granted to foreigners an obvious target. When in 2020, Beijing announced laxer entry–exit and currency transfer regulations for foreigners in the hope of attracting international talent, irritated netizens demanded the same rights for locals.[53] The following year, the article continues, perhaps to prove its *anti-imperialist* credentials, the government launched its *three illegals* (*san fei*) campaign, allegedly deporting over 40,000 foreigners on charges of illegal entry, employment, or residence. That hit the sweet spot: "We should have done this a long time ago," a widely supported social media comment read.[54] Propaganda and

---

[51] F.N. Pieke. November 2019. "How Immigration Is Shaping Chinese Society," *MERICS*. https://merics.org/en/report/how-immigration-shaping-chinese-society.

[52] MIPEX. n.d. "Migrant Integration Policy Index 2020." www.mipex.eu/china (accessed August 1, 2022).

[53] Q. Junya. May 2022. "Eventually, China's Borders Will Reopen. Will Foreigners Return?," *Sixth Tone*. www.sixthtone.com/news/1010282/eventually%2C-chinas-borders-will-reopen.-will-foreigners-return.

[54] J. Goldkorn and T. Garbarini. April 2020. "What Do Chinese People Think of the Recent Ban on Foreigners?," *SupChina*. https://supchina.com/2020/04/01/what-do-chinese-people-think-of-the-recent-ban-on-foreigners/.

public sentiment spiraled upward in a mutual embrace. The percentage of PRC citizens who said they would not want a foreigner as a neighbor doubled from 13 percent in 2013 to 26 in 2020, the World Values Survey reported.[55] Beijing's justification was further fight against the *foreign hostile forces* they had curbed with restrictions via China's 2015 National Security Law, 2016 Cyber Security Law, and 2017 NGO Law.[56] But many expats thought Beijing simply revoked their end of the Special Economic Zones deal.

"Cooperate or stop criticising"—Foreign Minister Wang Yi's orders were simple. When foreign executives, diplomats, firms, or associations protested, local officials were visibly stunned. Follow regulations and show humility: why was that so hard? If Mercedes-Benz, Marriott Hotels, and Dolce & Gabbana did it, so can any foreigner. But for reasons already mentioned, most expats in China were the rulemaking, as opposed to the meekly rule-following kind. Remember? To land and survive in a PRC-based position, they had already proven their determination, decisiveness, and flexibility. Most of them adhered to the *when you see something, say something* philosophy in the sincere belief that brave and honest discussion improved people, institutions, and communities. That, however, posed political risk in China's new environment, further limiting trust and interaction between expats and locals. "COVID changed China," Renata Santos told me. "At the executive MBA program, an Italian colleague said he hoped to change jobs after the program. But now, even if you graduate from the best program, and Tsinghua is one of the best, firms don't want foreigners anymore." As Angelo Puglisi had told me in the more serene summer of 2019: "You will always be a *'laowai'* in China."

Thriving in China's Walled Garden

Simple narratives go viral because they gift the illusion of understanding complex situations. Their power of contagion can multiply if they also

[55] T. Speelman. December 2020. "Chinese Attitudes Toward Immigrants: Emerging, Divided Views," *The Diplomat.* https://thediplomat.com/2020/12/chinese-attitudes-toward-immigrants-emerging-divided-views/.
[56] D. Shambaugh. 2020. *China and the World* (Oxford and New York, NY: Oxford University press), p. 350.

serve as proof to what people would like to believe. In the years between 2020 and 2022, as the COVID-19 pandemic intensified the already considerable controversies between China and the world, an *expat exodus*, the summary departure of foreigners from the People's Republic, became as contagious a meme as the virus itself. "China's pursuit of zero Covid driving expats away," *France24* announced in April 2022.[57] "Get me out of here: China's historic expat exodus," *The Australian*'s headline read a week later.[58] The underlying narrative of China's collapsing, or at least its stalling modernization and globalization reinforced Western views summarized by historian Niall Ferguson in an interview at the time. "Without free speech, how can you really have sustainable intellectual advance? That's a fundamental question that I don't think the Islamists or the Chinese have a good answer to."[59]

But the *expat exodus* meme served China's own version of the future as well. In the eyes of the Chinese Communist Party, its staunchest supporters, and many among China's native and even expat population, foreigners were leaving because the country's rise as an economic, scientific, and political superpower had made most of them irrelevant. The *three illegals* campaign had already been a harbinger of China's ebbing patience toward foreign guests who apparently overstayed their welcome. This narrative portrayed the previous 20 years of integration as a sort of gold rush for multinational firms, which, however, must give way to superior goals that loom larger than the economic interest of international investors and their agents. "The inconvenient truth is that Beijing doesn't care how much money global investors have lost," *Bloomberg Opinion* columnist Shuli Ren wrote in March 2022 in her piece "China Doesn't Care If It's Uninvestable—for Foreigners." "It does not care about short-term volatility. It does, however, have its eyes on the big prize of securing its real

[57] France24. April 25, 2022. "China's Pursuit of Zero Covid Driving Expats Away." www.france24.com/en/live-news/20220425-china-s-pursuit-of-zero-covid-driving-expats-away.

[58] W. Glasgow. n.d. "Get Me Out of Here: Inside China's Historic Expat Exodus," *The Australian*. www.theaustralian.com.au/web-stories/free/the-australian/get-me-out-of-here-inside-chinas-expat-exodus.

[59] N. Ferguson. April 2022. "The Utopian Myth of Equality," youtube.com, video. www.youtube.com/watch?v=niqHgJwx2Ck&t=10s.

economy."[60] Foreigners who disapproved could always book an exit flight, such voices implied.

Fortunately, viral views are seldom right. Their popularity is boosted by the internal contradictions of multifaceted issues—the kind of current events that confuse readers and make them wish for shortcuts to clarity. Foreigners in China, and the Chinese government's attitude toward them, is one such issue. Simultaneously with its crackdowns on various segments of the foreign population (teachers, visiting students, workers on temporary visas), Beijing eased the conditions of entry, employment, and entrepreneurship for highly skilled overseas citizens.[61] By that time, the Chinese government's *Thousand Talents Program* to lure top scientific minds into the People's Republic had run for over a decade—even though it had only managed to deliver less than half of the promised thousand talents.[62] In 2021, while grounded expats in China, international business travelers, entrepreneurs, and students anxiously awaited the reopening of PRC borders, Beijing announced further new measures to attract foreign talent. Premier Li Keqiang and Vice Premier Han Zheng attended the September 2021 ceremony of the Friendship Award, a recognition granted to a handful of high-profile foreign experts.[63]

Debates around that time, from government policy discussions to project meetings at China-based multinationals, often entertained themselves with the scholastic riddle whether China needed the world more than the world needed China, or vice versa. The puzzle had no straight answer—they seldom do. But it highlighted an essential characteristic of the PRC's relations with the outside world: the tendency of demarcations to create dynamism. Human activity is like water, spreading out evenly

---

[60] S. Ren. March 2022. "China Doesn't Care If It's Uninvestable—for Foreigners," *Bloomberg UK*. www.bloomberg.com/opinion/articles/2022-03-15/is-china-uninvestable-complaints-from-foreigners-won-t-sway-xi-jinping.

[61] KPMG China. April 2021. "New Policies to Attract Foreign Talent to China." https://home.kpmg/cn/en/home/insights/2021/03/china-tax-alert-09.html.

[62] G.S. Noi. January 4, 2022. "China-US Competition for Talent Hots Up," *The Straits Times*. www.straitstimes.com/opinion/china-us-competition-for-talent-heats-up.

[63] Xinhua. September 30, 2021. "China to Expand Channels to Attract Foreign Talent." www.news.cn/english/2021-09/30/c_1310220558_2.htm.

around the globe unless it hits obstacles: geographic barriers, regulatory restrictions, mutual mistrust between peoples, and so forth. When obstacles stop interaction, surplus mounts on one side and scarcity increases on the other. Eventually, whatever piles up on the surplus side will find its way over the top, through the cracks, erode the foundations, or demolish the barrier with a mighty roar. Like water, human curiosity and craving respects no boundaries. That was the invisible force that spurred 15th-century Jesuits to infiltrate a newly isolating Ming China, and 19th-century Great Powers to kick down the door of Qing isolationism. That is also the reason why China's current inward turn is likely to signal a new era of opportunity for enterprising expats.

It is undeniable that Beijing's lengthy and draconian response to the pandemic damaged both the size of China's foreigner community and the country's attractiveness as an expat destination. "Sentiment regarding current conditions is near rock bottom," The *Conference Board* reported the result of its mid-2022 survey. "The views of the China CEO group, which included 30 respondents to our initial survey are especially negative on present business conditions in China, with nearly all respondents saying conditions have deteriorated compared to six months ago and 40 percent saying they are substantially worse."[64] Around the same time I polled the people I had interviewed for this book, and found that only four out of 14 non-native executives still lived in China. Some of them managed their PRC operations from South-East Asia, some rotated to headquarters or elsewhere. Their previous positions were either passed to local managers or to expats earmarked to enter the country when possible.

Tables Turn But the Game Continues

Those who had witnessed the glory days of China's expat hubs were saddened to see departing expats vastly outnumber new arrivals. But a closer look at the PRC's immigration policies reveals that the short-term rotation of expats, and their thinning during the pandemic, was far from coincidental. "China's immigration management in the last decades has had a

---

[64] "Current Sentiment Gloomy, Outlook Uncertain," The Conference Board, published in May 2022.

narrow focus on migration's economic benefits and, more recently, immigration control," a *Sixth Tone* article quoted Leiden University researcher Tabitha Speelman. "Broader questions of migrant integration and societal diversity are hardly addressed in relevant laws and regulations. At the same time, pathways for permanent residence remain extremely limited, making it difficult for migrants to settle in China long-term."[65] The introduction of a new visa system in 2017 that categorized foreigners into more and less desirable ones based on education, job history, and Mandarin fluency, combined with COVID-19-related travel restrictions and visa freezes convinced pessimistic foreigners of an imminent end to China as an expat destination.

Widespread discussions about dilemmas like decoupling and who depends more on whom at least reinforced an inevitable conclusion: seemingly opposing parties (China and the United States, China and the outside world, and so on) were in fact part of one single ecosystem. Separation could be an optical illusion at best: China's recent economic rise depended on the West as much as major Western economies relied on China. Starting with the Western multinationals, for them, China had long offered refuge from trends at home like an increasingly expensive and reluctant blue-collar workforce and slowing consumption. Chinese people were as eager to make foreign-branded goods as to purchase them, while Western counterparts shopped for white labels and fought for four-day work weeks. In a characteristically mercantilist manner, Beijing used this exposure as leverage and set increasingly self-serving conditions to participation in the Chinese market. This in turn resulted in the ironic contradiction that while Western firms bitterly complained of an *uneven playing field* (a favorite term of EU Chamber publications), they simultaneously increased their China exposure.

By 2022, top multinationals relied on China for much of their global revenues, ranging from a tenth in the case of Daimler, HSBC, Merck, Siemens, Volkswagen, and others, and up to a fifth or more for Adidas,

---

[65] Q. Junya. May 2022. "Eventually, China's Borders Will Reopen. Will Foreigners Return?," *Sixth Tone*. www.sixthtone.com/news/1010282/eventually%2C-chinas-borders-will-reopen.-will-foreigners-return.

AstraZeneca, Atlas, and BMW.[66] China rose in the World Bank's *Ease of Doing Business* index, then rose faster, then busted the index, but multinational commitment remained. "No one complains because everyone is making good money," Luke Patay gave voice to many in his book *How China Loses*. "But most foreign companies are not growing as fast as their Chinese competitors. Market shares are stagnating, and some are falling."[67] Business in China got harder, but being bogged down in the PRC's regulatory and political swamp still got expat executives farther than a walk in a manicured park at home. The 2022 EU Chamber China *Business Confidence Survey* found that while 60 percent of member firms considered business in China harder than the year before, two-thirds reported revenue and profit increases after a weak 2021, and were ready to further expand their China operations.[68]

"Despite the negative outlook, expanding production in China remains a strategic focus," the Conference Board found in 2022. "Only 17 percent of the China CEOs say that reshoring to their home regions (US and/or Europe) to take advantage of new policies/investment incentives is underway, with none having actually done so yet."[69] Beijing's selective attitude to global business also granted unexpected opportunities for foreign businesses. For instance, China's retail network, mostly controlled by state-owned firms and a few monopolies like Alibaba and JD.com, has always struggled to supply a gargantuan and erratic market. Suitcase trading, known in Mandarin as *dai gou*, had been a lucrative black market and key networking resource. At a keynote I hosted in Shanghai, Shaun Rein told us what a highly appreciated gift a jar of manuka honey could make, both for its unavailability in the PRC at the time and its known properties of mitigating the harms of air and water pollution. Once China had

[66] T. Dams and X. Martin. April 2022. "Investors Beware: Europe's Top Firms Are Highly Exposed to China," *Clingendael*. www.clingendael.org/sites/default/files/2022-04/Report_Are_Europes_top_firms_highly_exposed_to_China.pdf.

[67] L. Patey. 2021. *How China Loses* (Oxford: Oxford University Press), p. 184.

[68] European Union Chamber of Commerce in China. June 20, 2022. "European Business in China Business Confidence Survey 2022," p. 6.

[69] The Conference Board. May 2022. "Current Sentiment Gloomy, Outlook Uncertain." www.conference-board.org/pdfdownload.cfm?masterProductID=39382.

erected the walls of *zero-COVID* measures, the *dai gou* sector ground to an inaudible halt, and shoppers reluctantly paid for imports whatever price their retailers saw fit. Among the biggest beneficiaries were European luxury brands, whose fans could no longer hop on business-class flights for some shopping in Paris, Milan, or worldwide duty-free outlets.[70]

The chief lesson for China was that economic development was not a linear and zero-sum hegemony-switching game as Marxist-Leninist textbooks predicted. That carrot would infinitely move forward with China's economic advancement, because integration granted foreign businesses a cut from each unit of domestic GDP. "As Jamie Dixon, CEO of JPMorgan Chase put it, 'the United States' (US) gross domestic product (GDP) per capita in 2019 was US dollar (USD) 65,000 while China's was USD 10,000," *EUROBiz Magazine* wrote in summer 2021. "Even if the US does a rather poor job at managing the economy (growing at two percent annually), US GDP per capita in 20 years will reach USD 85,000. Meanwhile, if China continuously does a good job managing their economy, GDP per capita in 2040 would still be under USD 35,000. though this will represent 30 per cent of global growth over that period."[71] As long as the PRC nurtures international ambitions, foreigners are by definition part of its secret. "China will always remain an irresistible market to foreign companies," Dan Wang of Hang Seng Bank China Chief Economist told *Sixth Tone* in 2022, but "China's market is growing so fast that relying solely on local talents won't meet the talent demand of the economy."[72] China and the world were in this together.

Realizing the need for foreign talent inspired Beijing's aforementioned campaigns to attract bright minds, but the bar was high. Already in 2018, less than 10 percent of foreign work visa holders were classified

[70] Financial Times. n.d. "Western Brands Aim for the Sky in Xi Jinping's China." https://amp-ft-com.cdn.ampproject.org/c/s/amp.ft.com/content/57ced15a-68fe-4b6c-883f-df71cd8ef250.

[71] J. Wuttke. May/June 2021. "President's Foreword," *EUROBiz*.

[72] Q. Junya. May 2022. "Eventually, China's Borders Will Reopen. Will Foreigners Return?," *Sixth Tone*. www.sixthtone.com/news/1010282/eventually%2C-chinas-borders-will-reopen.-will-foreigners-return.

as *high-level talents*.[73] It is unlikely that the *three illegals* campaign of 2021 would have improved that ratio. In other words, contrary to a simplistic *expat exodus* narrative, the inflow and outflow of talented foreigners coincided for at least half a decade, although departures seem to have exceeded new arrivals. That leads to a conclusion that is fairly typical for anything measurable in China: everyone was right in a way. Those who felt that the *golden age* was ending were right. "The threshold for ability to create value as a foreigner will continue to rise," the *China Business Review* wrote already in 2013. "Like in the United States, companies' default answer to the question 'do we need to hire a foreigner?' is usually 'no.'"[74] This remained true for the majority of expats anyway. But China's selective visa policies ensured that over time, those who remained would be elite talent by the party's definition. They claimed to see plenty of opportunity in China, and they were right too. "I'm now in advantage," a foreign pilot at Fuzhou Airlines told *The South China Morning Post* after most international crew quit or were dismissed.[75]

Many committed expats rode such migratory currents to better jobs, salaries, or benefits in recent years. "Our company had been in China for over ten years, but we only decided to place commercial operations here as the country became more important for our business," Renata Santos, one of the last expats to remain among my interview subjects, told me in early 2022. "Things became much more complicated then, and I was sent here to recruit and train local teams and align local business with headquarter operations." As it happened to many expat executives, as China gained economic weight, it became the Asia-Pacific center, and she found herself in charge of India, Japan, Malaysia, and Singapore as well. "Professionally speaking, it's better to stay here now: I practically

---

[73] X. Yi. January 2019. "Shanghai Home to Largest Foreign Worker Population in China," *China Daily*. www.chinadaily.com.cn/a/201901/16/WS5c3e-d0a9a3106c65c34e4d2a.html.

[74] C. Nelson. October 2013. "The Expat's Competitive Edge," *China Business Review*. www.chinabusinessreview.com/the-expats-competitive-edge/.

[75] South China Morning Post. n.d. "Coronavirus: Foreign Pilots at Chinese Airlines Head Home on Unpaid Leave as Demand Falls." www.scmp.com/news/china/society/article/3051437/coronavirus-foreign-pilots-chinese-airlines-head-home-unpaid (accessed July 12, 2022).

became CFO." She fulfilled a crucial need as one of the foreigners who, as Markus Baumgartner noted, knew where the money was. But expats do much more than guard the purse strings. They continue to serve as vital mediators between global organizations and their China operations, both in the physical and mental sense of the word. The more China's focus turns inward, the more important that bridging function will become for both multinationals and their local counterparts.

"Brazilian companies need someone on the ground," Renata Santos told me. "You cannot expect locals to stay in and work across an eleven-hour time difference. But you also cannot remote-control China operations from Brazil: local employees trust the company only if they have foreign managers close by." In other words, multinational companies can build most of the organizational pyramid on indigenous workforce, but they will always need expats to hold certain strategic cornerstones in place. Foreigners remain essential as personal emissaries of the China operations of multinational firms toward headquarters and worldwide branches, international clients and suppliers, at conferences and professional events. Early management localization strategies assumed that Chinese mangers would happily collect the necessary air miles, but reality turned out otherwise. While they proudly took leadership roles at multinationals in China itself, local managers proved more reluctant to work abroad than candidates from most other nations. Part of the reason were family obligations and practical concerns such as aversion to foreign food. But part of it was the hassle of visas and arrangements: in 2022, the PRC's passport mobility strength ranked at the 80th place internationally, between Botswana and Tunisia.[76]

The limited willingness and ability of Chinese managers to travel internationally resulted in a severe underrepresentation of the world's largest nation and most dynamic market in global business circles. In CEO World's 2022 list of the 200 most influential chief representatives, China featured with two executives, both heads of local companies (Pony Ma of Tencent and Daniel Zhang of Alibaba) as opposed to three from Japan,

---

[76] Arton. n.d. "Global Passport Index." www.passportindex.org/byRank.php (accessed July 12, 2022).

five from Australia, six from India, and 12 from France.⁷⁷ Most readers of the list would struggle to name Chinese equivalents of Satya Nadella of Microsoft or Sundar Pichai of Google, both naturalized U.S. citizens born in India. The pandemic also brought new sanctions on international trips for PRC passport holders, from restrictions on *non-essential travel* to withholding passport renewals.⁷⁸ "It's very ironic that we're striving to localise our management but then the management can't travel to our headquarters," EU Chamber China Director Joerg Wuttke told Reuters.⁷⁹ That increased the advantage of expat executives, who were usually both able and very willing to hop on a plane out of the People's Republic as long as the firm guaranteed their safe and timely return.

Beyond bridging the geographic distances that separate PRC branches from the rest of a global network of organizations, expats are also essential to narrow gaps in methods, mindsets, and cultures. In first-tier cities, multinational office towers, shopping malls, and bar quarters perfectly serve their intended functions of making people forget they are in China. But the further down one descends in the corporate hierarchy, the harder the communication becomes between locals and foreigners, for linguistic and cultural reasons alike. According to a 2020 survey by *The Diplomat,* nearly 60 percent of PRC citizens have never talked to a foreigner before.⁸⁰ The farther a community is from the Eastern coastline and its metropolises, the more likely that visiting foreigners receive a VIP treatment, complete with the obligatory distance-keeping. The strangely ambiguous attitude that Robert Bickers called *awkward confidence,* part curiosity and

---

⁷⁷ S. Ireland. January 2022. "The World's Most Influential CEOs And Business Executives Of 2022," *CEOWorld.* https://ceoworld.biz/2022/01/25/the-worlds-most-influential-ceos-and-business-executives-of-2022/.

⁷⁸ J. Horwitz and R. Lui. February 2022. "China Says Not Granting Passport Renewals for Non-Essential Travel," *Reuters.* www.reuters.com/world/china/china-says-not-granting-passport-renewals-non-essential-travel-2022-02-12.

⁷⁹ D. Kirton. May 2022. "European Businesses Fear More COVID Disruption in China," *Reuters.* www.reuters.com/markets/europe/european-businesses-fear-more-covid-disruption-china-2022-05-16/.

⁸⁰ T. Speelman. December 2020. "Chinese Attitudes Toward Immigrants: Emerging, Divided Views," *The Diplomat.* https://thediplomat.com/2020/12/chinese-attitudes-toward-immigrants-emerging-divided-views/.

part national pride mixed with "instinctive indignation at China's past humiliations and what they feel to be contemporary echoes of those" can utterly confuse foreign business visitors.[81]

To avoid cultural awkwardness and confusion, multinationals intuitively engineered their China operations into three-level organizational pyramids: expats on short-term rotations on top, long-serving foreigners and cosmopolitan locals right below, and then, the genuinely indigenous majority. The superstructure is essential to preserve the global character of the corporation and align it with headquarters, starting from wide strategic goals and down to performance targets, practical policies, and ad hoc emergencies. "I have known Chinese or Chinese-American people who could play this role, but I think they have to be out of China for long enough," Rachel told me. "There is an enormous difference in mindset between Chinese people who worked in China and those who did not. My job is essentially to bridge the GAP." Levels closer to the ground ensure that such policies are implemented in ways that suit China's multifaceted, diverse, and fast-changing reality. "You can use wide brushstrokes and say that expats must learn the language and understand the culture," Leigh said. "But China is nearly ten million square kilometres with a variety of cultures, and everything has its local character. That's why local market knowledge is so important."

Short-term visitors can do no more than dip a passing toe into China's mesmerizing complexity. Locals are too accustomed to its nuances to act as cultural interpreters. Longer-term expats, through bumpy rides past initial honeymoon periods, times of moody exile blues, and eventual reconciliations, get their bearings in China's vast and versatile terrain. With the country's growing importance in the strategies of global firms, their experiences enter a strategic reserve of lessons learned for the entire organization. "In 2006, the message from China CEOs was that China is different, so allow exceptions and let them do it their way," Laurie Underwood told me. "Today, the message is not so much that China is different, but that China comes first. China is doing things differently, but we might want to learn from them and bring those practices to other

---

[81] R. Bickers. 2012. *The Scramble for China: Foreign Devils in the Qing Empire, 1832-1914* (UK: Penguin).

markets." And once their time in China comes to an end, Dragon Suits become indispensable agents of sharing those lessons worldwide. "Living in China gives you an edge, because there are things happening here that cannot happen anywhere," Marie said. "It really gives you a different perspective of the world."

Upcoming *Dragon Suit* Trends

In mid-2022, a brief survey summary by a popular Shanghai restaurant guide went viral on WeChat, China's leading social and shopping app. The report bore the voluminous title *Bon App Poll Results: 40% of Expats leaving China soon.* The poll included over a 1,000 responses and represented a characteristic cross-section of the country's largest expat bubble, Shanghai. The typical respondent was a 30- to 50-year-old male from Europe or North America, employed at a corporation in the city and, in 70 percent of the cases, seeking a way out of China.[82] This demographic was exactly what Bon App founder Stone Shi, and the restaurants featured in his guide, were anxious to see depart. The protagonists of China's *golden age* for expats, as the Mercator Institute for China Studies had written in 2019, lived in *permanent impermanence* while China opened and closed again. "Many find it hard to remain at the right side of the law and have trouble navigating the linguistic barriers of the regulatory framework," the paper observed. "A growing body of research concludes that foreigners live segregated from Chinese society."[83] They, however, had been a blessing for business. Once they left, who would replace them?

In fact, China's permanently impermanent expat scene had been mutating for a quarter century by then, in tune with the nation's needs and preferences. The pandemic was simply the perfect time for claustrophobic contemplation on emerging worldwide mobility barriers. "How did the profile of successful expat executives change?" Laurie Underwood

---

[82] S. Shi. April 2022. "Bon App Poll Results: 40% of Expats leaving China soon," *BonAppOfficial.* https://mp.weixin.qq.com/s/2Id8HRZ6TTu6xHpjHwj-3A.

[83] F.N. Pieke. November 2019. "How Immigration Is Shaping Chinese Society," *MERICS.* https://merics.org/en/report/how-immigration-shaping-chinese-society.

asked me rhetorically in spring 2020. "We did comparisons between 2006 and 2020. One of the big differences was that current China CEOs have stayed longer in the country, have more China experience and speak better Chinese." Of course, in the age of *slowbalisation*, a term *The Economist* magazine invented in 2019 to describe the stalling globalization that would soon grind to a screeching halt, ambitious expats had to make tough choices. The PRC had matured into an indisputable mammoth market, but to put it simply, being in China meant not being anywhere else. A few years based there with frequent global travel was not an option anymore. "Many expats used to be here thinking 'if I spend three years in China, I can claim international experience,'" Markus Baumgartner told me. "Most of them are gone now, and they won't be missed."

There are reliable indicators to tell genuine *old China hands* from career tourists, experienced Dragon Suits told me in unison. One is the length of time spent in the country: while three years under one's belt sounded impressive around 2010, expatriates with a decade, two or more are far from exceptional in today's board rooms and conference halls. Another is language fluency, probably the surest measure of an expat's commitment to a China-based career. "Around 2004, almost no expat spoke Chinese," Markus continued. "Now, a lot of foreigners are quite good at it. In my opinion, that has a lot to do with respect." Laurie Underwood's research placed language fluency into a wider context. "China has become such an important market that companies invest into making sure that the CEO understands it really well. Apart from China CEOs who are actually Chinese, even among non-Chinese CEOs the Mandarin level was much higher in 2020 than fifteen years before. Some of them are truly fluent, making speeches and writing in Chinese." Finally, for an ultimate test, check their contracts. "Most foreigners used to stay for a maximum of five years," Tony Shi said. "Now, many of them give up their expat contracts and stay on local ones. At Benteler we have foreigners with both types of contracts."

Ironically, employers also told me about the disadvantages of placing expat executives with decades-long China experience in charge. "People don't understand how fast everything is changing in China," Rachel told me. "They still think Western, and especially US companies are more developed. When I came back to China after a few years of absence, it was like coming back to an entirely different country." That is not mere figure of speech. Around 2000, China started rebuilding its economy from near-zero, including macro-indicators like exports and outward investment and down to infrastructure quality and health care. Markus Baumgartner's experience is perhaps the most dramatic. "It was tough at the beginning. At the factory, water pipes regularly burst and everything kept breaking down. We didn't have a dentist in Yinchuan, so we had to fly the family to Beijing for treatment." Foreigners with such experience saw China at its worst and its best. If they have spent a few decades in the country, speak fluent Mandarin, and work on a local contract, to global headquarters they resemble local executives in many respects. But in addition to advantages, that status poses risks as well.

Mentally translating methodological, strategic, and cultural gaps between business locations is an essential function of Dragon Suits, and integration into the local society can interfere with that ability. "China is dynamic and exciting, every day is different and you can learn a lot professionally, but if you stay too long, you become what I call 'a China person,'" Rachel told me. "I know many of them: they marry locally, start a family, make their peace with the country and build their career and reputation on it." That identity can become a problem for several reasons. One that I often hear at global headquarters is that after an extended period in the country, *old China hands* become advocates of customizing the entire organization for China instead of executing global strategies in the PRC. As rational as it sounds to expats who personally witness the emergence of China as the single most important global market, that attitude often irritates the pride of headquarters—especially if they objectively have a lot to learn about China. That, in turn, can easily undermine the trust of global leaders in the expat in question, leading to a vicious circle of suspicion and disapproval.

New Horizons Beyond Shrinking Enclosures

Another hazard for long-serving foreigners is the inconvenient fact that changes in the PRC happen too fast not only for headquarters but for seasoned expats as well. Yesterday's hard-earned lessons are tomorrow's outdated stereotypes. As we saw earlier, the performance of even an individual manager depends on the systemic interaction between individual character, the corporate culture of the surrounding team and company, and that of the wider environment. As new generations of employees mature, China develops and even home countries change, each of these elements can be significantly different today from 20, 10 or even five years ago. As recently as the 2010s, droves of talented Westerners were offered positions in China as a chance to supercharge their typically mid-management careers and grow into global leaders under a powerful multinational brand. That proposition is exceptional today. But decade-long China veterans may not only lose touch with young foreigners from their home cultures, but also with radical changes that happened in China since their formative experiences in the country: remember how Chris, the luxury fashion CFO, related to social media. Like their predecessors did, China's next generation of expats must break brand-new ground.

The need for foreign talent is still there, as well as the interest from abroad to work in China. "Despite the expat exodus, we are seeing lots of enquiries relating to expats planning to move to mainland China for employment purposes," Jason Will of Asian Tigers Relocation wrote to me. "The economy here is too strong and has too much potential to ignore. And you cannot manage China operations from abroad—you need to be on the ground here." But COVID-19 disrupted the circular flow of migrant labor in the world, indirectly influencing expat destinations like China. "The pandemic has caused a 'hunkering down' of talent, who are opting to stay in their own countries—likely due to travel bans, concerns about safety, and other COVID barriers," a 2021 Universum Global employment study stated. "Many European countries, for example, are reporting talent shortfalls due to closed borders and migration shortfalls. Especially in the technical professions, areas like digitization, decarbonization, there will be big demand for qualified workers."[84] Beijing's clampdowns on youthful and emerging sectors made things worse. For instance, entering as a foreign language teacher, previously a top source of young expats, will be much harder after severe restrictions on private schools.[85]

[84] Universum. 2021. "World's Most Attractive Employers 2021." https://universumglobal.com/wmae2021/.
[85] Global Times. February 28, 2022. "Private Educational Institutions in China Are Slashed by About 90%: Ministry." www.globaltimes.cn/page/202202/1253438.shtml.

China's mounting economy will still attract plenty of worldwide talent and ambition. But as opposed to a previous *golden age*, large multinationals may not be the first choice of the best and the brightest. Instead, incoming foreigners increasingly choose to work for themselves. "While many highly paid expat executives and specialized workers are leaving in droves, a new generation of adaptable, entrepreneurial expats is emerging to replace them," one expert pointed out already in 2015. "Though the traditional expat job market is dwindling, new, more lucrative opportunities are emerging for those that are willing to pursue entrepreneurial or new market ventures. The start-up world of China is just taking off."[86] As gaps narrow between expatriate and local workers in terms of salary and employment (remember the popular switch to local contracts), the preferences of local workers can help predict future expat trends. "When thinking about where to work, MNCs (multinational companies) are not necessarily at the top of the lists," Laurie Underwood told SupChina in 2021. "Today, there are a lot of exciting Chinese companies to work for."[87]

Finally, multinational firms have to contend with an intensifying demographic shift in the composition of foreign residents in China. During the quarter century characterized by *reform and opening*, highly developed economies in Europe, North America, and East Asia (Japan and South Korea) enjoyed outsized shares among China's foreign population compared to their population sizes. At the time of the 2010 census, North America and the European Union together accounted for a similar percentage of foreigners in China as South and South-East Asia combined, although the population of the former two regions is merely two-fifth of the latter two. Ten years later, the 2020 census revealed a dramatically different picture. In 2010, Myanmar accounted for a mere 7 percent of China's foreign residents.[88] By 2020, that percentage rose to

---

[86] D. Redford. April 2015. "Expats in China Turn to Entrepreneurship," *China US Focus*. www.chinausfocus.com/political-social-development/expats-in-china-turn-to-entrepreneurship.

[87] G. James. December 2021. "Multinationals in 2021: The New Reality of Doing Business in China," *SupChina*. https://supchina.com/2021/12/15/multinationals-in-2021-the-new-reality-of-doing-business-in-china/.

[88] Z. Qian and S. Elsinga. January 2015. "Nali Lai de?—An Overview of Expat Demographics in China," *China Briefing*. www.china-briefing.com/news/nali-lai-de-overview-expats-china/.

nearly a third. Thailand, Pakistan, and other developing Asian economies showed similar gains, while immigration dropped from most rich nations, including the United States, EU, UK, Australia, Canada, and Japan.[89]

A dizzying array of changes occurred within the short span of a few years, but certain trends clearly emerge: China's foreign population is increasingly Asian and of modest means. Causes are multiple and resist simple causal explanations. One likely reason is that in recent years, China's reputation significantly worsened among advanced economies such as the United States, UK, EU, Australia, and Japan, but much less so in South and South-East Asia. In those countries, China's Belt-and-Road and similar outreach initiatives contributed to modernizing infrastructure, telecommunications, financial services, and even education, which resulted in renewed interest to work and study in China. Many countries in the region have youthful populations for whom China's development represents an opportunity that can support a steady career. In 2018, the top sources of foreign students in China were South Korea, Thailand, Pakistan, and India. At the sixth place, the United States contributed less than half the number of Thai students in the PRC.[90] Today's students will become tomorrow's expats.

A key difference between former and future generations of foreign workers is their attitude toward China's political and social system. Typical expats 10 years ago represented rich and advanced nations like the United States, EU member states, or Japan, and considered themselves agents of modernization and integration into a global order where, it seemed at the time, the PRC itself wanted to belong. Among China's incoming foreign workforce today, there are not only three times as many young immigrants from the rest of Asia as from Europe and the United

---

[89] Expat Focus. July 11, 2022. "Number of Foreigners in China, Results of 7th National Census." https://mp.weixin.qq.com/s?__biz=MjM5OTg2MTgzOA=
=&mid=2654317267&idx=1&sn=c790b7572d9186ac1fc15c3255db77d9&c
hksm=bcf401f28b8388e495d439dbd33c62d556744c1c65c6c100eeaea0ce63
fdc5b779a72e6b20ce.

[90] Ministry of Education, The People's Republic of China. April 18, 2019. "Statistical Report on International Students in China for 2018." http://en.moe
.gov.cn/documents/reports/201904/t20190418_378692.html.

States combined, but they often arrive thanks to the generous support of the Chinese government. The growth of student numbers from Belt-and-Road countries far outpaced all other segments in recent years, mainly due to state scholarships.[91] For those who arrive this way, China represents the next stage of development compared to their homelands, not a previous one. "I come from a poorly administered and highly unpredictable country," Muhammad Haroon from Pakistan wrote to me. "I try to relocate to China for the economic development, fast-paced technological advancements and opportunities for foreigners. Life is peaceful there."

Adding to a dramatic shift toward a mostly Asian foreign population in China is a powerful undercurrent: the return of ethnic Chinese talent previously lost to a century of civil strife and economic mismanagement. It is impossible to know, for instance, exactly how many foreigners with passports from advanced economies are actually former Chinese citizens. Immigration statistics from the United States, UK, Australia, and Japan suggest tens of thousands of such returnees. The People's Republic does not allow dual citizenship, which means that naturalized foreign passport holders enter the country as bona fide foreigners, with all the advantages and disadvantages of their status. "During the COVID pandemic, a lot of ethnic Chinese relocated to mainland China," Jason Will explained. "This created a new labour pool for employers." People of Chinese descent, especially from Asian countries, are another source of culturally agile foreigners. Already in 2014, a BBC article quoted a Guangzhou-based HR consultant whose clients asked for English-speaking candidates from Malaysia, Taiwan, Hong Kong, and Singapore who "cost less, still have the client-facing skills with the westerners, and yet can often also speak Chinese to a certain level."[92]

Foreign managers from such background will obviously relate and adapt better to circumstances that bothered previous expats, including Internet restrictions, political interference, and even pollution. Anecdotal evidence supports my own experience that they learn Mandarin and

[91] ChinaPower. n.d. "Is China Both a Source and Hub for International Students?.," https://chinapower.csis.org/china-international-students/.
[92] M. Durnin. February 2014. "China Is Still a Jobs Hotspot for Expats," *BBC*. www.bbc.com/worklife/article/20140212-get-hired-in-china.

integrate into local society faster and more willingly than expats from the West and even Japan or Korea. Sure enough, foreigners from any nationality see less of China's showcase expat lifestyle today than a decade ago. "We enjoyed the bubble for a while and went out with Brazilians here in Shanghai," Renata Santos told me. "But then we started new relationships. I was looking through photos we took with friends the other day, and ninety-five percent are Chinese now." However, picking up the local pace is much simpler coming from Jakarta or Hanoi than Paris or Rio. Entrepreneurial Westerners with near-fluent Mandarin still tend to settle in one of China's top cities with access to serviced offices, international schools, cosmopolitan food choices, global brands and entertainment, and other foreigners.

In fact, even Chinese fluency, a rare commodity among early expats and an admired feature of committed *China persons*, is seen differently by tomorrow's standards. Today, as a Beijing-based executive search professional told me, foreigners who speak good Chinese cannot hope to race ahead in the job market anymore: those who do not will fall behind. As Marion Campan, a former Communications Director of EF Education eloquently explained, "in China, you have plenty of people who speak Chinese, you have plenty of Chinese people who are super good at English and maybe one other language. What is it that you are going to bring? It's probably not going to be the Chinese language."[93] As multinational firms localize their management, gradually turning collaboration between their respective PRC branches into local business transactions conducted in Mandarin, and many new arrivals try their luck in a job market of waning legal and administrative expatriate privileges, what can the next generation of foreigners in China contribute?

"I have one simple message for future expats in China," Attila Hilbert of Danone told me. "This is one of the world's most competitive labour markets. If you come here, you must think through why you would be competitive here. What can Chinese people learn from you? Why would you be able to lead them? Why would they follow? Why would they take

---

[93] P. Frick and F. Kremer. "Running a service business as a flexpat with Marion Campan," *China Flexpat*, podcast. https://podcasts.apple.com/hk/podcast/china-flexpat/id1514659021?l=en&i=1000555702437.

your advice? What can you do better, especially if you don't fully understand their language and culture yet? If you were not commissioned by your firm, would anyone hire you here? If you can answer these questions, you are prepared." That describes a China where foreigners finally compare with locals on an equal footing for opportunities—or in fact start from the disadvantage of the PRC's selective immigration and employment regulations. It also signals the true end of a *golden age* for multinationals, and the expatriates they brought in to implement global strategies and steer foreign firms along the rising tides of China's unprecedented economic rise. The Dragon Suits of the future will truly arrive in China to learn, not to teach.

Epilogue: New *Dragon Suit* Patterns

Chinese people are not a carefree crowd. They know how to unwind, but usually have better things to do. As an Eastern European, I inherently judge representatives of other cultures by their sense of humor, and during my two decades in China, I only heard one indigenous joke I genuinely liked. It is about two rich tourists from the city who visit a mountain village. While passing a neatly arranged farmyard, they spot a darling little cat drinking milk out of a decorated porcelain cup. Barely able to breathe, they recognize the vessel as a Tang Dynasty antique, worth a fortune. Nearby, there is an old lady who is busily tending the garden. One of the friends suggests they make her an offer on the cup, but the other has a better idea. He approaches the lady, greets her, and bargains on the cat until she reluctantly agrees to part with the pet for a 1,000 yuan. The tourist pays, picks up the cat and, faking spontaneity, casually asks if he could also take the drinking cup to make the animal feel comfortable in her new city home. "No, that cup is not for sale," the old lady says. "That single piece of pottery has helped my family sell hundreds of cats!"

The story may sound funny for playing out the rich against the poor, the city against the country or modern arrogance against timeless wisdom. The tourists may be foreigners or Chinese visitors from a restless metropolis—the distinction makes little difference for the nation's majority in towns, villages, farms, huts, felt tents, or boathouses. Either way, the joke reveals perhaps the only consensus among China's conflicting and coexisting cultures, from Tao to Mao and up to now: accepting the essentially paradoxical nature of life. Taoist masters like Laozi saw the dueling of grounded *yin* and explosive *yang* forces as the only constant in the universe. Confucianism considered the human soul a battlefield of the dead and the living, of collective duty and personal honor. Two millennia later, Mao Zedong tried to forge a new national philosophy around his obsession with *contradiction*—the creative power of opposing forces in constant dialectic struggle. Foreign businesspeople in today's China dismiss this tradition as egg-headed philosophizing at their own peril. They will often find their local teams, clients, business partners, and friends accept contradicting statements as equally true. Surprisingly often, they are right.

Foreigners need no better example for paradoxes than their own status a quarter-century after China's ceremonial reopening. Initially, economic ambitions were firmly tied to welcoming foreign ideas, investment, technology, and people. Eventual success resulted in an identity crisis: should a modernized China further integrate or go its separate way? Does it still need foreigners, and why? The question sounds bizarre to most expats, and China's taste for dialectic contradiction does not help clarify it. Advocates of Chinese superiority see no irony in advocating the PRC's global outreach and claiming that it has no need for foreigners anymore. Beijing's policies simultaneously portray foreign business interests in China, and expats themselves, as a legacy of imperialist exploitation and the key to the country's future. Visa policies are eased, foreign residents honored and awarded, previously restricted economic sectors opened to foreign investment, diplomatic wars escalated, foreign firms boycotted and penalized, entry regulations revamped yet again. If international executives and firms want to make sense of it all, they must reach for China's traditional wisdom, accept the dialectic dance between ever-changing circumstances and their own reactions, and plan their activities accordingly.

Foreigners can learn from Chinese managers at multinational firms who, in true dialectic spirit, find themselves sitting at both sides of a proverbial table. Their local identity grants them insights and instincts unimaginable even to decades-long foreign residents with full Mandarin fluency. Their status at international firms, on the other hand, forces them to soberly scrutinize China from an external vantage point. "The last two years changed the way I see China," Tony Shi of Benteler told me in early 2022. "On one hand, it did not surprise me that our government managed the pandemic differently from the global mainstream. After all, our demographic and healthcare situation are also different. But the execution of those policies also revealed how much we must still learn in terms of management skills, especially on the lower levels of hierarchies." Such realizations inspire local and foreign managers at multinational firms to seek better combinations of indigenous and imported management methods. While politics and pandemics made Chinese and foreign politicians, diplomats, and even the wider public increasingly anxious about one another's intentions, foreign firms still serve as laboratories for blending the right mix of indigenous and international methods.

The pandemic years also changed the nature of mid- to high-level corporate decision making at foreign firms in China. Connecting virtually from their home offices at increasingly erratic hours, one after another of my coaching and consulting clients expressed a similar sentiment: this is not what they expected when they received their promotions. "The government did a great job to contain the virus itself, but the economic outlook and people's perceptions have worsened," Kurt Yu of Voith Group told me in 2022. "In theory I do the same job as before. In practice, it has become much more complex. I must deal with local COVID outbreaks, lockdowns and constant disruptions." At large global firms, foreign and local managers who find themselves in similar situations were promoted to their current responsibilities based on dramatically different performance criteria from what the present requires. On paper, most firms I know execute plans that were scripted years before the pandemic, down to detailed investment, production, and hiring targets. The reality resembles the very firefighting that managers were supposed to clean up and restructure into mature business practices when they assumed their leadership roles.

Many China-based expat managers I know grudgingly accept the constant flow of emergencies as a temporary nuisance, and hope for the speedy return of usual business as it was before the pandemic. I would not bet the firm's money on that scenario. China's emerging global ambitions, the ensuing resistance from incumbent economies, and eventually COVID-19 resulted in irreversible changes. Postpandemic paradoxes may seem similar to previous ones, but doing business with China will never be the same again. Dragon Suits in the second quarter-century of the new millennium, old and newly arriving ones alike, will find themselves surrounded by different circumstances. They may also find their own compatibility with China's business environment dramatically altered even if their temperament and work methods hardly changed. As a consequence of those new compatibility gaps, they will make different life choices as expats. Available options will be as ridden with paradoxes as before. Some will face painful dilemmas, others will go with the flow. Eventually, the unstoppable tide of human curiosity and ambition will create new currents and cut across new barriers: not better or worse, just different.

To start with wider trends, China's increasingly young and Asian foreign population will alter expat workforce dynamics. When multinational employers are unwilling or unable to localize certain management positions, especially when they already downsized expatriation budgets, hiring qualified Asian candidates on local contracts will be a reasonable alternative to expats on full packages. In some other cases, significantly less often than a decade ago, Western firms will prefer candidates who understand the language and culture of their headquarters and can play physical and virtual connecting roles. If current trends continue, such applicants will be rare on all levels of seniority. Entry-level talent will be scarce for several reasons. China's *zero-COVID* measures severely disrupted the inflow of foreign students and young professionals, who typically lacked the necessary expertise to earn privileges in China's points-based visa system and the significant sums required for an inward journey to the PRC, including COVID-19 tests, sky-high flight tickets, and relocation prices and quarantine costs. "People in the younger age tiers generally don't have these advantages," a 2022 article quoted an executive of publishing firm SmartShanghai.[94]

Expats in mid-career and senior brackets will fare little better, mainly because previously they were the most likely to settle in China with families. Whether their children were 14 months or 14 years old, parents and

---

[94] D. Morgan and Z. Ruiying. January 19, 2022. "China's Foreign Firms Are Running Out of a Key Resource: Foreigners," *Sixth Tone*. www.sixthtone.com/news/1009408/chinas-foreign-firms-are-running-out-of-a-key-resource-foreigners.

kids suffered equally under China's *zero-COVID* regime for an endless list of reasons. Entire families were grounded, complete with babies, toddlers, teenagers, pets, and all. China was more prepared for online education than many other societies, but not for years of erratic back-and-forth swaps between in-person and online classes. Internet restrictions undermined learning, contacting friends and family, entertainment, and more. Importantly, foreign families were never meant to stay in the country for years without business and recreational trips and crucially, home leaves. Each time cities eased restrictions somewhat, they had to make the devastating choice between staying in international isolation or leaving prematurely, and many voted with their feet. When they did, unlike their younger fellow foreigners, they typically found opportunities elsewhere. As the world slowly and joltingly went back to business and had to find ways around a China still in its beauty sleep, their expertise and networks were in high demand.

The sorest paradox that expats faced toward the end of the pandemic was that staying and leaving both seemed hard. Decades of polls clearly revealed the paramount reasons why expatriates were attracted to China. There, they had been able to quickly advance international management careers, participate in the thrilling saga of an emerging global economy, and both spend and save in ways that matched their ambitions. Expats who nurtured long-term visions in the country found it hard to accept the end of that era. They often lamented the erosion of previously thriving internal economies that supported them in top-tier cities. But the closure of their favorite restaurants and departure of their children's beloved teachers were just tips of looming icebergs. Below the surface, there was a growing disconnect between China's obvious developmental direction and the ideals of expats who had arrived years before. "China is becoming increasingly inward looking, nationalistic and ideological," Chris, the luxury fashion CFO told me. He echoed Markus Baumgartner almost verbatim: "It was during the second lockdown," Markus commented on events in 2022, "That the increasing isolation and trends towards nationalism in China occurred to me."

But if it was hard to stay, it was equally hard to leave. Expats built year-long projects and sometimes entire careers on a simple proposition of China's *reform and opening* vision: Beijing provides business hubs connected to a thriving domestic market, foreign businesses add global know-how, and fulfill demand. The foreign families that reluctantly packed their belongings had to leave unfulfilled dreams and ambitions behind. Expat life in China had treated them well, allowed them to realize their potential and plot the next stages of their personal and family ambitions. Few of them wished to return to the relatively confined and conventional milieu of their home countries. "Many expats want to stay in China after their assignments," Tony Shi already expressed in 2018. "One former manager told me his life in Germany is more difficult than here." That had been true about many foreigners before, and more so during the pandemic years. An unexpected return to headquarters in the midst of a crisis was not what they had envisaged when they accepted a China posting to supercharge their careers.

But a second round of interviews in 2022 also made me realize how easy it is to judge Dragon Suits as heartless career machines. "When I left China at the beginning of the COVID-19 outbreak in January 2020, I called China home," Judith told me. "I wanted to return within a few weeks, but in spite of holding a valid residency permit in Shanghai, I was not allowed to return because foreigners were banned from entering the country." Like many others who left for short business trips or the Chinese Lunar New Year holidays that year, she never returned. Many of those who stayed despite pandemic measures suddenly faced not only the impermanence of their presence in the country but also a fundamental change in their own attitude. Staying or leaving was not a simple question of tangible benefits anymore: it had become a question of loyalty. "In the spring of 2020, the firm offered us free tickets if we wanted to return to Brazil," Renata Santos told me. "At that time, I told Nicola: 'if we leave now, my team will never trust me again.' I told myself, perhaps I could use the pandemic as an opportunity."

Options and Opportunities

The mental and emotional struggle of expats in China is most apparent in the stories of foreigners who resolved to stay but eventually left anyway. Renata and Nicola repatriated to Brazil in mid-2022. By that time, only two of the foreign managers interviewed for this book, Fernanda

Barth and Marie, remained in the PRC. Some departures were timely and expected, true to the short-term nature of most expat assignments. Angelo Puglisi, Henrik König, and Christian had left before 2020, having completed their assignments. Rachel and Attila Hilbert left during the pandemic, but in line with previous plans. Other expats, however, left despite their earlier long-term commitments to their jobs in the country, including Briana, Judith, Rachel, Renata, and Markus Baumgartner. Their journeys are merely random examples among tens of thousands that are yet to be told in books, blogs, meeting rooms, and restaurants: expats whose contracts were not renewed, who resigned for the sake of their children's welfare and education, who left for a beach holiday and could never return, having their belongings shipped home by the same diligent local colleagues who once arranged their trips to China.

As consecutive waves of expats headed for the airport, it was hard to deny that China once again squandered an opportunity to create a faithful community of resident foreigners. With better immigration policies, closer attendance to essential expat services like taxation, social security, and education, and more reasonable mobility policies during the pandemic, some foreigners who shared their views in this book might have spent their retirement in the country. A new generation of locally born, Mandarin-speaking foreigners might have taken root, rejuvenating the former reputation of a once multiethnic and multicultural Chinese empire, and significantly boosting the PRC's global image. As it is, former Dragon Suits remain emotionally invested but hold mixed views toward China's affairs. "Recent years did not change my feelings towards Chinese colleagues, friends and people in general," Henrik König told me in 2022. "I will always appreciate their friendliness, openness and professionalism. But I also have major reservations towards government policies, especially regarding COVID-19. I simply cannot understand why they treated Chinese people that way and why they kept foreigners from entering China."

Some expatriates, like the rich visitors in the cat-selling joke, may grudgingly walk away from China with a life lesson and no treasure. Others depart with the bank account balances, professional recognition, or experience they always wanted. Still others will arrive. The country's economic clout seems likely to secure its attractiveness to international businesspeople. The pandemic years might have made business in China harder, but they rendered business in many other key locations next to impossible. The PRC's walled-around economy retained its internal dynamism: between 2020 and 2022, multinational firms enjoyed revenue growth levels unprecedented for at least a decade.[95] In some sectors of business, such as automotive and luxury retail, China is virtually the only significantly growing market in the world. In others like pharmaceuticals and manufacturing, it has developed into an irreplaceable pillar of global supply chains. Despite confusing regulations, emerging demarcations, and intensifying political risk, nearly all firms with an international profile will need to find someone who can translate their value propositions for China. *Dragon Suit* expertise will stay in high demand.

As new arrivals replace at least some of those who leave, the typical profile of successful expatriate manager will change according to the new circumstances. The last two expat managers interviewed for this book who remained in China beyond 2022 provide a useful contrast that may reveal future trends. Fernanda Barth spent nearly a decade and a half with Brazilian firm WEG in Nantong, a modest-sized city by Chinese standards. Her career represents a generation of foreign managers in China who steadily grew into mid- to high-level positions as multinational firms broadened their operations in the country. Maturing together with Nantong's foreign community seemed a safe bet: Fernanda's child was born around the time when the city's first international school was established near offices of firms like Merck, Microsoft, and IKEA. But although they might find themselves among the few indispensable expat executives in China, expats may also outgrow the opportunities provided by such settled paths. Their kids may prefer to study abroad. Their firms may prefer to localize their desired positions, or they may find that the next upward career step includes leaving China.

Contrast that with Marie's career which, over a similar time span, consisted of a handful of years spent at each of half a dozen successive Western multinationals at progressively higher-level positions in Shanghai, the PRC's top commercial hub. Although her job-hopping resumé is the nightmare of many recruiters, it seems likely that in China's volatile and

---

[95] European Union Chamber of Commerce in China. June 20, 2022. "European Business in China Business Confidence Survey 2022," p. 6.

politically charged business environment, successful expat executives will increasingly follow similar career trajectories. If they are in China already, they will trade in their experience with their existing or a prospective employer, for an expat or local contract, whichever makes sense. Those who are abroad, including the vital talent pool of worldwide managers with previous experience in China, can negotiate their terms of relocating to the PRC. Their bargaining position is likely to improve over time: China's relative isolation cuts succession at its root and reduces the number of experienced managers with each passing year. Meanwhile, the flow of investment, goods, and services between China and the world is likely to increase, which adds to the relative value of each expatriate with the language, professional, and cultural skills to do business in China.

In behavioral terms, the most successful profile for expats in the China of coming years is likely to require determination, risk tolerance, flexibility, and superb social skills: more politician and networker than technical expert. In cultural terms, ambitious expats must be able to operate and lead others in a whimsical and risky business environment where commercial and political stakes are significantly higher than in previous, more strategically oriented decades. Mediating between headquarters, international and local branches, suppliers, clients, and government bureaus will require a healthy balance between practical and social mindsets, to be equally confident in the realms of compliance and compromise. People with extensive overseas experience, third culture kids, and natives of diverse, especially nearby Asian cultures, will enjoy an obvious advantage. If, in addition, mobility in and out of China remains low, the country will increasingly become a haven for single expats. The more comfortable they are with China's permanent impermanence, characterized by lots of curiosity, but little trust between foreigners and locals, the healthier, happier, and more successful they can be.

With the help of behavioral mapping tools, experienced human resource professionals can easily identify the most suitable candidates for challenges of the coming years in China. One hazard, however, is that many multinational firms may select their next generation of expats according to the outdated requirements of a previous, steadier era of foreign business in China. As the pool of experienced applicants ebbs, it will also be tempting to localize most, if not all, management positions at foreign firms in the PRC. Decision makers who face that choice should recall the advice of seasoned Dragon Suits: expats remain essential in crucial areas of business such as knowing where the firm's money is, accessing data that local managers are unable or reluctant to handle, acting as cultural connectors between geographic locations, and so forth. As Renata Santos suggested, foreign firms need expats on the ground. The resulting demand for foreign talent in China opens avenues for enterprising employees and managers with an appetite for challenging assignments, whether they are already in the country or currently plot their entry strategies.

Business thrives on risk, and China's next upheaval may come at any time, in any shape. In 2021, due to Beijing's simultaneous shortening of the *negative list* of sectors closed to foreign investment and new restrictions on strategic industries such as energy and mining, multinationals suddenly needed lots of locally incorporated entities from which to conduct certain aspects of their business. That resulted in a sudden surge of foreign investment and new incorporations.[96] The next big chance to create new projects and import talent could be the introduction of nonindigenous COVID-19 vaccines in China, opening new sectors of infrastructure development or financial services to foreign investment. Or it could be draconian new restrictions on par with Internet controls introduced in 2008 and the 2022 tech clampdown, which calls for squads of able-handed crisis managers. Either way, new challenges will call for a new generation of expats better suited for a business environment fundamentally reshaped by the end of *reform and opening*, waves of localization, a global pandemic, or any other combination of the nation's endless dialectic upheavals. These new expats must speak the language and read the minds of their Chinese counterparts in a quite literal sense.

If the thousands of expats who matured during the *golden age* of foreign business in China are replaced mostly by local, occasionally by a new breed of foreign managers, will multinationals waste valuable experience

---

[96] T. Huang and N.R. Lardy. March 29, 2022. "Foreign Corporates Investing in China Surged in 2021," Peterson Institute for International Economics. www .piie.com/blogs/realtime-economic-issues-watch/foreign-corporates-investing-china-surged-2021.

with every departing manager? Personally, I see dissemination rather than waste. While under normal circumstances, expat executives tend to roam from one exciting location to another, post-COVID times inspire more cautious choices. All but one repatriating expat who appears in this book returned to their home regions: the exception was Attila Hilbert, who moved to the only other country he once marked as off-limits: Russia. That consolidation of global expertise is beneficial for firms doing business with China: Western headquarters have been woefully uninformed about the PRC since reforms began. Returning Dragon Suits can serve as in-house mentors in a long line of China-specific skills, from regulatory challenges to hard-earned intercultural leadership lessons that finally exceed the simplistic stereotypes of Confucian collectivism.

Wearing the Dragon Suit Wherever They Go

As virtual meetings shorten the preparation time for intercontinental negotiations from days to minutes, former Dragon Suits can also provide invaluable practical lessons on the technological, behavioral, and political skills necessary to engage China from afar. "Since internal mobility was less of a problem during the first year of the pandemic, Chinese people are less comfortable working online with external locations than we are now," Briana told me. "Personal communication still remains crucial. While I was away for months, my team postponed several important decisions until my return." As a leadership coach who often finds himself *ghosting* virtual business meetings as a silent observer, I can testify to the awkwardness of virtual communication between East and West. Asian participants are trained to be respectful listeners, and thus create unbearably long and awkward silences, which their more extroverted Western counterparts desperately fill with their own voice. Westerners mistake indirect Asian resistance for agreement, Asians interpret Western straightforwardness for personal insult. Next time, neither side may want to conference with the other, pretending that the invitation landed in their spam box.

Participants from different cultures can undermine entire projects without ever realizing it. Meanwhile, the solution can be literally at arm's reach. Managers with recent experience doing business in China, for instance, know a little secret about digitally engaging people there: WeChat. While

Chinese clients, suppliers, colleagues, and even bosses can be stiff as a board while using globally available conferencing applications, they act as a completely different, laid-back person while connecting with China's homegrown app. Former Dragon Suits might not even realize how many such tricks stay hidden up their sleeve until they help a colleague download a Chinese app with a few clicks, explain Mandarin naming traditions or demonstrate the country's abundant subcultures with the help of a map. However, there is another important caveat that may complicate the dissemination of experience amassed by former expatriates: the reverse culture shock of returning to one's home country.

A few years abroad is enough for expatriates to develop daily business habits that are incompatible with the practices of global headquarters. That, of course, is not unique to business: repatriating expats will find their driving and parenting styles clash with home habits too. In the first phase of readjustment, returnees will gaze in amusement at the routines, beliefs, and even spatial arrangement of their homelands. "When I first came back from China, Frankfurt seemed like a nice little village to me," Markus Baumgartner told me. Beyond buildings, they may find the human infrastructure irritating. Henrik König complained of too little *guanxi* in Germany: distance faded his Chinese relationships, while he found it hard to establish new ones in Europe. Christian Eh of Covestro complained of too much: he was unable to replace poorly performing suppliers to his firm, because relationships between firms in that part of Germany spanned generations. Rachel experienced a genuine reverse culture shock when she sent her kids to school in the UK. "In comparison to China, there is no respect for diligence here," she said. "Bullying is also a problem, but teachers are terrified of parents, so you have to be more terrifying than the bullies' parents to get some attention."

Similarly to the long-serving expats who try to introduce China-compatible practices at headquarters, returning Dragon Suits will find that unfavorable comparisons with China's dynamism and technological acumen are usually unwelcome in their home countries. When they do, they must remind themselves to approach their native cultures with the same patience and empathy that they once required from newly commissioned foreign team members in the PRC. They must accept the universal truth that most people in the world lack the multicultural mindset that became their second nature, and see their own approach as a unique skillset. "After seven years in China, my management style had changed, and I had to relearn ways to work with Europeans and Americans," Angelo told me. "I had to accept that what worked in China would often fail in Europe. We became outsiders in a way: both my girls have Shanghai as a place of birth in their passports. But I also realised that I could not have become a truly global manager without my time in Asia."

Finally, the PRC and its international business partners may soon find themselves in dire need of Dragon Suits willing and able to work *with* China but not *in* China. Challenges like Internet restrictions, political clampdowns, and the lack of international mobility hurt successful local businesses as much as multinationals. Predictably, those who have that option relocate abroad in pursuit of a post-COVID global market. Members of China's most affluent business elite left the country in droves that alarmed Beijing: they took with them not only their money but also their talent and connections.[97] Similarly, Chinese firms with a strong presence in foreign markets suddenly found themselves cut off from overseas offices, clients, suppliers, and consumers, and responded with moving some of their operations abroad.[98] Former China expats may play several important roles in a strengthening community of about 10 million immigrants and thousands of dynamic and innovative companies from China, scattered all over the world. They can help multinationals to engage overseas Chinese firms as customers, suppliers, or strategic partners. As entrepreneurs or consultants, they can play the same roles toward either Chinese or multinational firms. They might even find themselves recruited by a newly multinational firm from the PRC.

The *golden age* of multinational business in China may be over, but business with China is definitely in full throttle. Challenges may be mounting, or new ones may simply be replacing those we already know—which one is happening very much depends on where we get our

---

[97] Financial Times. April 18, 2022. "China's Wealthy Look to Leave After Shanghai Lockdown." www.ft.com/content/5f505cf6-4b2f-4f0e-8f74-128db1f01d9a.
[98] E. Cheng. July 12, 2022. "Chinese Companies Are Going Global as Growth Slows at Home," *CNBC*. www.cnbc.com/2022/07/12/chinese-companies-look-to-us-and-asia-as-growth-slows-at-home.html.

information. Or it may be both: that sort of mystery has always been part of the thrill of doing business with the world's most populous nation. As Walt Whitman once wrote about the human soul: it is large, it contains multitudes. But so do all other nations, as well as the companies, teams, and individuals whose job it is to overcome barriers and connect opportunities on opposite sides of negotiating tables, walls, borders, and continents. People on this planet have recently experienced unprecedented decades of peace, progress, prosperity, and consequently, overconfidence: many doubted that the development curves would ever slacken again. But in one respect, we underestimate ourselves: our ability to adapt. The coming years or decades may see ideological differences sharpen and conflicts intensify. But for longer than anyone can remember, people have talked and traded with one another, hoping for a good deal even if they agreed on nothing else. The stories of Dragon Suits are testimony to that invaluable human ability.

References

"Air quality and pollution city ranking." n.d. IQAir. www.iqair.com/world-air-quality-ranking (accessed July 12, 2022).

"China Foreign Direct Investment 1979-2022." n.d. *Macrotrends*, table 2, '% of GDP'. www.macrotrends.net/countries/CHN/china/foreign-direct-investment.

"China Presses Its Internet Censorship Efforts Across the Globe." n.d. *The New York Times*. www.nytimes.com/2018/03/02/technology/china-technology-censorship-borders-expansion.html (updated March 2, 2018).

"China's smog causes some expat families to live apart." n.d. *Bloomberg News*. www.expatinfodesk.com/news/2014/04/10/chinas-smog-causes-some-expat-families-to-live-apart/ (accessed July 12, 2022).

"Current Sentiment Gloomy, Outlook Uncertain." May 2022. *The Conference Board*.

"European Business in China Business Confidence Survey 2019." June 2019. *European Union Chamber of Commerce in China*, p. 34.

"How Many Foreigners Are Living in China?" n.d. Quora. www.quora.com/How-many-foreigners-are-living-in-China (accessed July 12, 2022).

"How Many Foreigners in China? 7th Population Census Tells." n.d. *Expat Focus*. https://mp.weixin.qq.com/s/z41mALLcni3Ei9rV_15o7g (accessed July 12, 2022).

"List of Sovereign States and Dependent Territories by Immigrant Population." n.d. *Wikipedia*. https://en.wikipedia.org/wiki/List_of_sovereign_states_and_dependent_territories_by_immigrant_population (accessed July 12, 2022).

"Living in mainland China: Your guide to expat life in mainland China." n.d. HSBC. www.expat.hsbc.com/expat-explorer/expat-guides/mainland-china/living-in-mainland-china/ (accessed July 15, 2022).

"Test if a site is blocked in China." n.d. Comparitech. www.comparitech.com/privacy-security-tools/blockedinchina/ (accessed July 12, 2022).

"The Great Firewall of China." n.d. *Bloomberg UK*. www.bloomberg.com/quicktake/great-firewall-of-china (updated November 6, 2018).

"Understanding U.S.-China Decoupling: Macro Trends and Industry Impacts." February 17, 2021. *China Center, U.S. Chamber of Commerce*, p. 3. www.uschamber.com/international/understanding-us-china-decoupling-macro-trends-and-industry-impacts.

"World Investment Report 2019, Special Economic Zones." n.d. *UNCTAD*, Chap. iv, pp. 142–145. https://unctad.org/system/files/official-document/WIR2019_CH4.pdf.

"Worldwide Survey of International Assignment Policies and Practices." n.d. *Mercer*. https://mobilityexchange.mercer.com/international-assignments-survey (accessed on July 31, 2022).

Al Jazeera. September 17, 2021. "Probe Finds World Bank Changed Data to Boost China Ranking." www.aljazeera.com/economy/2021/9/17/probe-finds-world-bank-changed-data-to-boost-china-ranking.

AmCham China. April 1, 2022. "COVID-19: Joint Survey Reveals Business Impact of Latest Outbreak." www.amchamchina.org/covid-19-joint-survey-reveals-business-impact-of-latest-outbreak/.

American Addiction Centers. n.d. "Global Drinking Demographics." www.alcohol.org/guides/global-drinking-demographics/ (accessed July 12, 2022).

Andrade, T. 2017. *The Gunpowder Age: China, Military Innovation, and the Rise of the West in World History*, Chap. 16, pp. 237–256. Princeton, NJ: Princeton University Press.

Andrews, P. 2020. "Pre-assignment Health Screening – Avoiding Failed Assignments." *Mercer*. https://mobilityexchange.mercer.com/insights/article/pre-assignment-health-screening-avoiding-failed-assignments.

Arton. n.d. "Global Passport Index." www.passportindex.org/byRank.php (accessed July 12, 2022).

Bandurski, D. n.d. "Tech Shame in the New Era," *China Media Project*. http://chinamediaproject.org/2018/04/11/tech-shame-in-the-new-era/.

BBC. January 12, 2018. "China Shuts Marriott's Website Over Tibet and Taiwan Error." www.bbc.com/news/business-42658070.

BBC. January 23, 2019. "'Racist' D&G Ad: Chinese Model Says Campaign Almost Ruined Career." www.bbc.com/news/world-asia-china-46968750.

BBC. November 17, 2016. "JP Morgan Pays $264m to Settle China 'Bribery' Probe." www.bbc.com/news/business-38013723.

BBC. November 23, 2018. "D&G: China Shopping Sites Pull Products in Ad Backlash." www.bbc.com/news/business-46312844.

Belbin, R.M. 1996. *Management Teams: Why They Succeed or Fail*. Oxford: Butterworth-Heinemann.

Bickers, R. 2012. *The Scramble for China: Foreign Devils in the Qing Empire, 1832-1914*, p. 311. UK: Penguin.

Bickers, R. 2017. *Out of China: How the Chinese Ended the Era of Western Domination*, p. 332. London: Allen Lane.

Bischoff, P. January 2022. "Internet Censorship 2022: A Global Map of Internet Restrictions." Comparitech. https://www.comparitech.com/blog/vpn-privacy/internet-censorship-map/.

Black, J.S. and H. Gregersen. MarchApril 1999. "The Right Way to Manage Expats." *Harvard Business Review*. https://hbr.org/1999/03/the-right-way-to-manage-expats.

Black, J.S. September 2019. "Why Foreign Firms Struggle to Break Into China." *INSEAD*. https://knowledge.insead.edu/strategy/why-foreign-firms-struggle-to-break-into-china-12421.

Bloomberg UK. August 18, 2018. "China Is Said to Freeze Game Approvals Amid Agency Shakeup." www.bloomberg.com/news/articles/2018-08-15/china-is-said-to-freeze-game-approvals-amid-agency-shakeup.

Bloomberg UK. March 24, 2022. "Experts See China Stuck in a Slowly Evolving Covid-Zero Loop." www.bloomberg.com/news/articles/2022-03-24/experts-see-china-stuck-in-a-slowly-evolving-covid-zero-loop.

Bloomberg UK. April 18, 2022. "China Meets With Foreign Chambers as Lockdowns Hit Business." www.bloomberg.com/news/articles/2022-04-18/china-meets-with-foreign-chambers-as-lockdowns-hit-business.

Bloomberg UK. April 19, 2022. "China Vows to Ease Supply Chain Woes in Foreign Chamber Meeting." www.bloomberg.com/news/articles/2022-04-19/china-vows-to-ease-supply-chain-woes-in-foreign-chamber-meeting.

Bris, A. and C. Cabolis. 2020. "IMD World Digital Competitiveness Ranking 2020." *IMD World Competitiveness Center*, p. 24.

British Chamber of Commerce in China. n.d. "British Business in China: Sentiment Survey 2020-21." www.britishchamber.cn/en/business-sentiment-survey/.

British Chamber. 2022. "British Business in China: Sentiment Survey 2021–2022." *British Chamber*, p. 13, 38. www.britishchamber.cn/en/business-sentiment-survey/.

Brown, K. 2018. *China's Dream: The Culture of Chinese Communism and the Secret Sources of its Power*, p. 42. Cambridge: Polity.

Bursztynsky, J. June 2022. "Apple Will Reportedly Move Some iPad Capacity to Vietnam After China Lockdowns." *CNBC*. www.cnbc.com/2022/06/01/apple-will-reportedly-move-some-ipad-capacity-from-china-to-vietnam.html.

C. Dwyer. May 2018. "The Gap Apologizes for Shirts Showing Map of China Without Disputed Territories." *NPR*. www.npr.org/sections/thetwo-way/2018/05/15/611278789/the-gap-apologizes-for-t-shirts-showing-map-of-china-without-disputed-territorie.

Chan, C. January 2016. "Why Some Chinese Speakers Also Use Western Names." *Deutsche Welle*. www.dw.com/en/why-some-chinese-speakers-also-use-western-names/a-18966907.

Chen, C.-C. and Y.-T. Lee. 2008. *Leadership and Management in China: Philosophies, Theories, and Practices*, p. 171. Cambridge: Cambridge University Press.

Cheng, E. July 12, 2022. "Chinese Companies Are Going Global as Growth Slows at Home." *CNBC*. www.cnbc.com/2022/07/12/chinese-companies-look-to-us-and-asia-as-growth-slows-at-home.html.

Chin, Y. Manuscript in preparation. "The Emergence of Chinese Global Executives." (accessed July 2022).

China Daily Show. August 15, 2012. "Why I'm Leaving China." http://chinadailyshow.com/why-im-leaving-china/.

China Economic Review. January 22, 2013. "Four Dishes and One Soup." https://chinaeconomicreview.com/four-dishes-one-soup/.

China Power. February 27, 2016. "Is China's Soft Power Strategy Working?" https://chinapower.csis.org/is-chinas-soft-power-strategy-working.

China Power. n.d. "Is China Both a Source and Hub for International Students?" https://chinapower.csis.org/china-international-students/.

Chung-Huang, N. 1958. *China Will Overtake Britain.* Peking: Foreign Languages Press.

Cimpanu, C. December 2019. "Two of China's Largest Tech Firms Are Uniting to Create a New 'Domestic OS'." *ZDet.* www.zdnet.com/article/two-of-chinas-largest-tech-firms-are-uniting-to-create-a-new-domestic-os/.

CNBC. July 20, 2017. "China Clamping Down on Use of VPNs to Evade Great Firewall." www.cnbc.com/2017/07/20/china-clamping-down-on-use-of-vpns-to-evade-great-firewall.html.

Covert, E. January 4, 2022. "China Beer Market Overview." *Statista.* www.statista.com/statistics/278566/urban-and-rural-population-of-china/.

Crane, B., C. Albrecht, K.M. Duffin, and C. Albrecht. 2018. "China's Special Economic Zones: An Analysis of Policy to Reduce Regional Disparities." *Regional Studies, Regional Science* 5, no. 1, pp. 98–107.

Cyrill, M. April 2016. "The 996 Work Culture That's Causing a Burnout in China's Tech World." *China Briefing.* www.china-briefing.com/news/996-work-culture-china-tech-sector-burnout/.

Dams, T. and X. Martin. April 2022. "Investors Beware: Europe's Top Firms Are Highly Exposed to China." *Clingendael.* www.clingendael.org/sites/default/files/2022-04/Report_Are_Europes_top_firms_highly_exposed_to_China.pdf.

Data Commons Place Explorer. n.d. "Gross Domestic Product Per Capita in People's Republic of China." https://datacommons.org/place/country/CHN?utm_medium=explore&mprop=amount&popt=Economic Activity&cpv=activitySource%2CGrossDomesticProduction&hl=en# (accessed July 31, 2022).

Deloitte. September 2020. *Sino-Foreign Joint Ventures After COVID-19 What to Expect?*, p. 5.

Denyer, S. January 2018. "Command and Control: China's Communist Party Extends Reach Into Foreign Companies." *The Washington Post.* www.washingtonpost.com/world/asia_pacific/command-and-control-chinas-communist-party-extends-reach-into-foreign-companies/2018/01/28/cd49ffa6-fc57-11e7-9b5d-bbf0da31214d_story.html.

Denyer, S. May 2018. "Gap Apologizes to China Over Map on T-Shirt That Omits Taiwan, South China Sea." *The Washington Post*. www.washingtonpost. com/news/worldviews/wp/2018/05/15/u-s-retailer-gap-apologizes-to-china-over-map-on-t-shirt-that-omits-taiwan-south-china-sea/.

Deutsche Welle. February 7, 2018. "Mercedes Bows to Chinese Pressure After Dalai Lama Instagram Post Prompts Outrage." www.dw.com/en/mercedes-bows-to-chinese-pressure-after-dalai-lama-instagram-post-prompts-outrage/a-42475537.

Devonshire-Ellis, C. November 2014. "Hong Kong Murders and Expatriate Psychological Issues in China." *China Briefing*. www.china-briefing.com/news/2014/11/04/can-recent-hong-kong-murders-teach-us-hr-issues-china .html.

Dicker, A. November 2021. "Western and Chinese Business Cultures." *The Ganbei Podcast*. Podcast. www.ganbei.tv/blog/transcript-western-and-chinese-business-cultures?categoryId=247144.

Dittli, M. April 2022. "China's Leadership Is Prisoner of Its Own Narrative." *The Market*. https://themarket-ch.cdn.ampproject.org/c/s/themarket.ch/amp/interview/chinas-leadership-is-prisoner-of-its-own-narrative-ld.6545.

Dolce & Gabbana. November 23, 2018. "Dolce&Gabbana Apologizes." Video. https://youtu.be/7Ih62lTKicg.

Durnin, M. February 2014. "China Is Still a Jobs Hotspot for Expats." *BBC*. www.bbc.com/worklife/article/20140212-get-hired-in-china.

Economy, E.C. 2018. *The Third Revolution: Xi Jinping and the New Chinese State*, p. 152. Oxford: Oxford University Press.

Education First. n.d. "EF English Proficiency Index: The world's Largest Ranking of Countries and Regions by English Skills." www.ef.com/wwen/epi/ (accessed July 12, 2022).

Esipova, N., J. Fleming, and J. Raw. n.d. "New Index Shows Least-, Most-Accepting Countries for Migrants." *Gallup*. https://news.gallup.com/poll/216377/new-index-shows-least-accepting-countries-migrants.aspx.

European Chamber of Commerce in China. n.d. "China's Covid-19 Policy and Russia's War in Ukraine Cause Severe Disruptions to European Business in China." www.europeanchamber.com.cn/en/press-releases/3431.

European Union Chamber of Commerce in China. June 20, 2022. *European Business in China Business Confidence Survey 2022*, p. 6.

European Union Chamber of Commerce in China. June 2021. *European Business in China Business Confidence Survey 2021*, pp. 1–17.

European Union Chamber of Commerce in China. June 8, 2021. *European Business in China Confidence Survey 2021*, p. 6–40.

European Union Chamber of Commerce in China. May 31, 2017. "European Business in China Confidence Survey 2017." *European Union Chamber of Commerce in China*, p. 30.

European Union Chamber of Commerce in China. September 9, 2014. "European Business in China Position Paper 2014/2015." *European Union Chamber of Commerce in China*, p. 5.

Expat Focus. July 11, 2022. "Number of Foreigners in China, Results of 7th National Census." https://mp.weixin.qq.com/s?__biz=MjM5OTg2MTgzO A==&mid=2654317267&idx=1&sn=c790b7572d9186ac1fc15c3255db77 d9&chksm=bcf401f28b8388e495d439dbd33c62d556744c1c65c6c100 eeaea0ce63fdc5b779a72e6b20ce.

Fabritius, F. and H.W. Hagemann. 2018. *The Leading Brain: Neuroscience Hacks to Work Smarter, Better, Happier: Powerful Science-Based Strategies for Achieving Peak Performance*. New York, NY: Tarcherperigee.

Ferguson, N. April 2022. "The Utopian Myth of Equality." youtube.com, Video. www.youtube.com/watch?v=niqHgJwx2Ck&t=10s.

Fernandez, J.A. and L. Underwood. 2011. *China CEO: Voices of Experience From 20 International Business Leaders*, p. 6–131. New York, NY: John Wiley & Sons.

Fernandez, J.A. and L. Underwood. 2020. *China CEO II: Voices of Experience From 25 Top Executives Leading MNCs in China*, p. 42–215. Oxford: Wiley.

Filippelli, G. and P. Gong. May 2018. "Aspiring Toward Healthy Cities in China." *Eos*. https://eos.org/editors-vox/aspiring-toward-healthy-cities-in-china.

Financial Times. April 18, 2019. "China Censors Ban Leica Name Over Tiananmen Square video." www.ft.com/content/7191da2c-6253-11e9-a27a-fdd51850994c.

Financial Times. April 18, 2022. "China's Wealthy Look to Leave After Shanghai Lockdown." www.ft.com/content/5f505cf6-4b2f-4f0e-8f74-128db1f01d9a.

Financial Times. August 11, 2021. "China Cracks Down on Post-Work Drinking and 'Harmful Karaoke'." https://amp-ft-com.cdn.ampproject.org/c/s/amp. ft.com/content/adc14a48-73ea-4baa-8638-9dec6138c758.

Financial Times. February 28, 2012. "Shanghai Netizens to Expats: Don't Mention the French Concession." www.ft.com/content/4378a9bf-6d5a-3c0a-a145-e73d7ab5a4f2.

Financial Times. July 17, 2022. "China's Zero-Covid Policy Has Had a Severe Impact on Its Stock of Global Talent." www.ft.com/content/fef5a71d-8a19-4f65-804e-42bfb02af083.

Financial Times. n.d. "China's Xi Calls for Wealth Redistribution and Clampdown on High Incomes." https://amp-ft-com.cdn.ampproject.org/c/s/amp.ft.com/content/87c3aa02-f970-48c8-b795-82768c9f7634 (accessed July 12, 2022).

Financial Times. n.d. "Western Brands Aim for the Sky in Xi Jinping's China." https://amp-ft-com.cdn.ampproject.org/c/s/amp.ft.com/content/57ced15a-68fe-4b6c-883f-df71cd8ef250.

Ford, P. March 2015. "Nokia Exit: Is China's 'Golden Age' of Foreign Investment Over?" *The Christian Science Monitor.* www.csmonitor.com/World/Asia-Pacific/2015/0309/Nokia-exit-Is-China-s-golden-age-of-foreign-investment-over.

France24. April 25, 2022. "China's Pursuit of Zero Covid Driving Expats Away." www.france24.com/en/live-news/20220425-china-s-pursuit-of-zero-covid-driving-expats-away.

France24. May 2008. "Anti-Carrefour Protests Hit China." www.france24.com/en/20080501-anti-carrefour-protests-hit-china-china-carrefour.

Fraser, I. February 2022. "Riding the Tiger—Scotch in China." *Whisky News.* www.whiskyinvestdirect.com/whisky-news/scotch-in-china-110220221.

French, P. January 2021. "Myth Busting: Shenzhen's Sleazy Past as Short-Lived Gangster and Gambling Hub Shum Chun." *The South China Morning Post.* www.scmp.com/magazines/post-magazine/long-reads/article/3117505/myth-busting-shenzhens-sleazy-past-short-lived.

Frick, P. and F. Kremer. "Running a Service Business as a Flexpat With Marion Campan." *China Flexpat.* Podcast. https://podcasts.apple.com/hk/podcast/china-flexpat/id1514659021?l=en&i=1000555702437.

Gallup. 2010. "Gallup Global Wellbeing the Behavioral Economics of GDPGrowth." https://news.gallup.com/poll/126965/gallup-global-wellbeing.aspx.

Gan, N. and S. George. December 15, 2021. "The Communist Party Thinks China's Prolific Censors Are Not Censoring Enough." *CNN Business.* https://edition.cnn.com/2021/12/15/tech/china-weibo-censorship-fine-mic-intl-hnk/index.html.

Ganbei. December 5, 2021. "The Gold Rush of International Banks 'Expansion in China'." Podcast. www.ganbei.tv/blog/ep-27-the-gold-rush-of-international-banks-expansion-in-china?categoryId=245717.

Glasgow, W. n.d. "Get Me Out of Here: Inside China's Historic Expat Exodus." *The Australian.* www.theaustralian.com.au/web-stories/free/the-australian/get-me-out-of-here-inside-chinas-expat-exodus.

Global Times. February 28, 2022. "Private Educational Institutions in China Are Slashed by About 90%: Ministry." www.globaltimes.cn/page/2022 02/1253438.shtml.

Global Times. March 26, 2021. "US-Led NATO Still Owes Blood Debt to Chinese People: FM." www.globaltimes.cn/page/202103/1219540.shtml.

Global Times. April 7, 2022. "GT Voice: Western Slander Won't Undercut Shanghai's Global Attractiveness." www.globaltimes.cn/page/202204/1258762.shtml.

Global Times. May 16, 2020. "China Readies Biggest Counterattack Against US." www.globaltimes.cn/content/1188493.shtml.

Global Times. n.d. "Boycotting Korean Firms, Products Over THAAD Triggers Ideological Conflict Online in China." www.globaltimes.cn/content/1036693.shtml (removed in 2022).

Godement, F. February 2022. "Xi Jinping as an Ordoliberal: China's Margins for Growth in 2022." *Institut Montaigne.* www.institutmontaigne.org/en/publications/xi-jinping-ordoliberal-chinas-margins-growth-2022.

Gold, S. September 2021. "World Bank Scraps Doing Business Rankings Due to Data Irregularities." *Devex.* www.devex.com/news/world-bank-scraps-doing-business-rankings-due-to-data-irregularities-101630.

Goldkorn, J. and T. Garbarini. April 2020. "What Do Chinese People Think of the Recent Ban on Foreigners?" *SupChina.* https://supchina.com/2020/04/01/what-do-chinese-people-think-of-the-recent-ban-on-foreigners/.

Goldsmith, J. May 2022. "Disney CEO Bob Chapek on the "Difficulty" of Getting Films Released in China." *Deadline.* https://deadline.com/2022/05/disney-ceo-bob-chapek-china-dr-strange-1235021804/.

Grammaticas, D. January 2013. "'Airmageddon': China Smog Raises Modernisation Doubts." *BBC.* www.bbc.com/news/world-asia-china-21272328.

Graver, J. W. 2016. *China's Quest: The History of the Foreign Relations of the People's Republic of China,* p. 290. Oxford and New York, NY: Oxford University Press.

Gu, H. and D. Stanway. September 2019. "Beijing Set to Exit List of World's Ttop 200 Most-Polluted Cities." *Reuters.* www.reuters.com/article/us-china-pollution-beijing/beijing-set-to-exit-list-of-worlds-top-200-most-polluted-cities-data-idUSKCN1VX05Z.

Hanes, W.T. and F. Sanello. 2002. *Opium Wars: The Addiction of One Empire and the Corruption of Another,* p. 160. USA: Sourcebooks.

Haywood, M. 2017. "Tainted Treasures: Money Laundering Risks in Luxury Markets." *Transparency International,* pp. 25–26.

He, L. January 2022. "China Is Still the Ultimate Prize That Western Banks Can't Resist." *CNN Business.* https://edition.cnn.com/2022/01/14/investing/china-western-banks-mic-intl-hnk/index.html.

He, L. April 2022. "Foreign Investors Are Ditching China. Russia's War Is the Latest Trigger." *CNN Business.* https://edition.cnn.com/2022/04/25/investing/china-capital-outflows-covid-ukraine-war-intl-mic-hnk/index.html.

Holch, G. July 2021. "Five Essential Qualities for China CEOs by Dr Laurie Underwood (East-West Leadership Webinar)." Video. www.youtube.com/watch?v=VIf1qC4B7rU.

Hong, H.-J. and Y.L. Doz. June 2013. "L'Oréal Masters Multiculturalism." *Harvard Business Review Press.* https://hbr.org/2013/06/loreal-masters-multiculturalism.

Horwitz, J. and R. Lui. February 2022. "China Says Not Granting Passport Renewals for Non-Essential Travel." *Reuters*. www.reuters.com/world/china/china-says-not-granting-passport-renewals-non-essential-travel-2022-02-12.

HSBC. n.d. "Living in Mainland China: Your Guide to Expat Life in Mainland China." www.expat.hsbc.com/expat-explorer/expat-guides/mainland-china/living-in-mainland-china/.

HSBC. October 2021. "Expat Explorer Survey 2021." *HSBC*. www.expat.hsbc.com/expat-explorer/.

Huang, J. January 2013. "Developing Local Talent for Future Leadership." *China Business Review*. www.chinabusinessreview.com/developing-local-talent-for-future-leadership/.

Huang, T. and N.R. Lardy. March 29, 2022. "Foreign Corporates Investing in China Surged in 2021." Peterson Institute for International Economics. www.piie.com/blogs/realtime-economic-issues-watch/foreign-corporates-investing-china-surged-2021.

Ide, B. March 2, 2017. "Chinese Media Call for Boycott of South Korean Goods." *Voice of America*. www.voanews.com/a/chinese-media-call-for-boycott-of-south-korean-goods/3746701.html.

Inglehart, R.F. 2018. *Cultural Evolution: People's Motivations Are Changing, and Reshaping the World*, p. 40. Cambridge: Cambridge University Press.

Ireland, S. January 2022. "The World's Most Influential CEOs And Business Executives Of 2022." *CEOWorld*. https://ceoworld.biz/2022/01/25/the-worlds-most-influential-ceos-and-business-executives-of-2022/.

Jacques, M. 2009. *When China Rules the World: The End of the Western World and the Birth of a New Global Order*. London: Penguin Books.

James, G. September 2021. "Too Much Work and Not Enough Sex Threatens China's New Population Plans." *Society & Culture*. https://supchina.com/2021/09/23/too-much-work-and-not-enough-sex-threatens-chinas-new-population-plans/.

James, G. December 2021. "Multinationals in 2021: The New Reality of Doing Business in China." *SupChina*. https://supchina.com/2021/12/15/multinationals-in-2021-the-new-reality-of-doing-business-in-china/.

Junya, Q. May 2022. "Eventually, China's Borders Will Reopen. Will Foreigners Return?" *Sixth Tone*. www.sixthtone.com/news/1010282/eventually%2C-chinas-borders-will-reopen.-will-foreigners-return.

Kania, E.B. February 2019. "Made in China 2025, Explained." *The Diplomat*. https://thediplomat.com/2019/02/made-in-china-2025-explained/.

Kim, C. and H. Jin. March 2017. "South Korea Struggles to Retaliate in Missile Spat With China." *Reuters*. www.reuters.com/article/us-southkorea-china-lotte-idUSKBN16G1FR.

Kinder, K. 2015. *Wonderlanded: Life as an Expat in China*, p. 3. Amazon LLC.

King, L., et al. 2009. *Environmental Sociology, From Analysis to Action*, p. 184. Maryland: Rowman & Littlefield.

Kirton, D. May 2022. "European Businesses Fear More COVID Disruption in China." *Reuters*. www.reuters.com/markets/europe/european-businesses-fear-more-covid-disruption-china-2022-05-16/.

Knape, C. November 2010. "Amway China Chairwoman: Dancing With Dragon Requires Give and Take." *MLive*. www.mlive.com/business/west-michigan/2010/11/amway_china_chairwoman_dancing.html.

Korczynska, E. 2018. *Made in China: Confessions of an expat*, p. 28–70. Amazon LLC.

KPMG China. April 2021. "New Policies to Attract Foreign Talent to China." https://home.kpmg/cn/en/home/insights/2021/03/china-tax-alert-09.html.

Kuo, K. January 2022. "Dan Wang on China in 2021." *SupChina*. Podcast. https://supchina.com/podcast/dan-wang-on-china-in-2021-common-prosperity-cultural-stunting-and-shortcomings-of-the-modal-china-story/.

Kuo, K. January 2022. "The Psychology of Political Discontent in China." *SupChina*. Podcast. https://supchina.com/2022/01/27/the-psychology-of-political-discontent-in-china/.

Kuo, K. n.d. "Mental Health Under Lockdown: A Clinical Psychologist in Shanghai." *SupChina*. Podcast. https://podcasts.apple.com/hk/podcast/sinica-podcast/id1121407665?l=en&i=1000565045048 (accessed July 12, 2022).

Kuo, L. April 10, 2014. "Six Years of Beijing Air Pollution Summed Up in One Scary Chart." Quartz. https://qz.com/197786/six-years-of-bejing-air-pollution-summed-up-in-one-scary-chart/.

Laband, J. May 2018. "Fact Sheet: Communist Party Groups in Foreign Companies in China." *USCBC*. www.chinabusinessreview.com/fact-sheet-communist-party-groups-in-foreign-companies-in-china/.

Lau, S. n.d. "Russia Crisis Gives EU a Grim Sense of What's to Come With China." *Politico*. www.politico.eu/article/china-xi-jinping-has-europe-eu-summit-russia (accessed July 12, 2022).

Lei, L. May 2015. "China Embraces Increasing Foreign Residents." *China Daily*. http://global.chinadaily.com.cn/a/202105/12/WS609b14c5a31024a d0babd49f.html.

Lin, B. "China's Economic Woes: A Conversation With Scott Kennedy." *CSIS*. www.csis.org/node/65721 (accessed July 12, 2022).

Livermore, D.A. 2009. *Leading With Cultural Intelligence: The New Secret to Success*, p. 70. New York, NY: Amacom.

Lovell, J. 2007. *The Great Wall: China Against the World, 1000 BC–AD 2000*, p. 272. New York, NY: Grove Press.

Lovell, J. 2011. *The Opium War: Drugs, Dreams and the Making of China*, p. 87. London: Pan Macmillan.

Lovell, J. 2015. "The Uses of Foreigners in Mao-Era China: 'Techniques of Hospitality' and International Image-Building in the People's Republic, 1949–1976." *Transactions of the Royal Historical Society* 25, pp. 135–158. Cambridge: Cambridge University Press.

Magnus, G. August 2021. "Going After the Private Sector: Xi on a Mission." *SOAS China Institute*. https://blogs.soas.ac.uk/china-institute/2021/08/24/going-after-the-private-sector-xi-on-a-mission/.

Martinez-Carter, K. November 2013. "The Best—and Worst—Countries for Expats?." *BBC*. www.bbc.com/worklife/article/20131122-an-expats-home-away-from-home.

McGregor, J. 2012. *No Ancient Wisdom, No Followers: The Challenges of Chinese Authoritarian Capitalism*, p. 42. Prospecta Press.

McKinsey Insights. May 24, 2019. "Why the Future Is Asian." *McKinsey Insights*. www.mckinsey.com/featured-insights/asia-pacific/why-the-future-is-asian.

McMunn, R. August 2014. "8 Tips for a Life in China." *Huffpost*. www.huffpost.com/entry/eight-tips-for-a-life-in-_b_5674838.

Mercer. n.d. "Worldwide Survey of International Assignment Policies and Practices." https://mobilityexchange.mercer.com/international-assignments-survey (accessed July 31, 2022).

Meyer, E. December 2015. "Getting to Si, Ja, Oui, Hai, and Da." *Harvard Business Review*. https://hbr.org/2015/12/getting-to-si-ja-oui-hai-and-da.

Meyer, E. 2016. *The Culture Map*, p. 36–90. New York, NY: Public Affairs.

Ministry of Education, The People's Republic of China. April 18, 2019. "Statistical Report on International Students in China for 2018." http://en.moe.gov.cn/documents/reports/201904/t20190418_378692.html.

MIPEX. n.d. "Migrant Integration Policy Index 2020." www.mipex.eu/china (accessed August 1, 2022).

Morgan, D. and Z. Ruiying. January 19, 2022. "China's Foreign Firms Are Running Out of a Key Resource: Foreigners." *Sixth Tone*. www.sixthtone.com/news/1009408/chinas-foreign-firms-are-running-out-of-a-key-resource-foreigners.

Morris, E. April 2004. "The Fog of War." Sony Pictures Classics, documentary.

Morris, S. and T. Kinder. July 21, 2022. "HSBC Installs Communist Party Committee in Chinese Investment Bank." *Financial Times*. www.ft.com/content/eac99fd9-0c30-4141-821a-45348f61c113.

Morrison, T. 2006. *Kiss, Bow, or Shake Hands: The Bestselling Guide to Doing Business in More Than 60 Countries*, p. 95–98. UK: Adams Media.

Musgrave, P. July 2018. "John Bolton Is Warning of a 'Clash of Civilizations' With China. Here Are the Five Things You Need to Know." *The Washington Post*. www.washingtonpost.com/politics/2019/07/18/john-bolton-is-warning-clash-civilizations-with-china-here-are-five-things-you-need-know/.

Nelson, C. October 2013. "The Expat's Competitive Edge." *China Business Review*. www.chinabusinessreview.com/the-expats-competitive-edge/.

Niewenhuis, L. May 2020. "Will Beijing Take Revenge on Qualcomm, Cisco, Apple, and Boeing?" *SupChina*. https://supchina.com/2020/05/18/will-beijing-take-revenge-on-qualcomm-cisco-apple-and-boeing-2/.

Noi, G.S. January 4, 2022. "China-US Competition for Talent Hots Up." *The Straits Times*. www.straitstimes.com/opinion/china-us-competition-for-talent-heats-up.

OC Tanner Institute. n.d. *2018 Global Culture Report*, p. 24. www.octanner.com/content/dam/oc-tanner/documents/white-papers/2018/2018_Global_Culture_Report.pdf.

Olsen, K. September 2014. "Businesses in EU Say China's Promised Reforms Moving too Slowly." AFP. www.industryweek.com/the-economy/article/21963586/businesses-in-eu-say-chinas-promised-reforms-moving-too-slowly.

Our World in Data. n.d. "The Value of Global Exports." https://ourworldindata.org/grapher/world-trade-exports-constant-prices (accessed July 12, 2022).

Our World in Data. n.d. "Women's Economic Opportunity Index, 2012." https://ourworldindata.org/grapher/womens-economic-opportunity-2012-index (accessed July 30, 2022).

Overholt, W.H. 2019. "Hong Kong: The Rise and Fall of the 'One Country, Two Systems'." Harvard Kennedy School. www.overholtgroup.com/media/Articles-Hong-Kong/Rise-Fall-of-One-Country-Two-Systems.pdf.

Paine, L.S. June 2010. "The Globe: The China Rules." Harvard Business School. https://hbr.org/2010/06/the-globe-the-china-rules.

Palmer, J. April 2018. "China Threatens U.S. Airlines Over Taiwan References." *Foreign Policy*. https://foreignpolicy.com/2018/04/27/china-threatens-u-s-airlines-over-taiwan-references-united-american-flight-beijing/.

Palmer, J. August 2017. "China Is Trying to Give the Internet a Death Blow." *Foreign Policy*. https://foreignpolicy.com/2017/08/25/china-is-trying-to-give-the-internet-a-death-blow-vpn-technology/.

Patel, D. August 27, 2021. "The Semiconductor Heist of the Century." *Semianalysis*. https://semianalysis.com/the-semiconductor-heist-of-the-century-arm-china-has-gone-completely-rogue-operating-as-an-independent-company-with-their-own-ip/.

Patey, L. 2021. *How China Loses*, p. 117–184. Oxford: Oxford University Press.

PBS NewsHour. November 22, 2019. "China: Power and Prosperity." Documentary. www.youtube.com/watch?v=oIF-ujSeQho.

Peraino, K. 2017. *A Force So Swift: Mao, Truman, and the Birth of Modern China, 1949*, p. 134. New York, NY: Crown Publishing Group.

Pieke, F.N. November 2019. "How Immigration Is Shaping Chinese Society." *MERICS*, Exhibit 2. https://merics.org/en/report/how-immigration-shaping-chinese-society.

Price, D.C. 2016. *Bamboo Strong: Cultural Intelligence Secrets to Succeed in the New Global Economy*. London: DCP Global Limited.

Qian, Z. and S. Elsinga. January 2015. "Nali Lai de?—An Overview of Expat Demographics in China." *China Briefing*. www.china-briefing.com/news/nali-lai-de-overview-expats-china/.

Radelet, S. 2016. *The Great Surge: The Ascent of the Developing World*, p. 35. New York, NY: Simon & Schuster.

Rajagopalan, M. May 2016. "China to Relocate 2 Million People This Year in Struggle to Banish Poverty." *Reuters*. www.reuters.com/article/us-china-poverty-idUSKCN0Y10LF.

Rautela, A. April 2020. "China to Ban Online Gaming, Chatting With Foreigners." TalkEsport. www.talkesport.com/news/china-to-ban-online-gaming-chatting-with-foreigners.

Redford, D. April 2015. "Expats in China Turn to Entrepreneurship." *China US Focus*. www.chinausfocus.com/political-social-development/expats-in-china-turn-to-entrepreneurship.

Refer China. August 13, 2021. "What Leads to the Downfall of Wall Street English in China?" www.referchina.com/2021/08/What_Lead_to_the_Downfall_of__Wall_Street_English_in_China__43806.html.

Ren, S. March 2022. "China Doesn't Care If It's Uninvestable—for Foreigners." *Bloomberg UK*. www.bloomberg.com/opinion/articles/2022-03-15/is-china-uninvestable-complaints-from-foreigners-won-t-sway-xi-jinping.

Reuters. April 2008. "LVMH Denies Tibet Support, Sees No Chinese Boycott—Report." www.reuters.com/article/idINIndia-33081720080416.

Reuters. December 7, 2021. "Travel Curbs Are Biggest Challenge for British Firms in China—Survey." www.reuters.com/world/china/travel-curbs-are-biggest-challenge-british-firms-china-survey-2021-12-07/.

Richelle. October 2017. "After FIVE Years in China, I'm Finally Moving On." *Adventures Around Asia*. www.adventuresaroundasia.com/leaving-china/.

Robinson, R. December 2020. "2020 Year in Review. Beijing to Bali to Beijing and Back—or—Hindsight Is 2020 ;-)." *LinkedIn*. www.linkedin.com/pulse/2020-year-review-beijing-bali-back-rich-robinson/.

Russell, B. 1922. *The Problem of China*, p. 52. Abingdon-on-Thames: Routledge.

SAMPi. October 24, 2018. "China Expat Population: Stats and Graphs." *SAMPi*. https://sampi.co/china-expat-population-statistics/.

Schell, O. and J. Delury. 2013. *China's Long March to the Twenty-first Century*. London: Little, Brown.

Schneider, J. October 20, 202. "China Fines Sony ¥1M for Announcing a Camera on a Controversial Date." *PetaPixel*. https://petapixel.com/2021/10/20/china-fines-sony-%C2%A51m-for-announcing-a-camera-on-a-controversial-date/.

Schuman, M. 2020. *Superpower Interrupted: The Chinese History of the World*, p. 68. New York, NY: PublicAffairs.

Scofield, A. n.d. "New Research Shows Expats Earning Up To 900% More Than Local Employees." *Expat Focus*. www.expatfocus.com/employment/new-research-shows-expats-earning-up-to-900-more-than-local-employees-3159 (accessed July 12, 2022).

Sha, L. April 2018. "The Real Cost of Air Pollution in China." *CKGSB Knowledge*. https://knowledge.ckgsb.edu.cn/2018/04/13/environment/economic-effects-of-pollution-china/.

Shahbaz, A. and A. Funk. 2019. "Freedom on the Net 2019." *Freedom House*, p. 25. https://freedomhouse.org/report/freedom-net.

Shambaugh, D. 2020. *China and the World*, p. 26–364. Oxford and New York, NY: Oxford University press.

Shi, S. April 2022. "Bon App Poll Results: 40% of Expats leaving China soon." *BonAppOfficial*. https://mp.weixin.qq.com/s/2Id8HRZ6TTu6xHpjHwj-3A.

Shih, G. October 2019. "Response to NBA Executive's Hong Kong Tweet Shows the Rift Between China and U.S." *The Washington Post*. www.washingtonpost.com/world/nba-rockets-face-backlash-from-chinese-fans-after-tweet-in-support-of-hong-kong-protesters/2019/10/07/68e9ad24-e902-11e9-bafb-da248f8d5734_story.html.

Shindelar, W. May 3, 2016. "6 Myths Vs Realities of Living in China, Written by an American Expat." *Matador Network*. https://matadornetwork.com/abroad/6-myths-vs-realities-living-china-written-american-expat/.

Shroff, M. October 2021. "China: Sunset of Localized Version of LinkedIn and Launch of New InJobs App Later This Year." *LinkedIn*. https://blog.linkedin.com/2021/october/14/china-sunset-of-localized-version-of-linkedin-and-launch-of-new-injobs-app.

Silver, L., K. Devlin, and C. Huang. October 2020. "Unfavorable Views of China Reach Historic Highs in Many Countries." *Pew Research Center*. www.pewresearch.org/global/2020/10/06/unfavorable-views-of-china-reach-historic-highs-in-many-countries/.

Smith, G. and L. Lim. "Gimme, Gimme, Gimme a Han After Midnight: China's Masculinity Crisis." *The Little Red Podcast*. https://podcasts.apple.com/hk/podcast/the-little-red-podcast/id1136685378?l=en&i=1000560480404 (accessed July 12, 2022).

Soo, Z. November 2021. "Yahoo Pulls Out of China, Citing 'Challenging' Environment." *Yahoo news*. https://news.yahoo.com/yahoo-pulls-china-amid-challenging-110457049.html.

South China Morning Post. n.d. "Coronavirus: Foreign Pilots at Chinese Airlines Head Home on Unpaid Leave as Demand Falls." www.scmp.com/news/china/society/article/3051437/coronavirus-foreign-pilots-chinese-airlines-head-home-unpaid (accessed July 12, 2022).

Speelman, T. December 2020. "Chinese Attitudes Toward Immigrants: Emerging, Divided Views." *The Diplomat*. https://thediplomat.com/2020/12/chinese-attitudes-toward-immigrants-emerging-divided-views/.

Stripe. April 4, 2017. "Alipay Terms of Service." https://stripe.com/alipay/legal#prohibited-business-list.

Tang, F. April 2022. "China's European Firms Warn 'On-Off Economy', Covid Lockdowns Cloud Business Outlook." *China Macro Economy*. www.scmp.com/economy/china-economy/article/3173287/chinas-european-firms-warn-economy-covid-lockdowns-cloud.

Textor, C. February 2022. "Urban and Rural Population of China From 2011 to 2021." U.S. Department of Agriculture Foreign Agricultural Service. https://apps.fas.usda.gov/newgainapi/api/Report/DownloadReportByFileName?fileName=China%20Beer%20Market%20Overview_Beijing%20ATO_China%20-%20People%27s%20Republic%20of_01-04-2022.

Thaerigen, S. n.d. "Podcast #81 First China job—Better Job—Own Business." *China Flexpat*. (Podcast). https://podcasts.apple.com/hk/podcast/china-flexpat/id1514659021?l=en&i=1000550923269 (accessed July 12, 2022).

The Conference Board. May 2022. "Current Sentiment Gloomy, Outlook Uncertain." www.conference-board.org/pdfdownload.cfm?masterProductID=39382.

The Economist. July 6, 2019. "Cheerleaders and Police Usher in a New Era of Trash-Sorting." www.economist.com/china/2019/07/06/cheerleaders-and-police-usher-in-a-new-era-of-trash-sorting.

The Economist. July 11, 2019. "Supply Chains for Different Industries Are Fragmenting in Different Ways." www.economist.com/special-report/2019/07/11/supply-chains-for-different-industries-are-fragmenting-in-different-ways.

The Economist. October 17, 2017. "A Geopolitical Row With China Damages South Korean Business Further." www.economist.com/business/2017/10/19/a-geopolitical-row-with-china-damages-south-korean-business-further.

The Economist. October 19, 2017. "A Geopolitical Row With China Damages South Korean Business Further." www.economist.com/business/2017/10/19/a-geopolitical-row-with-china-damages-south-korean-business-further.

The International Bank for Reconstruction and Development and the World Bank. June 1, 2009. "Doing Business 2010." www.doingbusiness.org/content/dam/doingBusiness/media/Annual-Reports/English/DB10-FullReport.pdf.

The New York Times. March 2, 2018. "China Presses Its Internet Censorship Efforts Across the Globe." www.nytimes.com/2018/03/02/technology/china-technology-censorship-borders-expansion.html.

The New York Times. n.d. "Billions in Hidden Riches for Family of Chinese Leader." www.nytimes.com/2012/10/26/business/global/family-of-wen-jiabao-holds-a-hidden-fortune-in-china.html (accessed July 12, 2022).

The New York Times. n.d. "China Is a Minefield, and Foreign Firms Keep Hitting New Tripwires." www.nytimes.com/2019/10/08/world/asia/china-nba-tweet.html (accessed July 12, 2022).

The New York Times. n.d. "Versace, Givenchy and Coach Apologize to China After T-Shirt Row." www.nytimes.com/2019/08/12/fashion/china-donatella-versace-t-shirt.html (accessed July 12, 2022).

The New York Times. October 21, 2021. "China Is a Minefield, and Foreign Firms Keep Hitting New Tripwires." www.nytimes.com/2019/10/08/world/asia/china-nba-tweet.html.

The World Bank. 2020. *Economy Profile China, Doing Business 2020*, p. 4. www.doingbusiness.org/content/dam/doingBusiness/country/c/china/CHN.pdf.

Towson, T.J. and J. Woetzel. 2014. *The One Hour China Book: Two Peking University Professors Explain All of China Business in Six Short Stories: Volume 1*, p. 5. Cayman Islands: Towson Group LLC.

Tse, E. and P. Pan. August 2014. "Is the Golden Age Over for Multinationals in China?." *South China Morning Post*. www.scmp.com/comment/article/1581467/golden-age-over-multinationals-china.

Universum. 2021. "World's Most Attractive Employers 2021." https://universumglobal.com/wmae2021/.

van der Chijs, M. March 2013. "Why I'm leaving China." *CNN Business*. https://money.cnn.com/2013/03/26/news/economy/china-business-pollution/index.html.

Wang, D. January 2022. "2021 letter." *blog*. https://danwang.co/2021-letter/.

Wei, S. December 2014. "Inside the Firewall: Tracking the News That China Blocks." ProPublica. https://projects.propublica.org/firewall/.

Wei, L. and B. Spegele. May 2022. "China's Top Two Leaders Diverge in Messaging on Covid Impact." *The Wall Street Journal*. www-wsj-com.cdn.ampproject.org/c/s/www.wsj.com/amp/articles/chinas-top-two-leaders-diverge-in-messaging-on-covid-impact-11653486508.

Wikipedia. n.d. "List of Sovereign States and Dependent Territories by Immigrant Population." *Wikipedia*. https://en.wikipedia.org/wiki/List_of_sovereign_states_and_dependent_territories_by_immigrant_population (accessed July 12, 2022).

Wilson, G. February 23, 2017. "How to prepare employees for international assignment success." *ECA International*. www.eca-international.com/insights/articles/february-2017/how-to-prepare-employees-for-assignment-success.

Woetzel, J. July 2019. "China and the World: Inside the Dynamics of a Changing Relationship." *McKinsey Insights*. www.mckinsey.com/featured-insights/china/china-and-the-world-inside-the-dynamics-of-a-changing-relationship.

Wong, B. December 2021. "The West Needs to Understand That China's People Are Not a Monolith." *Nikkei Asia.* https://asia.nikkei.com/Opinion/The-West-needs-to-understand-that-China-s-people-are-not-a-monolith.

Woodley, N. November 2014. "Prime Minister Tony Abbott Praises Chinese President Xi Jinping's Commitment to Democracy, But Tourism Industry Not Convinced by FTA." *ABC News.* www.abc.net.au/news/2014-11-18/praise-for-chinese-president/5898212?nw=0.

Wübbeke, J., M. Meissner, M.J. Zenglein, J. Ives, and B. Conrad. December 2016. "Made in China 2025." *Mercator Institute for China Studies*, papers on China 2, no. 74.

Wuttke, J. May/June 2021. "President's Foreword." *EUROBiz.*

Xinhua. September 30, 2021. "China to Expand Channels to Attract Foreign Talent." www.news.cn/english/2021-09/30/c_1310220558_2.htm.

Yan, B. and Z. Goh. June 2022. "Tesla's China Output Decline Trending Deeper Than Musk Forecast, Data and Internal Memos Show." *Reuters.* www.reuters.com/business/autos-transportation/teslas-china-output-decline-trending-deeper-than-musk-forecast-data-internal-2022-06-09/.

Yeung, J. n.d. "Hong Kong and Shanghai Lose Their International Luster as Covid Restrictions Bite." *CNN.* https://edition.cnn.com/2022/04/22/china/china-hubs-shanghai-hong-kong-covid-intl-hnk-mic/index.html.

Yeung, Y., J. Lee, and G. Kee. May 15, 2013. "China's Special Economic Zones at 30." *Eurasian Geography and Economics.* www.tandfonline.com/doi/abs/10.2747/1539-7216.50.2.222.

Yi, X. January 2019. "Shanghai Home to Largest Foreign Worker Population in China." *China Daily.* www.chinadaily.com.cn/a/201901/16/WS5c3ed0a9a3106c65c34e4d2a.html.

Yuchen, Z. April 2014. "Expats Seek Breath of Fresh Air Outside Big, Smoggy Cities." *China Daily USA.* http://usa.chinadaily.com.cn/china/2014-04/11/content_17425595.htm.

Yufei, Y. February 2022. "When Beijing's Skating Rinks Were Battlefields." *Sixth Tone.* www.sixthtone.com/news/1009514/when-beijings-skating-rinks-were-battlefields.

Zani, M. n.d. "Harnessing Clinical Science to Identify Talent: The Predictive Index." *The Silicon Review.* https://thesiliconreview.com/magazine/profile/harnessing-clinical-science-to-identify-talent-the-predictive-index (accessed July 12, 2022).

Zavoretti, R. 2016. "Is It Better to Cry in a BMW or to Laugh on a Bicycle? Marriage, 'Financial Performance Anxiety', and the Production of Class in Nanjing (People's Republic of China)." *Modern Asian Studies* 50, no. 4, pp. 1190–1219.

Zeng, D.Z. February 2015. "Global Experiences With Special Economic Zones: With a Focus on China and Africa." The World Bank.

Zhang, Z. and K. Huang. December 31, 2021. "Tax-Exempt Fringe Benefits for Expatriates in China Extended till End of 2023." *China Briefing*. www.china-briefing.com/news/tax-exempt-benefits-for-expatriates-in-china-extended-end-2023/.

Zhang, Z. December 2019. "China's 2019 Market Access Negative List: What Investors Need to Know." *China Briefing*. www.china-briefing.com/news/chinas-2019-market-access-negative-list-whats-new-attention-investors/.

Zhou, L. January 2015. "China's Overseas Investments, Explained in 10 Graphics." World Resources Institute. www.wri.org/insights/chinas-overseas-investments-explained-10-graphics.

Zhou, S. January 2021. "Will China Fall Into the 'Middle Income Trap'?" *Contemporary China Studies*. https://link.springer.com/chapter/10.1007/978-981-15-6540-3_3#DOI.

Zhou, T. March 2021. "Leveraging Liminality: The Border Town of Bao'an (Shenzhen) and the Origins of China's Reform and Opening." *Cambridge University Press*. www.cambridge.org/core/journals/journal-of-asian-studies/article/abs/leveraging-liminality-the-border-town-of-baoan-shenzhen-and-the-origins-of-chinas-reform-and-opening/45A171DCD475824FD726C999250845D2.

Zhou, Q. August 2021. "Will Foreigners Be Subject to China Social Insurance in Shanghai?" *China Briefing*. www.china-briefing.com/news/will-foreigners-be-subject-to-china-social-insurance-in-shanghai/.

About the Author

Gábor Holch spent his last two decades as a Shanghai-based intercultural leadership consultant, coach, trainer, lecturer, and speaker, mostly working for multinational clients in the Asia-Pacific and Europe.

After his studies in languages and philosophy, then graduate studies in diplomacy, he joined intergovernmental security organization OSCE, and worked in the former Yugoslavia until he moved to China in 2002. There, he established his Shanghai-based management consulting practice, became a Mandarin-language Certified Management Consultant (CMC) and advised, coached, or trained thousands of managers in various combinations of intercultural and leadership skills. He has served over a 100 firms, including AkzoNobel, Bayer, BMW, Nissan, Nokia, Patek Philippe, PepsiCo, Peugeot-Citroën, Porsche, and Walt Disney.

Gábor delivers keynote speeches on intercultural leadership and expat existence. His writing includes two books in English, another two in his native Hungarian, and about a 100 articles in print and online.

Gábor and his wife Yimin split their time between Shanghai, Budapest, and Barcelona. His grown stepdaughter Tingting lives in Ottawa.

Index

OTHER TITLES IN THE INTERNATIONAL BUSINESS COLLECTION

S. Tamer Cavusgil, Michael Czinkota and Gary Knight, Editors

- *Strategic Development of Technology in China* by Kelly Luo
- *Adjusting to the New World Economy* by Michael Czinkota
- *Global Trends and Transformations in Culture, Business, and Technology* by Hamid Yeganeh
- *The Business of Relationships* by Joan Turley
- *The Chinese Market Series* by Danai Krokou
- *Trading With China* by Danai Krokou
- *The Chinese Market* by Danai Krokou
- *The Chinese e-Merging Market* by Danai Krokou
- *Creative Solutions to Global Business Negotiations, Third Edition* by Claude Cellich
- *Exporting* by Laurent Houlier and John Blaskey
- *Global Trade Strategies* by Michel Borgeon and Claude Cellich
- *Doing Business in Germany* by Andra Riemhofer

Concise and Applied Business Books

The Collection listed above is one of 30 business subject collections that Business Expert Press has grown to make BEP a premiere publisher of print and digital books. Our concise and applied books are for...

- Professionals and Practitioners
- Faculty who adopt our books for courses
- Librarians who know that BEP's Digital Libraries are a unique way to offer students ebooks to download, not restricted with any digital rights management
- Executive Training Course Leaders
- Business Seminar Organizers

Business Expert Press books are for anyone who needs to dig deeper on business ideas, goals, and solutions to everyday problems. Whether one print book, one ebook, or buying a digital library of 110 ebooks, we remain the affordable and smart way to be business smart. For more information, please visit www.businessexpertpress.com, or contact sales@businessexpertpress.com.

www.ingramcontent.com/pod-product-compliance
Lightning Source LLC
Chambersburg PA
CBHW061153220326
41599CB00025B/4463

* 9 7 8 1 6 3 7 4 2 4 8 5 8 *